Lecture Notes in Computer Science 1675

Edited by G. Goos, J. Hartmanis and J. van Leeuwen

Springer

Berlin
Heidelberg
New York
Barcelona
Hong Kong
London
Milan
Paris
Singapore
Tokyo

Jacky Estublier (Ed.)

System Configuration Management

9th International Symposium, SCM-9
Toulouse, France, September 5-7, 1999
Proceedings

 Springer

Series Editors

Gerhard Goos, Karlsruhe University, Germany
Juris Hartmanis, Cornell University, NY, USA
Jan van Leeuwen, Utrecht University, The Netherlands

Volume Editor

Jacky Estublier
Laboratoire Dasault Systèmes/LSR
Actimart, 2, Allée de Roumanie, 36610 Gieres, France
E-mail: jacky.estublier@imag.fr

Cataloging-in-Publication data applied for

Die Deutsche Bibliothek - CIP-Einheitsaufnahme

System configuration management : 9th international symposium / SCM-9, Toulouse,
France, September 5 - 7, 1999. Jacky Estublier (ed.). - Berlin ; Heidelberg ;
New York ; Barcelona ; Hong Kong ; London ; Milan ; Paris ; Singapore ; Tokyo :
Springer, 1999
 (Lecture notes in computer science ; Vol. 1675)
 ISBN 3-540-66484-X

CR Subject Classification (1998): D.2, K.6, K.4.3

ISSN 0302-9743
ISBN 3-540-66484-X Springer-Verlag Berlin Heidelberg New York

Typesetting: Camera-ready by author
SPIN: 10704193   06/3142 – 5 4 3 2 1 0   Printed on acid-free paper

Preface

This workshop series is now over ten years old, which is a pretty long time for a very focussed topic: Configuration Management. The first conference took place in 1988 (Grassau, Germany) and the topics were focussed on version control and rebuilding.

Many people consider that SCM is one of the few areas of software engineering that can be considered to be really successful. Products, that more or less fulfill their purpose, exist, and everybody agrees that they are now mandatory for a successful software project.

Indeed, during the second half of the nineties, SCM has entered a maturation phase, in which good commercial products have been incorporating many of the features designed and discussed at previous conferences of this workshop. With the generalization of commercial products, the question now is: What are the objectives of a scientific workshop on this topic? Is there any more research to be done in SCM today?

This ninth volume in the series reflects pretty well the current state and mood in the CM community. There are an unprecedented number of papers discussing the current state of the art and trying to identify research directions (session 6). On some core topics, like versioning (session 3), and following SCM8 tracks, papers present work on unified models. Versioning models, after years of raging discussions, now seem to have found a consensus.

Nevertheless, SCM is facing new challenges, and new solutions are required to manage systems consisting of tightly integrated hardware and software, dynamic systems that change at run-time, or non-traditional artifacts such as Web sites. Moreover, new solutions are required to deploy complex systems within large organizations, to support development teams from multiple disciplines, located in different settings, and constrained by important quality and time objectives.

The following papers do not propose new solutions to all these issues (session 5), but at least make an effort to identify the new needs and challenges of SCM in such a context (sessions 1 & 3). We believe there are still many aspects to be addressed and enhancements to be made in the area of System Configuration Management.

June 1999   Jacky Estublier
                                                                                          General Chair

CONTENTS

5. NEW DEVELOPMENTS
Chair: Geoff Clemm

6. RESEARCH STATUS AND FUTURE DIRECTIONS
Chair: Boris Magnusson

TUTORIAL
Chair: Annita Persson

AUTHOR INDEX

Content Change Management: Problems for Web Systems

Susan Dart

ology Strategies, Inc., 1280 Bison Ave, PMB-510,
Newport Beach, CA. 92660. USA
sdart@susandart.com
www.susandart.com

Abstract: Behind the facade of a web site, lies the task of managing its infrastructure and content. This is driving the Internet economy into a Web crisis. The software community has experienced a similar crisis and knows that configuration management (CM) is a key player in resolving it. Nine challenges facing web systems are presented. As the entire world becomes "webified", content problems will be magnified. While traditional software CM provides a static solution (such as via a centralized development methodology creating batched, planned releases), content CM will provide a dynamic solution (via distributed, real-time updates) in response to user traffic monitoring. It is imperative that the lessons learned from CM be applied to web tools. Otherwise, the Web community is doomed to experience all the delivery, quality and complexity problems that have plagued the software community.

1 Introduction

The World Wide Web (WWW) is a unifying force bringing the world closer to together: Regardless of race, color, creed, skills, educational background, computer platform, browser, nature of business, geographical location, and job position, we all "look" the same. Business is being transformed into E-commerce. Such revenue is expected to hit $220billion by 2001 (says International Data Corp.1999). Behind the facade of e-commerce though, the Web Crisis is looming [1]. That crisis is the exponential proliferation of web content that was created, and is maintained, without any expertise in data management techniques – the proliferation of "hacked together" web-based systems developed without any rigorous approach and kept running via a continual stream of patches. Companies are desperate to "webify" their business applications. The Internet "gold rush fever" is encouraging business start-ups centralized around the WWW. With the advent of many, low-cost publishing tools that are very easy to use, web system creation is now so simple that anyone without programming skills can create one.

The demand for content creation and maintenance is escalating at an unmanageable rate. Some analysts (Merrill Lynch Co. 1999) have predicted that by the year 2002, the market revenue from content management tools will be around $5billion. And, even when we have it under control, content has a multiplier effect, a snowball effect, where we will further exploit new ways of using content. First generation web systems have focused on providing access to any piece of information around the world. The next generation web systems will focus on knowledge management:

-- managing the semantics of, or concepts of, content, rather than just the raw information.

For now though, we see the shortcomings of first generation web systems. There are problems with information being published on the web site at the wrong time and information that is inaccurate, top secret, corrupt, inconsistent, unauthorized, unchecked, garbage, stale, or inappropriate. These can have devastating consequences for companies such as millions of dollars lost in revenue, lost customers, and lowered stock prices (such as with software crash [13].) The causes are easily linked back to lack of: well-defined processes, testing, cross-checking of information, authorized changes, security checking, or responsibility for co-ordinated changes. Essentially, the problems stem from poor configuration management (CM) practices. The first generation of web systems were crafted from immature tools and languages, and inexperienced staff. To properly provide Change Content Management (CCM) -- CM for web systems -- we will have to go beyond the capabilities traditionally provided by industrial-strength software CM tools because the challenges presented by the emerging web economy are exceptional.

This paper is designed to raise questions about CCM for web so that we can understand the new demands placed on companies by web systems. A web system is a generic term for an application that can be accessed via the WWW. It fundamentally consists of **content** (its data, such as a document), **application server** (for executing actions on the data, such as updating document), **access** (its interface, such as the client's browser) and the **web server** (supporting the applications; common ones include Apache, Internet Information Server and Enterprise Server). **The biggest challenge for the WWW community is how to build maintainable web systems that are highly responsive to immediate, high-volume change.**

This paper defines the kinds of resources in the WWW environment that are used in web systems, specifies the classes of web systems being developed, identifies the many challenges that companies are facing in their efforts to understand CCM, highlights capabilities provided by software CM and web CCM tools and ends with recommendations for approaching the solutions.

2 The World Wide Web Environment

Web systems can be huge, with millions of pages, many interconnections and with incredibly high hit rates. Consider Figure 1 which highlights the many kinds of resources throughout the WWW that can be a component of a web system. Figure 1 shows that users can be connected to the network via a **thin client** or a **fat client**. A thin client means application code is resident on the server, rather than on the client (fat client). A firewall determines the kind of access, encryption and security levels. **Web servers** provide much of the application code and can have **accelerators** for caching dynamic pages in order to improve user access time. The network can be specialized into an Intranet, Extranet or **Virtual Private Network**

(VPN). An **Intranet** is an internal network behind a firewall that allows only users within the company to access it. An **Extranet** allows outside partners to have access to the Intranet. A **VPN** is a secure and encrypted connection between two points across the Internet. It acts as an Intranet or Extranet except it uses the public Internet as the networking connection rather than a company's own wiring. This enables, for instance, a company's branch offices to be inexpensively connected via the Internet.

Attached to the network can be other types of networks such as **Storage Area Networks (SANs)** and **Portals**. SANs are networks that pool resources for centralized data storage. They may include multiple servers working against a centralized data store built with redundant hardware such as RAID (high volume storage) devices. **Portals** (such as Yahoo!, AOL) are full-service hubs of e-commerce, mail, online communities, customized news, search engines and directories, all suited to the particular needs of an audience. Portals are evolving into corporate enterprise portals. Such portals for instance, enhance corporate decision making by integrating the company's applications thereby removing barriers that exist between business units.

Other resources that can make up web systems are: **DBMS (Data Base Management Systems)**; workflow applications used for optimizing business processes, such as **ERP (Enterprise Resource Planning)** tools (e.g., SAP, PeopleSoft, Baan); database applications such as **OLAP (OnLine Analytical Processing)** systems which allow users to perform "multi dimensional" analysis on data via their browsers; **document management** tools [9] for providing access into shared libraries of documents; **imaging systems** for optical character recognition of documents; **data warehouses** containing terabytes of data; (Data warehouses provide common interfaces to variant databases); **multi-media databases** for holding archives of music, speech, videos; **mainframes** which contain approximately 70% of legacy data for large companies; **data-marts** which are data warehouses with their own unique interpretation of business data to suit certain functional needs of a business unit; and, **non-PC devices**, such as pagers, personal digital assistants (PDAs), webTV, and smart phones.

Web systems are made up of various combinations of the resources shown in Figure 1. Each of the resources imply content that can be dynamically added, changed, deleted, accessed, manipulated, along with their relationships and hyperlinks. CCM will need to control the static content which goes into the web system along with the dynamic content that is created during execution of the web system. Different kinds of web systems are being developed which affect the nature of CCM.

3 Types of Web Systems

It is difficult to classify the types of web systems being built today because, of course, there is no universal blueprint for such systems, the design is still an immature art and the systems themselves are evolving fast. But, for the purposes of opening up discussions about CCM, we need to understand the types of "architecture" of web systems with respect to content creation. In a broad sense, a web system which is visible via its web site, either acts as a provider of information or is an application. But the applications can be of different types.

From a content perspective, we are interested in types of web systems which have data points where data can be added, changed, deleted, accessed or accumulated. Once we understand the types of applications, we can then determine the nature of its CCM needs, its development processes and types of tools needed to properly maintain it. A web system can be categorized as having the properties of one or more of the following classes:

1. **Informational**: information sites with read-only usage, commonly called "Brochureware" e.g., information presented on a site that gives details about a company and its products. First-generation web systems are this type and are static.

2. **Delivery system**: download content to user or resource e.g., download upgrades or plug-ins

3. **Customized access**: access is via a customized interface or based on user's preferences e.g., my customized view of my ISP's (Internet Service Provider's) home page, or favourite portal

4. **User-provided information**: user provides content by filling in a form e.g., subscription to a magazine or registering for a company's seminar

5. **Interactive**: Two-way interaction between sites, users and resources e.g., business-to-business

6. **File sharing**: remote users collaborate on common files e.g., users co-ordinate schedules

7. **Transaction oriented**: user buys something e.g., buys books or travel tickets

8. **Service provider**: rentable applications; user rents an application on a per user, per month basis e.g., virus scan program

9. **Database access**: user makes queries into a database e.g., supplier looks up catalog of parts

10. **Document access**: libraries of online documents are available e.g., view corporate standards

11. **Workflow oriented**: a process has to be followed e.g., order entry automation

12. **Automatic content generator**: robots or agents automatically generate content e.g., "bots" scour the WWW to bring back specific information such as best price on products.

Given these classes, it becomes obvious that content can essentially be created by anyone or any other resource: from the content designer, the webmaster, any user or another database or device or other web system. From a CCM perspective, it is straightforward to capture content that makes up a released baseline since that is static content, but what about content that is created or changed dynamically? This raises four key questions then: (1)] What constitutes a configuration item for a baseline with static and dynamic objects? (2) How can dynamic baselines be captured? (3) Now that the user of the web system participates in the creation or changing of a baseline, how does that affect the definition of the CCM lifecycle? (4) Are CCM requirements different for each class of web system? These are some of the questions being asked by webmasters, developers and CM managers.

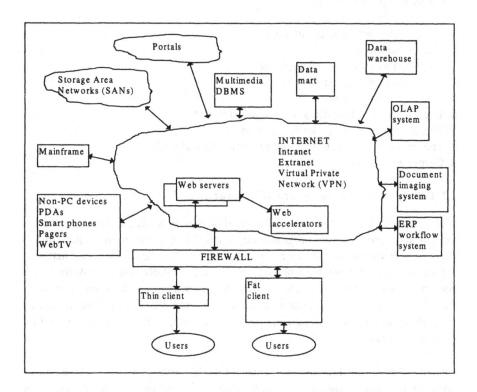

Fig. 1. The Web Environment

4 Enterprise Challenges for Web Systems

CCM is not really a problem for small, static web systems managed by a few developers. But it is for medium and large, enterprise systems that involve many content developers creating many pages that will have a high hit rate involving high-volume database accesses and updates every minute. For instance, the NASDAQ stock exchange system [2], is a web system of types 1, 4, 5, 6,7, 9, 10 and 12, and was built to sustain 12 million hits per day with 8 web servers per database server. When the stock market goes "crazy", the NASDAQ site gets 20 million hits per day. Its content must be completely accurate, and it changes within seconds. Boeing [3], with a web system of types 1, 2, 4, 5, 9, 10, and 11, has 1 million pages hosted by 2300 Intranet sites on more than 1000 web servers.

Developing and maintaining such large systems with large volumes of content, offers many challenges to companies. These challenges span technical, people, process and political issues. The major ones obvious today are the following, and are described in detail below.

1. The dynamic, active nature of content
2. Variant explosion
3. The free-form style of development
4. The performance effect of content
5. Scaleability of content
6. The urgency and frequency of change to content
7. The outsourcing and ownership of content
8. The immaturity of tools, techniques, standards and skills
9. Corporate politics.

4.1 The Dynamic, Active Nature of Content

Web content is dynamic because it is created on-the-fly based on a user's or agent's request. It is active because programs are executed in response to the request and to the user's environment (browser and plug-ins on the client side). For instance, HTML is static but when combined with active controls (such as ActiveX), it becomes dynamic such as when the web site gives users feedback on the type of data they are supposed to enter to make sure the input complies. Content can be generated and changed in real-time such as with tables, forms, database queries, documents, and code.

Content is made up **data objects**, **component libraries** and **code**. These can be static or dynamic, singular or a collection, compiled or interpreted, source or binary code. Objects include documents, images, streaming video and audio, files, or tables. Code can be active controls and scripts such as: ActiveX controls, Java, C++, VisualBasic, HTML, DHTML, XML, VRML, OLE controls, Active Server Pages (ASP), Java applets., VBScript, JavaScript, and ISAPI, CGI, and Perl scripts. Scripts, or behaviours, can be attached to web objects allowing, for instance, the user to alter attributes, such colour, positioning and font size on objects or execute applications. Component libraries are reusable code to be used as toolkits. Examples are JavaBeans, Microsoft Foundation Classes and Lotus' eSuite of business applets.

An applet or a control is a compiled binary file that a field in the HTML references. A script is executable code in a readable source language that can be embedded directly in the HTML tag. In essence, an object becomes a container for various pieces of content, all of which, need to be under CM control.

We are moving towards container-based, or a component bundling approach to software development. This means CM techniques need to account for embedded scripts and customized components. Also, the executing environment needs to be taken into account. For example, if a browser doesn't support a certain scripting language, then the behavior of the web system will be different. Also, HTML files can be manually touched up. Scripts can be easily changed because they are interpreted whereas applets or controls typically are compiled. This assumes of course, that the source code can be accessed which isn't the case when components are bought and reused in their binary form. Hence, changing or recompiling isn't an option sometimes. Executing code may require a series of steps. For example: a Java file is compiled into platform-independent bytecodes; these are then processed by a JIT (Just In Time) compiler to yield fast native instructions for a particular platform. All the above objects types, their relationships to intermediate forms, and all the tools, need to be tracked for good CM practices.

Web pages are dynamically created which means that any CM control must too be of a dynamic nature. For example, an .asp file (Active Server Page which is a combination of static HTML and VBScript) is recognized; the VBScript is interpreted with the appropriate database or related files being accessed; then the server creates the full HTML on-the-fly thereby dynamically generating the web page which is then displayed. How is all this data tracked for CM purposes? How is a dynamic baseline captured? To add complexity, hyperlinks can be created on the fly to point to documents for instance. This then changes the original baseline. Also, dynamically generated pages can be customized using ActiveX, CGI scripts, JavaScript and DHTML frames.

But there is more. Content has meta-data associated with it that must be captured:

• The **separation of content and format**. Companies have standard templates into which content is published. These templates are part of the released baseline

• **External structure** information, such as the hierarchy and relationship of web pages

• **Internal structure** information, such as embedded objects

• **Hyperlinks** to internal or external pages, static or dynamic

• **Task objects** that indicates some activity must happen to an object, such as update the content

- **Transaction**, such as this data is involved in carrying out an e-commerce activity

- **Security** information attached to each objects

- **Audit logs** related to the activity on each object

- **Tool compatibility** information such as the version of the browser for which this object is valid

- **Bill of materials**: the artifacts used to create the baseline (tools, tool options, data, files)

- **Generated** or converted files, such as a Word document that is converted into HTML

- **Validation rules**, such as a form requires input validation for each field

- **Handler rules**, such as a data base access request invokes certain tools and operations.

There are obviously many properties about content that need to be captured. Ideally, a company should have a well-defined CM data model that captures all the properties and relationships of content. With that, configuration items, baselines and releases can be defined.

4. 2 Variant Explosion

Web systems imply a variant explosion problem. Consider that web systems are either created from scratch, are re-designed or merged web systems, or are web-enabled legacy applications. In many cases, companies must live with all these systems in parallel. Thus, a company could easily have a nightmarish number of versions of their latest baseline. For example, it has 4 variants of its main application available at all times: [1] The "demo" version which is a partial "web-enabled" baseline of the original legacy code with a minimal set of functionality as this is the textual version [2] a full version that is the same as the first where all functionality is available since it is the graphical version [3] the true web version which is a completely redesigned form of the application ideally suited to the web rather than merely web-enabled legacy code, and [4] the original legacy system for non-web use.

Each variant must work with 2 different browsers (Internet Explorer and Netscape Navigator) including the latest three versions of those browsers – and support 5 different languages for international use. Hence, we have $(1 * 5) + (3 * 2 * 3 * 5)$ = 95 potential variants. Then add in variants for non-PC devices such as pagers, PDAs and smart phones that have "micro browsers", and the number of variants escalates further. Most companies have different teams working on separate variants without much communication, reuse or change propagation across common code. With the variants, come all the complexity of parallel development support for simultaneous changes and concurrent baselines, along with significant change propagation to selected variants thereby demanding change set support [10], more sophisticated change tracking along with help desk support and of course, much better release planning and change scheduling. The ramifications are dramatic. Variant management and change propagation have long plagued software companies.

4.3 The Free-Form Style of Development

Web system development is different from traditional software development [7,8]. This is due the nature of the tools, languages, skills of the developers and the dynamic nature of the Web environment. There is tremendous pressure on developers to "code-and-publish". And the web tools support this free-form style of development. Also, the skill set of the developers is quite limited with typically no experience in software engineering. They are guided only by the capabilities of the tools and languages which, as we know from software engineering practices, cannot be adequate.

Scripting languages (such as JavaScript, Jscript, Tcl, VBScript) are changing the way that applications are developed. Most of these are interpretive languages or use JIT (Just In Time) compilers. This leads to a style of "change on the fly". There is no process in between creating content and publishing it. Programming has gone from a process-oriented compiler based approach, to a combine components, mix in some new code and publish! Essentially, this squeezes down the change cycle time dramatically because all sense of process is eliminated. This enables a faster rate of change which is a real benefit for web systems but provides greater opportunity for errors through lack of testing and content co-ordination and authorization of change. The question becomes: how can testing, system integration, load testing and release management processes be inserted into the code-and-go paradigm to enable proper CM? Some companies use staging areas for testing before publishing to a live site whereas many do not.

The complexity of web system development can be seen from Table 1. The major phases are highlighted along with who assumes responsibility for those steps. There are at least 9 key steps involved in getting the web system functioning. At each point, CM issues come into play such as, which release or version of the web system is being changed or published or tested or registered or validated for security purposes or being monitored for hits or performance improvements. Without CCM practices and tool support, all these activities become fraught with errors. Automated workflow along with role based activities must be supported in web tools.

1.	MAJOR ACTIVITY IN WEB SYSTEM	WHY DOES THE WORK
2.	**Design and creation**	Web Team or IT Dept. or Outsourced
3.	**Infrastructure** support: servers, network connections, databases	Outsourced to network management company, or hosted by IT Dept.
4.	**Testing** e.g., compatibility of content, link accuracy, viewable by all kinds of browsers	Web Team or IT Dept.
5.	**Publishing** of content	Business Units or Web Team or IT Dept.
6.	**Registering** of sites on search engines	Web Team or IT Dept.
7.	**Security** checking: access control, hacker analysis, virus detection	Web Team or IT Dept or Security Consultant
8.	**Monitoring: traffic** performance: intelligent load balancing and web page redesign; replication; web accelerators/caching; traffic shaping capacity planning	Web Team or IT Dept.
9.	**Maintenance**: content evolution via changes, enhancements, deletions, redesign	Content experts or Web Team or IT Dept.

Table 1. Typical web system lifecycle phases

4.4 The Performance Effect on Content

Performance – particularly response time to a user's request -- plays a major role in influencing content design. High performance web systems have continuous traffic monitoring. Users must have immediate access to quickly-changing content under any load situations. If access times are not acceptable, a company makes a decision to either, install web accelerators which enable caching to improve performance, or, they redesign the content for better access. For instance, at the Olympics site [11], traffic monitoring showed bottlenecks for users by having to navigate too many pages to get to the right content. The web site was redesigned on-the-fly to make access much easier and speedier along with adding caches.

Web accelerators, or caches, are beginning to play bigger roles in performance enhancement with content being designed to take into account, caching techniques for accelerators. But a dependency results between the content baseline and the version of the caching algorithm and server that are used. Also, server crashes (such as with the E*trade brokerage site crashes which shut out users who lost money through lack of trading access) must be catered for in contingency plans. This means content must be replicated across servers which in turn, means synchronization and distribution of real-time updates.

4.5 Scalability of Content

The Olympic [11] and NASDAQ [12] web systems are huge in terms of number of pages (million), amount of traffic (millions of hits per day), and number of database and web servers. Millions of pages cannot be reasonably stored in a flat, file system. Databases are obviously required for storage and are being redesigned to suit web access. Some database companies are redesigning their products so that web applications are stored directly in the database, such as Oracle's WebDB. This helps with scalability, reliability and administration. It is likely that first generation web systems will be redesigned to use web-enabled databases. This means that CM capabilities must be integrated and synchronized with database facilities.

4.6 The Urgency and Frequency of Change

The web enables the paradigm of change at the speed of thought. The mind set is typically: I see a problem and can, or need to, fix it immediately because it is globally visible. Corporate embarrassment or even worse, litigation, needs to be avoided. There may be no time to follow through a normal change lifecycle (such as with a change request, Change Control Board, change authorization, edit, testing and re-release). Because the change can be done so easily, process is often bypassed. All the benefits then of change tracking are lost. Repeatability will be a difficult benefit to achieve. Roll-back of a site may be the only options for companies. But, the corporate need of keeping the web site accurate, takes top priority. There are changes that may need to be propagated across all pages of a web site, or just a few pages. For example, simply changing a copyright notice, may involve changing each of the one million pages, whereas other changes may involve a select set of pages so an incremental publishing capability is required along with ways of organizing files into partitions to enable incremental updates. A company needs to define its classes and priority of changes and decide what process should be followed for each type of change.

4.7 Outsourcing

Outsourcing is a significant trend for industry, especially for web system creation, and sometimes maintenance. It is done for many reasons: to reduce operating costs, share risks with others, access leading-edge technology without having to purchase the infrastructure for it, use expertise not found in-house, do things more quickly, and to focus more on a company's own core competencies. But outsourcing does require distributed management techniques along with doing CM with a third-party.

Easy-to-use web tools and specialized commercial-of-the-shelf tools (such as OLAP, ERP, document management) are helping to change the political infrastructure of companies. For instance, business units no longer are forced to rely on the Information Technology (IT) department in order to get things done. They go out and buy the best tool that suits their need, bypassing IT. They can even go out and rent the infrastructure for supporting the tools, and outsource its administration. This complicates issues of who has responsibility for what, how to maintain control and visibility over outsourced changes, and can a business unit guarantee that a quality process was followed for the outsourced work.

4.8 Immaturity of Tools, Techniques, Standards and Skills

Engineering techniques for web systems are still in their infancy. Tools, standards, and skill sets are maturing albeit slowly. Each month, new tools and new versions of tools are being released that support easier ways of building web systems. As a result, companies have to maintain different tool technologies in parallel. Standards (such as XML (eXtensible Markup Language) from World Wide Web Consortium, or WebDAV from the Internet Engineering Task Force) are slowly being developed which in turn, will affect the tools. There are many web technology tools that enable easy publishing of content without team co-ordination or process. Because of the many choices, large companies will end up having their business units using different tools. To get some control over how content is developed, and to ensure that quality processes are followed in publishing content, companies will have to define standards and guidelines. These standards will pertain to style templates, component libraries, tools, languages, servers, testing processes, and CM.

Web systems require developers and content experts for their creation and maintenance. Many web developers have little background in software engineering. Content creators can be human resources personnel, marketing people, accounting staff, etc. people whose core competence is not software. Their web skills then are totally dependent on their knowledge gleaned from the web tool set and any training class they attended. This implies that the tools need to have interfaces that suit the content writer yet have excellent CM processes embedded to make up for the lack of software skills.

4.9 Corporate Politics

There is confusion in companies these days as to who should have the right to publish content to the web site. For instance, business units publish independently from the IT department. Essentially, there is lack of control as to what goes up, when, and how it has been tested and does it conform to standards? This is particularly a problem when the web system has content that must be co-ordinated and validated as a whole with other departments (such as Accounting, Marketing, Personnel, etc.) or with other applications. Who assumes responsibility for the accuracy of the information on the web site? Who assures that quality control processes have been followed before information is published to the site? Who is responsible for making changes? Who assumes the cost of change? The role of the

IT department is changing dramatically – from an infrastructure provider – to that of a strategic advisor and standards producer. Many functions traditionally done by IT (such as network administration) are now being outsourced. Outsourcing will significantly change the modus operandi of IT departments. And web creation is mostly outsourced these days. All in all, companies face a delicate balancing act in trying to rein in the proliferation of web systems while still leaving employees freedom to meet their business needs.

5 Software CM is a Major Part of Content Change Management

Everything that the software community has learned about CM can be applied to the CCM problems. Software CM spans a significant spectrum of activities and roles within a company [5, 6] and Table 2 highlights the main goals of CM. The software CM tool vendors are adding CCM capabilities to their tools.

GOAL	EXPLANATION
Identification	Identifying uniquely all content
Control	Version control of all objects including baselines
Status accounting	Tracking the status of all work on all objects
Audit and review	Keeping an audit trail, confirming all processes followed
Cost-effective production	Fast and quick builds of software releases
Quality automation	Ensuring all testing, notifications, signoffs, reviews are done
Teamwork optimization	Enabling teams to work in parallel effectively
Enabling change	Containing the explosion of changes

Table 2. Goals of software configuration management

Web tool vendors are beginning to realize that CM practices need to be incorporated into their tools Advice on good web design [4] is beginning to highlight the importance of CM but only in the sense of version control of files. On the other hand, web engineering advice [12] completely ignores CM. Table 3 lists some of commercial software CM tools.

Software CM vendors are taking different approaches to CCM support in their tools. Some, such as StarTeam are web-enabled and have purchased web technology companies with the intention of tool integration. Others such as TrueChange have decided to build a completely new software CM tool for CCM. Others such as Continuus and MKSIntegrity, have added on CCM support. The former's offering, WebSynergy and WebPT, provide a web front-end into all of its existing CM process-oriented capabilities as well as web authoring tools with transparent access to files. The latter's offering, WebIntegrity, integrates its version control facilities with an authoring tool.

6 Web Technology Tools

Web tools are marketed for web authors or web developers. As to what constitutes a CCM tool, that is not totally clear and there is no consistency in functionality across the tools. Suitability for large-scale development seems to determine whether it is a CCM tool or just an authoring tool. Tools are first generation ones (with respect to CCM support) with only one product (DynaBase) claiming that it provides configuration management facilities. Some tools are geared to large-scale web production although it is not clear how scaleable these tools are yet. Half a million components seems to be the maximum so far. Table 4 lists some commercial CCM tools. If there are any similarities or trends, they would be: support for web languages, command line interfaces, templates for separating content from formatting, version control of files, roll-back of complete sites, minimal workflow support for publishing authorization, audit logging, event triggers, commercial database interfacing, drag-and-drop component reuse so that minimal programming is required, role support for authorizations, minimal change tracking and concurrent site production (for multiple releases).

CM TOOL	VENDOR	WEBSITE
Continuus	Continuus	www.continuus.com
ClearCase	Rational	www.rational.com
Harvest	Platinum Technology	www.platinum.com
Perforce	Perforce Software	www.perforce.com
PVCS	Merant	www.merant.com
Source Integrity	MKS	www.mks.com
SourceSafe	Microsoft	www.microsoft.com
StarTeam	Starbase Corp.	www.starbase.com
TeamConnection	IBM	www.ibm.com
TrueChange	True Software	www.truesoft.com

Table 3. Some Commercial Configuration Management Tools

Some noteworthy features include: TeamSite provides visual differencing for examining two versions of content side by side. Tasks can be assigned to authors using notifications. Authors can be notified when content is published on the web. Content is moved to a staging area each time it is changed or receives approval to be published. Drumbeat gives developers guidance on targeting code to specific browsers thereby providing variant creation support. In Raveler, teams can be set up with pre-configured worklfows. StoryServer supports static and dynamic versioning. Overall, more CM support needs to be provided to support CCM needs.

7 Conclusion

The web environment provides the opportunity to connect many different resources. Whilst the resultant web systems are easily created, they are complex systems offering many challenges for CCM. We need to understand the problems that companies are having with web systems in order to properly define their CCM requirements. Then we still need solutions to questions such as: What are good content development and change processes for teams developing large-scale web systems? Are there different processes depending on the type of web system, size of company, volume of web data? Can the types of web systems be categorized into classes or architectures? Will component libraries be indicative of these architectures? What factors affect the definition of the CM process and CM items? Do we need system models, data models, architectures of web sites in order to fully capture the appropriate CM meta information?

CONTENT TOOL	VENDOR	WEB SITE
ArticleBase	Running Start	www.runningstart.com
DreamWeaver	Macromedia	www.dreamweaver.com
Drumbeat 2000	Elemental Software	www.drumbeat.com
DynaBase	Inso	www.inso.com
Frontier	Userland	www.userland.com
FrontPage98	Microsoft	www.microsoft.com
Fusion	NetObjects	www.netobjects.com
Raveler	Platinum Technologies	www.raveler.com
StoryServer	Vignette corp.	www.vignette.com
TeamSite	Interwoven	www.interwoven.com

Table 4. Commercial Web content development tools

Second generation web systems will focus on knowledge management and hence need sound engineering principles, such as CM, behind them Given the many challenges, much of the solution will have to be embedded in the tools because the skill set of the developer cannot be guaranteed. This means that the CM processes will have to be implemented in the web tools rather than relying on manual procedures. Along with excellent variant support, change tracking, and change propagation (especially via change sets). CM is becoming an issue for all companies because, in order to survive beyond the first decade of the new millenium, companies must "webify" their applications.

References

1. Murugasen, S., Deshpande, Y.: Proceedings of ICSE99 Workshop on Web Engineering. International Conference on Software Engineering, Los Angeles, USA (May 1999)
2. Hutcheson, M.: The NT Application That Wouldn't Die (NASDAQ.COM). In: Enterprise Development. 1,1 (Dec. 1998)
3. Sliwa, C: Maverick Intranets: A Challenge for IT. In: Computerworld (March 15, 1999)
4. Siegel, D: Secrets of Successful Web Sites : Project Management on the World Wide Web. Haydn Books, Indianapolis, IN, USA (1997)
5. Dart, S.: The Agony and Ecstasy of CM. A half-day tutorial given at 8TH International Workshop on Software CM, Brussels Belgium (July 20-21, 1998) http://www.cs.colorado.edu/~andre/SCM8/dart.html
6. Dart, S.: Not All Tools are Created Equal. In: Application Development Trends (Oct. 1996) 7pp http://www.adtmag.com/pub/oct96/fe1002.htm
7. Gellerson, H. Gaedke, M.: Object-oriented Web Application Development. In: IEEE Internet Computing (Jan/Feb 1999) 60-68
8. Lockwood, L.: Taming Web Development. In: Software Development Magazine (April 1999)
9. Dart, S: The Dawn of Document Management. In: Application Development Trends (Aug. 1997)
10. Dart, S.: To Change Or Not To Change. In: Application Development Trends (June 1997)
11. Iyengar et al.: Techniques for Designing High-Performance Web Sites. In: IBM Research (March 1999) 17pp
12. Powell, T.: Web Site Engineering. Prentice Hall, NJ, USA (1998)
13. Bloomberg News: Net Shares Battered Amid Signals That Web's Expansion Is Slowing. In: Wall Street Journal (June 15, 1999)

Experiences: Distributed Development and Software Configuration Management

Ulf Asklund[1], Boris Magnusson[1], and Annita Persson[2]

[1] Dept. of Computer Science, Lund University; P.O. Box 118, SE-221 00 Lund, Sweden
{Ulf.Asklund | Boris.Magnusson}@cs.lth.se
[2] Ericsson Microwave Systems AB; SE-431 84 Mölndal, Sweden
Annita.Persson@emw.ericsson.se

Abstract. Distributed development occurs more frequently today than only some years ago. Distributed development states new demands on Configuration Management and used processes. This paper describes experiences from more than ten different Swedish companies in the area of distributed development and software configuration management. We present definitions, experiences and hints on Software Configuration Management from three different aspects; four cases of distributed development, architecture, and working methods in some key-areas.

1 Introduction

Large companies and organizations have for a long time had access to global networks, but the rapid development of the Internet has brought about a dramatically increased access to such services. This results in such a degree of accessibility that it is expected at almost all kinds of work, not least in software development. Groups of developers are now able to work all over the world on the development of the same system. From different locations they may need to modify thousands of different files and sometimes the same files, within a single product. The potential is considerable due to the increased possibility of using personnel and competence in a more efficient, flexible and comfortable manner. At the same time, this new technique has caused considerable changes of the organization of the work place in many other respects, as well as in this one. The way in which the work has been divided and the handling of the interactions between different groups and individuals has been largely affected by the fact that the staff is geographically dispersed. This creates new demands on the tools and the systems used for handling the coordination of the development, especially with concurrent development. Much of these demands, but not all, are within the area of Software Configuration Management, which is the subject of this report. Other systems for communication and management are of course also affected if the staff are geographically scattered over great distances, but they are not the primary focus here.

SCM is targeted towards two target groups; *management* and *developers* [Fei91], which have resulted in several different definitions of SCM. The main objective for supporting *management* is to document and provide full visibility of the product's present configuration and on the status of achievement of its physical and functional requirements. Guidelines to fulfill these objectives are documented in standards like MIL-STD-973 [MIL], and ISO 10 007 [ISO95]. *Developers* need support to synchronize their work and to be aware of what other developers are doing, etc. Support which aims at coordinating them towards a mutual goal.

A central problem is the management of the history and development of documents and programs over time as well as the management of branches and to support merge. SCM was originally developed under the more or less explicit assumption that the people as well as the files are situated at the same geographical location. This applies to the tools that have been developed as well as to the working processes used. The general opinion on the functionality associated with SCM has been formed from this assumption. The support for management as well as for developers are tasks that gets even more complicated when the staff is geographically dispersed.

Some aspects of system development, such as the creation of a general picture and a context, the communication between developers and groups, have remained manual and without direct tool support [AM97]. A part of the requirements is covered by individual documents, specifications, and formal meetings where important decisions are made. But an astonishingly large part of this requirement of information for synchronization, within, as well as between groups, is covered by informal contacts between developers, during discussions, at review meetings, during coffee breaks, in the corridor and so on. When people working closely together are geographically disperse we need to consider how these additional aspects may be supported in the working method and in tool support. The closer together people work (despite the geographical distance) and the more dependent their various tasks are, the more apparent the lack of support will be.

A good strategy during all development is to try to limit the dependency between the developers, especially if they are situated at different locations. This is often already done during the structuring of the product to be developed. The system is divided into modules or components, which are then developed by different groups separately. However, it turns out that despite good structuring, dependencies between the components remain. This becomes clear not least when interfaces need to be modified or when the components are to be integrated. These are examples of situations when one, although one has tried to avoid it, requires an overview and synchronization between the groups mentioned above.

Much of the discussions in this paper is not limited to software, but may be applied to other products and documents. We will hence denote configuration management as CM rather than SCM.

This paper presents a part of the results from a project sponsored by the Association of Swedish Engineering Industries (VI), with the aim of focusing on the area of CM in connection with distributed development. The study was based upon interviews at 11 Swedish companies with experience in the introduction of distributed development. The full result can be found in [Ask99a, Ask99b]. Our experiences from the project can be grouped into three parts: classification of situations of distributed development, client-server architecture of CM-tools, and working methods. We demonstrate guidelines from the companies which can be used by other companies to better understand their situations and give them practical tips how to deal with these.

Section 2 contains a number of examples where different situations of distributed development may arise in a company. Section 3 describes different client/server architectures and their advantages and disadvantages regarding distributed development. Currently used methods and tools, how they are being used at the different companies and their experiences in doing so is presented in section 4. Conclusions ends the paper.

2 Five Cases of Distributed Development

Distributed development may arise due to several different reasons. During the investigation four cases were identified. The companies interviewed recognized the cases and could describe how they dealt with the distribution aspects related to each case. The classification also facilitated a discussion regarding suggestions of solutions. The different cases that have been identified are: (1) Locally (for comparison), (2) Distant work, (3) Outsourcing, (4) Co-located groups, and (5) Distributed groups.

The different cases occur individually or in combinations. For instance there may be groups which are normally connected, but which may occasionally be distributed.

2.1 Locally

A fast network is characteristic of a place of work where everyone is situated locally, allowing complete development and test environments for all developers. It is fairly easy for the project groups to communicate and synchronize their work, by formal meetings as well as by more informal encounters such as at the coffee table. Informal meetings also create a team spirit, which in turn increases the probability that the established CM process is observed.

From a CM perspective:
- A common file system.
- Complete development and test environment.
- Synchronization can to a certain degree be achieved through meetings. In particular, problems that arise can be solved through direct communication.
- Good awareness of what others are doing (group awareness).
- No particular security problems (external networks are virtually unused).

2.2 Distance Working

Modem, CD/Tape, Laptop computer

This kind of distant work is brief work being performed elsewhere than the usual place of work. Home working as a complement to the daily work being the primary example.

When developers work at home (or elsewhere) on a more regular basis or for longer periods of time, a situation similar to that for distributed groups arises, see further below.

A limited computer utility and a relatively slow means of communication with the world around (for instance by data modems to the usual place of work) is characteristic of distance working. Despite this, there is a desire to be able to start working quickly, as the total working time on each occasion is short (typically a few hours in the evening), which means that it must be possible to set up the working environment quickly. As the daily contacts remain, the possibility of informal communication and maintaining the team spirit is more or less the same as in the local situation.

Two common modes of working are: (1) Individual files are brought home and worked on locally, or (2) remote login to the place of work and the home computer is being used as a terminal.

From a CM perspective:

- Bringing home individual files results in the work being done locally outside of the control and support of the CM system. The degree of impairment this can lead to partially depends on which CM model the tool supports [Fei91]. For instance no support is offered as to the awareness of what others are doing simultaneously. In addition, testing is made impossible.
- Login at a terminal is similar to the local case. The slower connection makes the work somewhat heavier going for the developers. Then there is also a tendency that they may not follow the working models the way they should (for instance to make a complete test of all platforms before check-in).

2.3 Outsourcing

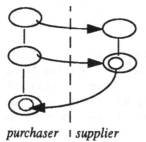

copying of the test environment

possible updating of the test environment

delivery of component

purchaser ı supplier

Instead of developing everything by yourself or buying existing components (COTS - Commercial Off The Shelf) you may have a third party develop them for you. This is usually called outsourcing (or subcontracting) and gives, compared to COTS, a greater control of the development of the component, albeit at a higher price.

Outsourcing is based on a close collaboration between the supplier and the purchaser. Consequently it is often possible for the developer/supplier to test the component in an environment similar to the target environment prior to delivery. The purchaser then usually provides the test environment.

The purchaser is ultimately responsible for the product and possible error/change management can be reflected in changed demands on the component towards the supplier. As with any order, it must be clear what should be delivered, but in this case it is further complicated by the fact that the demands as well as the environment may change.

From a CM perspective:

- The purchaser must be able to integrate new versions of the component into the product, which itself may have developed since the latest release of the component.
- The supplier should be able to manage the updating of the development and test environments.
- The purchaser and the supplier do not necessarily have the same CM tools, which might make the updating (in both directions) difficult.
- At delivery of a source code, the generation tools must also be consistent between the purchaser and supplier.
- With changed demands, the connection between the version of the demand and delivery must be clear.

2.4   Co-located Groups

Developers at different affiliated companies usually belong to local groups or projects. The division of the work has already been determined at the structuring of the project/product to prevent too much dependency between the different groups. The product is divided up into sub products, which can be developed by different project groups. The division makes it possible to do most of the development locally within the groups without the requirement for much communication with other groups. Within the group and between groups in the same place, the situation is the same as with local development. Groups in different places normally only have access to the latest stable versions produced by the other groups. Due to the geographical distance, potential problems will inevitably be more difficult to solve. Therefore, updating and distribution between the groups requires more effort and administration, these may be considered as internal deliveries and therefore tend to come more infrequently. Cooperation between the groups may be facilitated if the work is planned in phases of which everyone is aware. Conversely the redistribution or division of the work is more difficult to perform afterwards.

From a CM perspective:

- The files are stored in different file systems, but (ideally) in the same CM system. Large companies sometimes have different CM systems in their different affiliated companies.
- When the locations are permanent, each local group should be able to work within a complete development environment and with the possibility of testing.
- The groups deliver (release) sub-products between them rather than develop together.

- There are often few or no unplanned daily contacts between the groups. The contact is limited to e.g. weekly meetings, which may be actual physical meetings or telephone/video conferences.
- It is important to maintain the knowledge of the development status between the groups.
- Change management of common components, such as interfaces, is of particular importance.

2.5 Distributed Groups

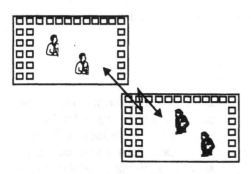

Distributed groups means that the members of the group are also distributed, i.e. that the people working in the same project, perhaps even in the same files, are geographically dispersed. The possibility of daily communication by formal as well as informal meetings is lost even *within* the group. Projects working towards the same product usually use some common libraries or components. Changes in these are unusual (simply because they are common and changes are difficult to manage), but sometimes inevitable. If group members at different places want to make changes at the same time they face a situation similar to that for the updating of interfaces where there are "connected groups" but in this case the problems apply to all files.

The situation with distributed groups can usually be avoided, by considering separate individuals as very small connected groups for example. Despite these efforts, there are cases when the groups need to work more closely together although they are still distributed. The obvious example is when people included in one group, have to travel around to other groups for various reasons. Of course there is a desire to be able to continue working with the usual project, this will then be done as a distributed group. A similar situation arises when staff are moved to new projects but often need to be consulted on the old project. People with special competence are often included in several groups, which can be at different locations.

From a CM perspective:
- It is important that the members of the group receive information about what the others in the group are doing, how the project is developing, its status, which changes have been done and by whom etc.
- It is important to support the sharing of files and concurrent, simultaneous changes.
- Solutions using "locking" and exclusive access to files work poorly as it is difficult to solve situations where group members, located at different sites, must wait for each other.

2.6 Discussion

The situation of local development is of course preferable from a CM point of view, as it is easier to manage than the cases of distributed development. However, there are several other good reasons for the use of the different situations outlined above.

The situation with connected groups usually results in the work being planned in a manner such that the dependency between groups in different places is minimized.

The situation with distributed groups is usually not desirable, but rather the planning of the work, the complete system construction, the division into components and so on aims to avoid this. However, it can be anticipated that such a situation arises as a consequence of the break up of connected groups.

An additional example is in using remote places of work, i.e. a place of work situated closer to home than the "real" place of work, which is therefore used most of the week. The situation is a combination of distance working and distributed groups. Typically, formal meetings work, but informal ones, either partially or completely, fail to occur.

3 Six Possible Architectures

To meet the demands arising from different situations (the four cases above), one can in a number of different ways, locate workstations and repositories/servers in these places, in different architectures. We will therefore from now on call a geographic place (e.g. the same house), equipped with repository/server and a number of work places, a "site". Developers with workstations but without a repository/server are therefore not a site. The different architectures being discussed are: (1) Locally to a server, (2) Remote login, (3) Laptop computer to a server, (4) Several sites by Master-Slave connections, (5) Several sites with differing areas of responsibility, and (6) Several sites with equal servers.

3.1 Locally to a Server

All developers are situated locally and work via a rapid network towards the same server.

3.2 Remote Login

A single server towards which everyone works. Those situated at a different location than where the server is located, work towards the server by "remote login", "telnet", or other similar protocols. Technically a developer then works as if situated locally but is limited by a slower (and possibly a less reliable) connection, for instance over a modem or Internet.

3.3 Laptop Computer to a Server

The server towards which everyone works, but in contrast to remote login, some of the product's files are copied to be then worked on locally. Updating and synchronization of the files is typically done on a daily basis. The work is performed without support by the CM tool. If a CM tool is available on the laptop computer, then a situation as outlined in chapters 3.4 or 3.5 may arise.

3.4 Several Sites by Master-Slave Connections

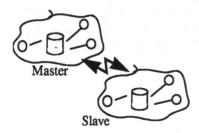

A version of a connected sub-system is copied from a master to another (slave) server where it is further developed. This architecture is commonly used without support from a common CM tool and therefore the version history is not included at the copying stage, nor at the following synchronization stage, at "delivery" back to the master. To avoid a complicated merge situation a sub-system copied to a slave server can not be changed at the master or any other server. If both servers have the same CM tool, and it supports this architecture, these limitations can be eliminated or at least reduced. Irrespective of this, the requirement for updating is usually relatively infrequent (weeks, months). A situation like this may occur with outsourcing for instance.

3.5 Several Sites With Differing Areas of Responsibility

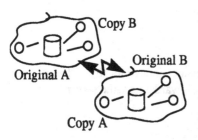

Different sites are responsible for different sub-systems. The division can be based on the responsibility for certain files or certain variants. The variant concept must be the same for all of the files on the servers. For those parts that a site is not responsible for, the information can only be read. Synchronization is achieved by the changes in the original being transferred to the copy. Examples of such protocols are ftp, www, e-mail or those within the CM tool. Synchronization is often done automatically and at close intervals (time scale of hours) or when needed, i.e. when changes have been made. It should be noted that a site can have the original of one sub-system and at the same time have copies of others. This means that updating can occur in both directions between servers holding the originals for different sub-systems.

Compared to the master-slave architecture, this is a more permanent division and the synchronization is usually done automatically and therefore more frequently.

3.6   Several Sites With Equal Servers

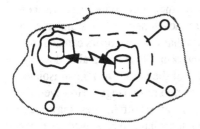 This is an architecture where several equal servers are located at different sites. These are automatically synchronized at close intervals (hours, minutes, seconds) and all of the servers have (with very little delay) the same information. The result is that a developer can work at any site (towards the server at that site) without noticing any difference. The dotted line symbolizes how the servers at the various sites are being synchronized, the outer limit symbolizing a virtual site within which everyone works.

3.7   Discussion

The division in different architectures can serve as a guide when planning the introduction of distributed development, and as a basis for the analysis of the consequences and limitations of different solutions. The different examples may also serve as a guide for the manual management of the situation and to understand what different CM systems can offer. Of course, it will never be very easy to use an architecture until there is tool support.

The situation of remote login is often used in manual management. Situations in which temporary branches need to be merged will most likely increase, therefore a tool supporting this function would be of great value. The same principle applies to the situation with simple use of a laptop computer. There are also simple tools for supporting the synchronization of directories with files existing on the server as well as on the laptop computer, e.g. File Assistant for Macintosh [Mac]. The Master-Slave connection is a situation that is directly supported by the tools Teamware [Team94], which was developed to support this particular architecture. Similarly ClearCase Multi-Site [Clear98], Continuus [Con98], and PVCS Replicator [PVCS99] support the architecture in which there are sites with differing areas of responsibility. Finally we conclude that the ideal situation with equal servers, is unfortunately not covered by any of the commercially available systems.

The interval between updates will impact on when changes can take effect and thus controls the degree of awareness in and between the groups.

4   Working Methods in Two Key-Areas

In this chapter two areas are indicated where a distributed development affects the working mode and gives rise to situations which must be solved in order to obtain an effective and problem free development. The areas being discussed are: (1) Concurrent development and awareness and (2) Change management.

For each area we give our definition of the area and examples of problems that may arise or be magnified by geographical separation, we report on the experiences from the interviewed companies, as well as advice and practical guidance.

4.1   Concurrent Development and Awareness

To shorten the development time, companies are increasingly developing more of their software in a concurrent manner, i.e. a number of developers make simultaneous changes to the same product. A prerequisite for this is that the developers can and may make simultaneous changes. By letting developers work in different parallel development branches they can, despite the concurrent nature of the work, work in an isolated 'sandbox' and in that way avoid using each others temporary changes. However, the isolation results in the possibility that, without being aware of it, they may make changes that are in conflict with each other. These conflicts have to be solved when the branches are subsequently merged into a common development branch.

Concurrent development can be achieved at different levels. At the system level, sub-products or different functions are developed in parallel (concurrent system development), and at a lower, more detailed level, several developers can make simultaneous changes in different versions of the same file (concurrent software development). The lower the level, the greater the possibility for a high degree of concurrent work, but the greater the risk of conflicting changes.

There are two main ways of reducing the risk of conflicts:

- A good product structure makes it possible to make dependencies obvious and distribute the work to different parts of the product. The more independent the parts are of each other, and the better their interfaces are described, the smaller the risk of conflict. It is then relatively easy to distribute the areas of responsibility, as different parts of the product, to the different developers or project groups.
- A high degree of awareness of what other developers/project groups have worked with and are currently working on. Concurrent development on a low, detailed level requires more awareness than on a higher level. With concurrent working at the system level, knowing if/when an interface is being changed may be enough, whereas two developers working in the same module would probably like to know if/when the other starts working in the same file.

Awareness is mainly achieved through formal and informal meetings, e-mails between developers and through CM tools. In a distributed situation much of the information obtained through the informal meeting disappears, in addition, the formal meetings become less frequent and may be performed as telephone and video conferences rather than sitting around a table. Other aspects, such as cultural differences and time zones, also reduce the possibility of good communication. To increase the degree of awareness in a distributed situation it is therefore required that this reduced communication is compensated for by an adjusted working model and CM tool support.

An implemented process can for instance send e-mails under certain predefined conditions, one can see who created new versions, when and so on. However, the support for increased awareness is sensitive; for instance, too large a number of messages intended to increase awareness can hinder more than they help. That may be the case if small changes far down in a sub-project, result in messages being given to developers working higher up in the product structure.

Experience of concurrent development

Well defined tasks result in increased awareness in the sense that a person knows what the others should be working with; this is an important aspect with collaborations over long distances. It also reduces the risk for misunderstandings, e.g. due to cultural differences. However, it gives no "real" awareness through system support, i.e. what actually happened yesterday, or what is happening right now. By defining the tasks for each developer one does not decrease the reasons for concurrent work at lower levels either.

Another common technique is to allocate *exclusive areas of responsibility* (e.g. a set of files/modules). Especially during *new development* this is often possible, by having a suitable product structure, and to split the work between developers such that they become responsible for different parts of a product. Clear tasks and well-defined interfaces result in the work, particularly between locations, being done quite independently. Despite this, awareness is important and companies are now looking for a greater connection between development at different locations, with a possibility of seeing on a daily basis how work is progressing, rather than as now with a regular follow up of, for example, once a week. Since only one person is allowed to make changes in a file due to the division of responsibility, branches at the file level are rarely used.

During *maintenance* it is more difficult to make the same division of responsibility. Instead of breaking down associated tasks, e.g. change requests, into too small pieces which should be performed by different people in their respective areas of responsibility, it is better to enable a developer who notices a simple error in another persons module to, at least temporarily (possibly in an own branch), quickly correct the error in order to be able to test his own changes. This is particularly important when the developers are situated in different locations (although it may be more difficult to achieve). The person responsible for the module should then be informed that somebody else has made a proposal for a change, to be able to decide whether it should be integrated (merged) into the main branch.

When the division of responsibility is too great, it easily becomes too static and therefore limits the developers in what they can do. Some people also believe that the working mode according to "new development" outlined above is only caused by an inadequate support for distributed development and that it is a concession in order to get simpler CM management in the absence of branches. Instead of this, the normal working mode should be that every new functionality is implemented by a responsible person, who then implements the complete change in all affected files. It should also be stated that the maintenance of, and further development of a product are the greatest part of its life cycle (at least 80% according to some sources). Therefore the formulation of tools and processes just for new development rather than for further development/maintenance is a common, and in this respect, serious mistake.

To prohibit concurrent development at the file level for example, means that two developers will not be able to simultaneously make changes in the same file. In contrast, it is possible for the two to organize the work in sequence and implement their changes one after the other, i.e. there is dynamic locking of the files. Areas of responsibility result in a static division where (always) only one of the developers is allowed to make changes in a particular file. The strict allocation of exclusive areas of responsibility is thus a firmer synchronization for the developers than just prohibiting concurrent development at the corresponding level.

Some companies use a pure checkout/checkin model with locking at the file level and do not allow the creation of branches, even during maintenance. As several files often have to be changed to implement a complete change request, a "deadlock" between two developers may arise when they both want to change files which the other one has already locked. If one has locking without branches, a method to solve all arising deadlocks must be created. The most common method in local development is that the developer who has got the longest time before his deadline (manually) reverses his changes, after which the other developer can complete his change request. In some way (without direct tool support) the waiting developer becomes aware that he can continue, the previous changes are repeated and the change request is completed.

In many companies there is a fear of concurrent working at a lower level (module or file). It is unclear whether this fear is due to the fact that they want to keep the positive aspect of clear areas of responsibility ("only the one understanding the code can make the changes"), or whether it is due to a fear of loosing control of what is happening in the project and who does what. These fears are to a large part due to poor tool support for awareness.

One conclusion that can be made is that two sub-products (in a well-structured product with normal dependencies) can be developed more quickly and easily if they are both developed at the same location rather than at different locations. However, it is still an open question as to exactly what support is required by the CM tool to avoid this difference or even whether it is possible to avoid it. In addition to awareness support, which was discussed previously, many tools lack an overall picture of how the system as a whole is developed. For each individual file one can see which versions are included as well as the differences between them. In contrast, configurations (the product and the sub-product) are described in a configuration file and usually lack version graph of its own where one easily can see how they have developed. In addition, a version graph would clearly show if, for instance, a certain sub-product was at that moment being developed concurrently by several developers.

Practical guidance

- Replicate the information at the different development locations so that everyone can work towards a local server. Synchronize the replicates regularly and frequently, preferably automatically using tool support.
- Do not lock files to prevent simultaneous development, particularly if the lock restrains developers at other locations. Instead, make it possible for the developers to create a temporary branch themselves. The branch should then be merged with its original branch as quickly as possible and finished.
- Create a good product structure that gives an early, natural division of the work. A good structure decreases the need for branches. Where branches are still

being used, a good structure reduces the risk of conflict at the subsequent merge.

- Do not use too strict a division of work with people being responsible for individual files or modules. This easily leads to static and inflexible change management where several change requests affecting the same files, cannot be managed concurrently, particularly if the same change request may affect areas of responsibility in several places.

4.2 Change Management

The management from error report to actual changes must work even when the error reports as well as the actual changes are being made in a distributed organization. Figure 1 shows an example of an architecture for the reception, storage and division of a change request. The local support, for example in the form of the sales organization, receives error reports and put them in a central database. The variant with only one central support also exists, but a local department usually has a better level of contact with the customers, knows their installations better and can directly manage human errors, incorrect installations and such like. A central decision forum (e.g. CCB - Change Control Board) processes the different requests (e.g. by criticallity and urgency) and allocates them to the correct development location. The actual allocation can be implemented by anything from letting the request stay in the central database and just changing the status of an attribute, to physically sending the request to a local database. The development locations also deposit error reports in the central database, for instance when errors are discovered during a test.

What differs in the distributed architecture described compared to local development, is that the development locations are geographically separated. This may lead to:

- it becoming more difficult for (the central) decision authorities to meet as they consist of representatives from e.g. the development locations. If they meet

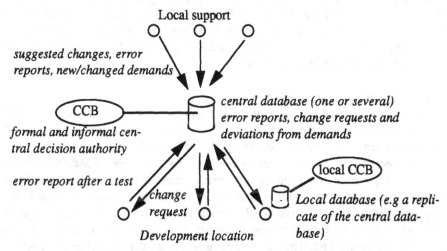

Fig. 1. The role of the database in change management

infrequently, it may result in a slower turn-around time for the projects and a slower reconnection of changes that have been done. To increase the meeting frequency, telephone conferences rather than real meetings are arranged. However, telephone conferences are not as effective and the risk of misunderstanding is greater.

- a need for local decision authorities as a supplement to the central ones to compensate for the point made above.
- that local databases are created. To increase the availability, replications of the central database are made.

Maintaining error corrections to a released product can be done in the products own maintenance branch. It is then important to also make those changes in the main development branch and possibly in other released products containing the same error. Additional products have to be checked to see whether a correction would be relevant. Also, with distributed development, when products are now owned and located at different sites, collaboration on the reuse of the actual error reports as well as the use of the final error corrections is important.

It is also important that each change refers back to (or starts out from) a bound configuration. Following the introduction of the change, a reference as to which configuration the change has been introduced should be included.

The management of changes is described in the CM plan and should follow a procedure defined therein, examples of such a procedure can be found in [Whi91]. With distributed development, it is possible that there are several decision forums with differing areas of responsibility and perhaps also at different locations (see above). The CM plan must clearly describe how these forums should cooperate and how much synchronization there should be between the local decision making authorities.

As we have previously concluded, the awareness of what is happening at other sites is reduced with distributed development and there is a risk that an individual does not feel as loyal to the products derived from other places as to their own. I.e. there is a strong need for team building and as much support as possible that makes it easy to follow the correct procedure, both in the form of a clear procedure outlined in the CM plan as well as in the form of tool support. This should e.g. be through awareness and strong support for the merge of different product branches whilst maintaining the ability to track what has already been done.

Experiences of change management

Change requests can be managed by both formal and informal decision forums. One example of a formal forum is the CCB. Examples of alternative names for error reports include: incident report, defect, trouble report, and anomaly.

It is common that a central database is used for error reports and many people stress the importance of a common error management system. However, distributed local databases for error reports also exist. The advantage of local databases is that they are easily accessible to both developers and project management. However, in the cases where the same request is stored centrally as well as locally there is a risk that they may be inconsistent. The risk is particularly great if it is unclear as to who is allowed to make changes in these databases. Automatically synchronized databases are rarely used.

Another risk is that the people responsible for the project keep their own error lists separate from the common database. Such lists tend not to be made public for other products, which of course impairs the possibility of cooperation and reuse. The best way of avoiding this is (again) by having a well-defined working mode and tools supporting the process.

An alternative to a central database is to divide the database into several parts, each managing different types of reports. For instance, one of the companies has four levels of databases: (1) "CCRP - Customer Complaint Report" which stores complaints from external customers via the sales organization, (2) "PMR - Product Maintenance Report" which manages error reports in released products, (3) "PPR - Pre-release Problem Report" which stores error reports in beta releases and (4) "CR - Change Request" which stores change requests.

There are several reasons for such a division, one being that the different databases can be implemented using different tools adapted to each developer, e.g. CCRP in LotusNotes for customers and sellers, PMR and PPR in Oracle, and CR using RCS for the developers. They may also have different distribution. CCRP and PMR are global whereas PPR and CR are internal. However, this results in a certain degree of overhead and it must be possible to fully track the movement of a message between the different databases.

Change management must follow strict routines. Errors discovered in a product will result in change requests in one or several components, at one or several places. It is also important to have clear rules as to who closes/finishes a change request when the error has been corrected. This is particularly important if the changes are performed in different locations, which makes it more difficult to control whether things that should have been done, have actually been done. It must be possible to follow up these matters and the status of each change must be made public. For instance, one of the companies have a www interface for their Oracle database to increase their accessibility via the intranet.

Another company has introduced support into their system to keep changes together belonging to the same change request. If a change request affects several modules, which therefore have to be modified (new versions created), a new version of a module cannot be used in a particular configuration until all of the modules are finished. In that way, the use of inconsistent module configurations is prevented.

In large projects, hierarchical CCB's may be necessary, i.e. central as well as local ones both being responsible for their own developed product. Only matters affecting several CCB responsibility areas are managed in the central CCB. This reduces the burden on the central CCB, which may find it difficult to have as frequent meeting as otherwise required.

Practical guidance

• Regularly check all opened, ongoing change requests and their status.

- The CM plan should describe the change management process. With distributed development it is particularly important to carefully describe how changes are finished (closed).
- In cases when relocated projects have their own CM plans, it is good to have a generic CM plan to which the project's CM plans refer, indicating differences from the generic CM plan.
- Avoid using several different databases for the same kind of change requests. For example, the product management and the software development should not have separate databases for error reports, and the project leaders should not have their own lists separate from the database.
- Let each change refer to the bound configuration in which the error was discovered as well as the configuration in which the change is implemented.

5 Conclusions and Implications for SCM Research

We have demonstrated, by using a number of examples, different situations when distributed development may arise in a company. We classified some different cases of distributed development and highlighted their specific merits. Furthermore, we have described different architectures and working processes. By using company interviews as the underlying information, we demonstrate guidelines and characterize the currently used methods, how they are being used at the different companies and their experiences in doing so. We believe that theses classifications and practical hints can be used by a company to better understand its situation and how the new requirements should be treated. For example can a self evaluation, based on the defined cases, be used as a first step towards the introduction of the suggested routines and tools into an existing environment.

We have also noticed that current tools not fully support distributed development. There is a strong connection between the different work situations described and the architectures. Here, the situation with distributed groups is problematic as, in practice, it requires the most advanced architecture, i.e., symmetric servers, which is not yet supported by existing CM tools. Thus in finding oneself in this situation, one is forced to manage it by partially manual methods.

It is evident that allowing concurrent work is key to efficient work in distributed development. However, the potential merge problems at the file level makes many companies use a more conservative strategy. There is thus a need for techniques to support merge in a better way that provides overview and flexibility during the process.

The trend seen is an increase of all cases of distributed development. Higher demands on lead-time due to shorter time-to-market implies higher demands on concurrent development. Many companies have, or are planning to, implement tool support for distributed development. To date companies have found themselves in different situations with geographically distributed developers. We see now, however, that distributed development is a more planned situation for a better use of resources independent where they are located.

Acknowledgments

This work has been supported by NUTEK, the Swedish National Board for Technical Development, and VI, the Association of Swedish Engineering Industries.

References

[AM97]   U. Asklund and B. Magnusson. A Case-Study of Configuration Management with ClearCase in an Industrial Environment. In Proceedings of SCM7 - International Workshop on Software Configuration Management, R. Conradi (Ed.), Boston, May 1997, LNCS, Springer Verlag.

[Ask99a]   Ulf Asklund. Distribuerad utveckling och Configuration Management. Project report nr V040073, The Association of Swedish Engineering Industries, http://www.vi.se

[Ask99b]   Ulf Asklund. Configuration Management for Distributed Development - Practice and Needs. Licentiate thesis, Dept. of Computer Science, Lund University, Sweden. 1999. http://www.cs.lth.se/~ulf

[Clear98]   http://www.rational.com/products/clearcase

[Con98]   http://www.continuus.com

[Fei91]   P. Feiler. Configuration Management Models in Commercial Environments. Technical report CMU/SEI-91-TR-7, Software Engineering Institute, Carnegie Mellon Institute, mars 1991.

[ISO95]   ISO 10 007 Quality management - Guidelines for configuration management, European Standard

[Mac]   http://www.macevolution.com/

[MIL]   MIL-STD-973, Military standard 17 April 1992; Notice of change MIL-STD-973 13 January 1995

[PVCS99]   http://www.intersolv.com

[Team94]   TeamWare user's guides, Sun Microsystem, 1994.

[Whi91]   David Whitgift. Method and Tools for Software Configuration Management. ISBN 0-471-92940-9. John Wiley & Sons. 1991.

Applying Software Configuration Management in Web Sites Development: A Case Study

Matteo Leoni[1] , Michele Trainotti[1] and Andrea Valerio[2]

[1]WebPower Networking Solutions s.n.c., via F. Filzi 10/2
38060 Aldeno (TN) - Italy
Matteo.Leoni@webpower.net
Michele.Trainotti@webpower.net
[2] COCLEA s.n.c. via Magazol, 32
38068 Rovereto (TN) - Italy
Andrea.Valerio@coclea.it

Abstract. Due to the need of making quick business and reducing the time-to-market, a small enterprise does not generally rely on solid and highly methodological software engineering bases. However, the necessity for clear and replicable methodologies for electronic archiving of the history of software products has been individuated by WebPower as a milestone for achieve better quality and satisfy the increasing number of customers. To this purpose, a Process Improvement Experiment, co-founded by the European Union and aimed at the introduction of Configuration Management in the software development process (mainly Web sites), has been conducted. The experiment will be briefly outlined and some first results presented and commented.

1   Introduction

The recent explosion of Internet and the fact that every day more and more people and organisations are connected to the global network have produced an incredible growth of the information technology and telecommunications fields. The market constantly demands better services and higher quality, and the software companies respond with new or modified products. The software life cycle has to be controlled in all its phases, in particular in the *delivery* and *maintenance* activities.

Configuration Management (CM) is a solution, consisting in the application to the software process of procedures, standards and practices, for monitoring and managing the evolution of the product. It can thus be part of a total quality program, for example in the framework of ISO 9000 certification. The benefits of CM can be fully expressed also when the software product is an Internet-based application such as a Web site, etc. Actually this market and the related architecture are very dynamic and, due to the lack of global standardisation, increasingly complex. Moreover, each product is tailored on the customer needs and often requires a frequent update.

WebPower s.n.c. is a small Italian company involved in this Internet-related business. Despite the company dimension, the management had grown the opinion that a more dynamic response and better satisfaction of the customers can be achieved through better software engineering practices, and as a first milestone, in the use of proper configuration management methods and tools. In this paper we report on the SPICE project, a Process Improvement Experiment (PIE) co-founded by the European Union and aimed to the introduction of configuration management in the development and maintenance process of a typical WebPower product.

2 Initial Context and Execution of the Experiment

The software development process of WebPower is highly dynamic and based on the skill of the single programmer. The programming languages and implementation methodologies are very heterogeneous and problem-specific; frequently, a more traditional top-down approach (C and HTML languages) coexist with the event-driven object oriented one (C++ and Java). The resulting code is thus very often *scarcely documented, scarcely traceable* and *heterogeneous*. In general, it lacks a proper action plan for the projects and there is not an archive of historical information concerning the evolution of products.

The SPICE project is a direct response to the lack of well organised software process tracking and monitoring activities; it aims to increase the product quality, decrease the development and maintenance costs and time, and obtain a better exploitation of human resources.

The project was studied to be minimally invasive: the starting development environment and daily practices were analysed to provide the frame in which to insert a suitable CM method. Various methods proposed in literature, together with the consideration of the guidelines identified by different standards (IEEE [1,2] and SEI CMM [3]) were considered. An adequate set of CM guidelines was produced, prescribing only the strictly necessary requirements for the achievement of our goals. A reasoned analysis of the market, lead to the choice of Visual Source Safe (VSS) by Microsoft as CM tool. It is based on the check-out/check-in model where the files, grouped as "projects" into directories, are the basic items.

Suitable training was then started; it was crucial for the experiment since it can motivate people, presenting benefits/advantages of the new techniques and tools. Subsequently, the application of CM to a typical WebPower project, the development of a complete Web-site for a company that wishes to open a commercial activity on the net, was started. A suitable project layout was defined in order to match the requirements of the CM tool: in particular we found the need for a uniform naming convention of the various basic project units (components) and for the directories where the project will be stored. The application need to be considered in term of interacting subsystems framed in a tree structure. The definition documents were introduced in the system with the check-out/check-in paradigm.

The team worked to the translation of the design documents into executable code with the same procedures, checking-out the assets they have to work on in their private environment and re-introducing them in the public space with the check-in procedure. As a result, each time a new artefact or a new version was ready, it was commented and versioned in the system and we have a complete trace of the evolution and of the main activities carried out during the project.

3 Analysis of the Results

During the experiment, a continuous monitoring based on the Goal-Question-Metrics proposed by Basili [4] has been conducted. We present here a first analysis of the collected data and of the achieved results.

As expected, an extra effort was necessary in the execution of the CM procedures: we can estimate in 20-30% the initial overload given by the combined effect of the introduction of the CM procedures and tool. This could be due to the learning process and to need to prepare the naming schema, the archive structure and setting up the environment for the use of the tool. In the design phase we highlighted a slightly less incidence in the performance of the process, and in the implementation phase the CM procedures had an influence estimated less than a 10% of the total effort employed.

Even if the tool demonstrated to be sufficiently robust and efficient, we have to argue a possible deficiency in handling big-sized Web site projects since these objects differ from traditional software products for which VSS is created. In a Web site we have in fact a small number of software components and many pages of information, both static and dynamic, possibly interacting through a database. The effects of the PIE on the organisational environment have been limited and confined to the baseline project where CM was experimented. SPICE showed that CM introduces a few changes in the daily work, in particular considering the new practices for the planning and recording the relevant activities influencing the product under development. These include the definition of the project structure, the identification of the configuration items and the use of the support tool for storing and retrieving the artefacts.

A significant aspect regards the importance of a formal definition of roles and responsibilities for what concerns the CM. The IEEE 1042 standard indicates in details role and responsibilities that have to be considered, but in a small organisation we must consider that very often there are no resources that can be allocated full-time on CM activities. That is why a distributed mechanism for responsibilities was implemented: each people were responsible for one or more specific activities, and a centralised control intervention was required only in specific and critic situations.

We found fundamental to grow up self-consciousness in each person of its role and responsibility in the organisation, since the software process is still mainly based on the work of the people. The impact on the culture of the people involved in the experiment was quite relevant; the core of CM can be synthesised with the words 'plan what you want/must do and record what you plan and do'.

This approach has a great impact on a small sized firm; the schedule is often very strict, and support activities (including planning and documenting activities) are seldom carried out completely. CM imposes a way of work based on planning and recording every activity and this is a remarkable benefit we feel we have achieved in this experiment.

Another important lesson we learnt relates to the motivation of people. CM is a support practice that could be seen as an overhead by personnel, in a way similar to metrics and measures. There could be resistance to its adoption and this can negatively influence the success of the project. In our context we acted through the motivation of people and the definition of a CM method adequate to our context, strictly centred on the objectives we had. Personnel reported during the experiment that they gained a broader perspective on the software process. The SPICE staff has grown specific competencies and expertise on software engineering and, in particular, on CM issues, important achievement, in a small company, where the production and its rhythms are the primary concern. Besides, the introduction of CM stimulates people to think to their daily routine, to better structure and organise it. The personnel are the most important resource of WebPower and a strong motivation and involvement of it is a necessary condition for the success of the organisation.

We think these key lessons learnt during the project are an important knowledge source for other small and medium size organisations in Europe that want to introduce CM in their process. Even if they cannot be generalised, the experiences we made represent a starting point for others, and some hints and suggestions are likely applicable to their situations.

4 Conclusions

Some results of a Process Improvement Experiment aimed at the introduction in WebPower, a small Italian software company, of Configuration Management (CM) practices and tools, have been presented. The impact of the experiment on the organisation of WebPower has been analysed and described.

The next step in SPICE will be the quantitative analysis of the information gathered during the experimentation, deepening a cost-benefit evaluation, too.

These figures will allow deciding how the achieved results, lessons learnt and the new acquired tool VSS will be integrated inside the software process of WebPower.

After the completion of the experiment, the maintenance process for the product developed during the experiment, will be monitores in order to analyse the effects of configuration management as a support method and tool in the medium term.

Acknowledgements

The SPICE project is co-financed by the European Commission under the framework of the Esprit ESSI PIE (reference: 27418).

References

1. 'IEEE Standard for Software Configuration Management Plans', 1990, IEEE/ANSI Standard 828-1990.
2. 'IEEE Guide to Software Configuration Management', 1987, IEEE/ANSI Standard 1042-1987
3. Paulk, M., Curtis, B., Chrissis, M., Weber, C., 'Capability Maturity Model for Software – version 1.1', Technical Report, Software Engineering Institute, 1993.
4. Victor Basili, 'Software Modeling and Measurement: the Goal-Question-Metric Paradigm', *Computer Science technical report CS-TR-2956*, University of Maryland, 1992.

Software Configuration Management Risk Analysis before Relocating the Porting of Product's Family

Marjan Simonič[1], Jozsef Györkös[2], Ivan Rozman[2]

[1] Hermes SoftLab, Litijska 51, 1000 Ljubljana, Slovenia
Marjan.Simonic@hermes.si
[2] University of Maribor, Faculty of Electrical Engineering
And Computer Science, Smetanova 17,
2000 Maribor, Slovenia
{Gyorkos, I.Rozman}@uni-mb.si

In a real life example selected from a number of experiences that HERMES SoftLab has had, we show what major challenges software development companies face when establishing a virtual enterprise due to the need to relocate part of the porting of product's family. The analyses of what we have experienced to be the major Software Configuration Management (SCM) related risks are given, why sometimes such efforts fail, and what the key factors are to success with guidelines for addressing such SCM risks. We point out major problems that often arise but also advantages of doing business this way. We show that a late transition from one to more dislocated sites brings additional challenges when not planned correctly from the beginning. In this we assume the usage of a modern configuration management tool.

1 Introduction

Software engineering is still one of the most rapidly growing industrial areas. The lack of skilled engineers has become one of the biggest issues in the leading software engineering countries over the past few years (Presently, just the USA has a need for approximately 300.000 software engineers as mentioned in [17]).

One of the solutions to this problem is to bring into their business contracts foreign companies that take over parts of the software development and maintenance. Because doing this may also significantly reduce costs due to a cheaper labor force in countries like India it is of no surprise that more and more companies are looking for ways of establishing a so-called virtual enterprise. An example of such virtual enterprise is depicted in figure 1.

However, if this is really such a great thing to do, then why isn't it a common practice and not just a trend for doing business? The answer is straightforward. There are many serious risks associated with doing business this way.

The processes a company or a team has developed might be extremely well suited for their current needs, but in this new situation, they are probably largely inadequate. They can be even among the reasons for a future failure unless some serious changes take place. Majority of companies usually starts working on a project at a single location without much thinking about the possible ways for the future expansions of their business. Therefore, adapting them to geographically dispersed locations may cause them many unexpected problems.

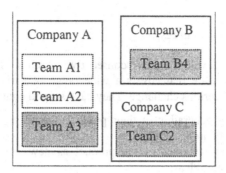

Fig. 1. *Teams A3, B4,* and *C2* from the respective *companies A, B,* and *C* work on the same joined project. They have agreed upon their roles, and might even use a single organization chart. Regardless of how far apart the teams (companies) are they could constitute successful virtual enterprise

Based on the experience that HERMES SoftLab has had, we learned that the importance of software configuration management (SCM) can never be stressed enough as a key factor in the successful transition of work to relocated sites. In the following sections, we use a common real life example from HERMES SoftLab to show what the SCM related risks are, what troubles can be expected on both sides, and how to avoid them.

2 Related Works

Traditionally, SCM related risk analysis has been associated with the introduction of new CM tools to a company. Susan Dart and Joe Krasnov in their paper [7] present potential problems based on a number of experiences. There are several works: [4], [10], ... that discuss *parallel development across distributed environments* in general or in a specific way. However, these papers usually focus on the technology rather than presenting complete CM solutions with associated activities. The authors of paper [7] have shown that the percentage of technology-related issues is as low as 10-25%. Mostly they also assume that we start applying the CM solution right from the beginning when no or possibly, a simple version control tool was used.

We focus on risks associated with such a decision to relocate a part of the software development and maintenance when a company has already set up a modern CM tool and CM processes but only for one site.

3 A Real Life Challenge

Let's describe an example of an increasingly common situation that many successful software development companies find themselves in increasingly often.

3.1 Lack of Human Resources

A company that has developed many consecutive versions of a successful product family of system software that covers a wide range of variations of a number of platforms must face a serious challenge. They have several contractual obligations:

– support of existing generation of their products on all supported platforms with patch releases for a number of years,
– introduction of new releases of the product as new versions of the pertinent operating systems are released,
– releases of the product on some brand new platforms.

Nevertheless, they also have to think about the future. They need to start working on the next generation of the product's family soon enough to stay competitive in the marketplace of the future.

Their major problem is that they do not have enough available human resources to do it all. What should they do?

3.2 Possible Innovative Solution

They may consider moving parts of their business to some other company. All together, it is also a chance to lower their costs by choosing a company from India, for example.

They can achieve that by gradually transferring all current generation-related work in order to be able to focus completely on the development of the next generation product. However, they first have to make sure the transition can be done successfully. So the best idea would be to start porting the product to a newer version of an already supported operating system (OS) and only when successfully completed, the rest could follow. Thus, the engineers from India would be able to become familiar with the product's source code, SCM, existing processes, the product itself, etc. After the first release, the probability of failure would be significantly reduced. We can look at it also as some kind of trial project. Successful completion would be the key for a long-term relationship between companies.

Until all the current generation tasks are not completely transferred to this relocated site, the development and maintenance will take place in a way simultaneously. While the off-site team works on a product port to support the new OS release on platform X, our company would still need to be engaged on several simultaneous projects. For example, porting to some new platform Y, preparing patches with fixes of escalated or otherwise critical bugs. The last stage would be to completely transfer current generation-related responsibilities to this company and focus exclusively on a product's new generation.

3.3 Risks

Parallel development across two or even more dislocated sites, distributed work, and parallelism may seriously endanger the project. Since such transfers would entail many risks, both companies need to make sure it's done as smooth as possible and certainly without any negative impact on their customers. In the following section, we analyze SCM-related risk.

4 SCM Risk Analysis

At that point, those in the company would need to ask themselves many questions. We believe that when preparing for distributed ports, special attention needs to be paid to the following major SCM-related issues listed below. We analyze them with the purpose of describing why you have to consider these issues most of all. We give guidelines what both companies should do in order to reduce SCM risks and how to accomplish the relocation of the porting as smoothly as possible. We show that there are many more SCM risks than purely technological.

4.1 Technological Issues

Undoubtedly, they have to raise technological issues first. They have to be sure that their CM solution supports multiple-site capabilities. Even if it does not, there is still large probability nowadays that there is an available, add-on product from their CM solution vendor that should add this additional functionality without a wider negative impact.

As discussed in a number of papers: [1], [2], ... automated CM tools have been accepted as a necessity for software development enterprises. Thus, let's assume the company has been using such tool when developing the current generation of its product's family. Let's assume it supports distributed development teams as well. Therefore, we can avoid dealing with serious technological problems when preparing the transition in the case of the example using simple version control solutions.

Searching for Solution. However, the road to success is still not clear. Below is a list of a few questions that should definitely be asked:

- Would the way both of us used to do it need to be changed?
- Could we expect repository synchronization problems?
- What other infrastructure would need to be set up in place on both sites?
- How the tool supports parallel development of files shares with other distributed sites? Is simultaneous development in the not-owned branches allowed?

Unfortunately, as we can see, it is not just enough to know that the tool we have supports simultaneous parallel development across multiple sites. We have to understand how this is supported and what could be other potential technology-related risks. Authors of the paper [7] have shown that the percentage of technology-related issues is as low as 10-25%. Therefore, one has to focus on mitigation of a whole set of risks and not just the obvious - technological ones.

4.2 Additional SCM Customization / Automation Scripts

However, having a perfect CM tool won't just make distributing the ports painless. Modern CM tools are designed to fit into wide variety of environments. Since nearly every organization is different, it is simply not possible for vendors to develop such CM solutions that would not require any customizations, or the implementation of additional scripts.

In order to automate often-repeated manual tasks, a company might have invested a lot of effort. Very often, such scripts, usually in a form of triggers or pre/post-operations, become almost built-in features of their CM technology where no one remembers what might actually be behind it. And even if they have it very well documented, there are still plenty of possibilities that the scripts may be either machine or platform dependent or have some other site specifics built in.

Solution. Our experiences have proven that even careful checking in advance does not secure a smooth transition. Testing of tools in simulated new distributed working environment is the only secure way to go. Of course, it may very well be that everything is up and running shortly after an intervention or two, but here we have to stress the importance of proper design and implementation. Just a little more time spent when preparing such automations can save as a lot of troubles, if the distributed environment might be required in the future. Although this is very common statement in software development theory, it seems to be quite natural to overlook potential future usage in order to have it done just a bit sooner.

4.3 Build Automation

A basic message from the previous section can be applied to this almost literally. It is rarely the case that only manual builds take place. Especially in the case of parallel development on several platforms at once, there is often a need for nightly builds, thought this is usual in other development situations as well. On top of that, special care has to be taken in establishing and maintaining baselines, sometimes even automatic merges. For these purposes, special scripts still have to be implemented regardless of what build or release management our CM technology has integrated. Since with modern complex software products is often the case, several compilers, linkers and other tools have to be run before a complete product is built. It may be possible that a complete build process is even distributed over several different machines.

An Example. The contract company an ocean or two away wants to start with upgrade of some product to a newer version of the operation system. The first thing to do is to reproduce the build of the product on an already supported OS version. By repeating the build, they can be at least sure that whatever problems they might experience later during the build, the process itself is not a cause of them.

Possibilities. They can decide to do remote builds and use the same old build machines or configure their own machines to be able to execute the builds locally. Both options have some positive and negative sides. When settling for the remote option, there are plenty of chances that something might go wrong. The telephone lines might be down. Something could go wrong with one of the remote machines. As it might be the case that there is a 10-hour time difference, there is practically no way that somebody could reboot such a machine. The only thing they can do is wait. Even without mentioning other scenarios, it is clear that completely depending on remote site hardware is a serious option only in very special cases. So, what is left? Build environment just has to be replicated.

Risks. When planning for replication of the existing development environment arise many risks associated with the build process arise because of the "site" dependencies (different machine names and/or configurations, special build users/permissions are required, etc). As one could note, they closely relate to some risks related to configuration identification.

4.4 Packaging

It is extremely rare that developers are allowed to be creative when preparing packages nowadays. Almost every platform has its own specific packaging tool. Therefore, several extra *configuration* files are required to make it work. Binaries, documentation and other product files often need to be at special locations before the packaging can be started. In order to speed up this process or often to automatically produce additional information about the produced packages, many companies develop or sometimes even buy additional tools. The output of such *packaging* tools may be much more than a newly created packages at a specified location. Packages may be automatically archived, baselined, etc. Extra web pages with information about the contents of the packages, the dates of creation, the configuration specification, Release notes, etc may be created.

Risks. The more complex the software to be ported is and the more refined process automation is, the more careful we have to be when preparing to replicate the whole SCM environment at multiple sites. Again, the reasons are hidden environmental dependencies, not enough documented descriptions of customized processes or, at the bottom end, the absence or the turnover rate of knowledgeable engineers.

However, there is always a way to ignore the existing infrastructure, processes, tools, etc, and to focus on the development of new processes, add-on tools, and scripts at each new location in the virtual enterprise. Unfortunately, this would require significant effort, not to mention that virtual enterprises prefer to have common processes across all geographic locations, which has numerous advantages especially when long-term relationships are planned.

4.5 Configuration Identification

We believe that proper configuration identification is an extremely critical activity. The company that is mentioned in this report should worry about it the most especially in the earliest stages of transition. Among other things, a successful replication of the development environment completely relies upon it. Only a 100 % replication is the guarantee for success.

Risks. We have to remember that the company is not at the beginning of preparing SCM strategy. Configuration items (CI) had been selected a long time ago before they even considered establishing such virtual enterprise. However, all they had had to worry about at that time was single location development. We all know that a selection of CIs should not be any different when development takes place at one site than in the case of multiple sites. Nevertheless, in practice, it is still hardly the case. From our experience, we learned that major CIs-related risks are as follows:

1. Some engineers tend to avoid using CM tool whenever possible and secretly stick with at least a few *private files*. Especially, various source files needed for creating different product documentation are often critical! Before going distributed, you have to ensure nothing is missing in a shared software development library (SDL) repository. Such files might have gotten by unnoticed before but now the problem will get high visibility.
2. Least attention is usually paid to all the *tools we need to make the product*: compilers, linkers, translators, utilities, ... and to summarize, a bunch of various, often publicly available programs. These tools and utilities were often installed on machines years ago and they are taken for granted now. From our experience with major software companies, such information is often lost or not evident enough, especially when talking about noncommercial utilities. When dealing with only one site it would hardy become an issue since backup, nearness of other installed machines and concentration of knowledgeable engineers is often a guarantee for solving such problems quickly. However, when preparing for relocated ports, it is no longer a simple issue.
3. Due to the complexity of SCM when dealing with product's family the following CI-related issues are often raised:

   - versioning schema of the product's files,
   - versioning schema of the product itself,
   - naming conventions for the various identifiers, baselines, branches,
   - agreement regarding the locations for storing new files in shared SDL repository.

Now, all that becomes much more visible than it used to be. Good documentation, especially a software configuration management plan (SCMP) is crucial. Unless there is a clear common understanding of how to handle all that and availability of useful documentation, both sites will face serious problems for a while. Organizing phone/video conferences whenever one of the above issues is not clear will not bring long term success. When the new company starts messing around in a now shared SDL repository without a good enough understanding of the concepts previously used, it may suddenly become pretty confusing for both sides.

4.6 Configuration Control (CC) with File Merges

Since the development on both sites will take place simultaneously for some time until the current generation of the product's family is completely taken over by contract company, this topic becomes a serious challenge.

There are several risks associated with it. Certainly, we would not like to be fixing the same bugs or implementing the same enhancements repeatedly just because the code was not in the same branch, for example.

However, there is no need to look at the CC and file merges much differently as done before. Unless there are some technological issues that would require them to do it differently from how they used to when there was only one site, nothing needs to change. Of course, a little more coordination would be required. However, otherwise, all the processes may exist as they presently are. Our experience has shown that when all parties understand and follow the existing procedures for changes, there is very little to be afraid of, as modern CM solutions offer good support for CC.

Merging. When both sites have made changes to the same file, the merging has to be initiated and performed according to previously agreed procedure, which would still need to be defined. Since [4] gives an extensive in-depth analysis of possible solutions and even methodologies on how to solve this issue we believe that it should not be too hard to find the right solution that would suit ones needs.

Change Configuration Board (CCB). Although the contract company may even take over all port-related work, both companies will still need to take part in deciding what has to be implemented and sometimes even how to do it. As porting software is about changes, both sides have to put a lot effort in making the changing process as efficient as possible.

Poor CC Implementation Risks. If the procedures for configuration control, branching and merges were not properly implemented before, it could cause a lot of pain to both sides now. Although the problems may not have been that visible in the past, a confused history of the files' changes and irregular merges will become serious challenges when trying to coordinate further work. The more previous development history, baselines and merges are confusing, the less chances are that both companies will be able to proceed with success in the long run.

Again, detailed SCM plans and/or other documentation are necessary. Strictly following procedures during everyday activities is extremely important as well. Having that entirely in mind will enable both companies to work efficiently. Especially the one that is not yet familiar with the product will work much easier and consequently cheaper, thus making virtual enterprise a success story.

4.7 Configuration Status Accounting (CSA)

Through an efficient CSA, all essential and important information regarding SCM activities are distributed to the involved staff. Making smart decisions may become much easier with the proper CSA. Lab and test environments need a rapid and simple change process. The difference between dealing with one or multiple sites can become a serious obstacle for the existing implementation of CSA. We have to think about making changes to the existing solution to make it work transparently on both sites.

Since CSA solutions often include World Wide Web publishing on the companies Intranets, they have to find a way both to integrate the Intranets and to overcome companies' firewalls. Although there are first signs of commercial solutions available on the market that promise to overcome all such problems, some effort still has to be put to make it work with the existing CM solution.

4.8 Configuration Audits (CA) and Reviews

Primarily CA should make sure that all CIs are present and available in baselines. As the analysis in configuration identification section has shown, it is one of the most critical potential risks for not being able to reproduce the build. When preparing for relocated ports, a careful CA should be among first things to do.

Since this issue will become increasingly important as distributed parallel development proceeds, a substantial effort needs to be invested in assuring the future reproducibility of the builds and packages.

4.9 Configuration Management Plan (CMP)

The CMP would have to be upgraded with several topics. Here we want to mention defining a set of new procedures regarding who should authorize what, when and how.

All standards related to CM clearly specify that planning is the key to success. But there are plenty of companies out there that still believe that preparing a CMP is waste of time and money though they may have the most powerful set of CM tools. Since different certification programs require some sort of documented CMP, many of those companies have prepared brief documentation just to fulfil the formal requirements in some way. However, the quality of the CMP and existing processes is really challenged when a company is about to start such transition.

4.10 Additional Soft Issues

Here we would like to stress the importance of some other soft issues that we have to mention as well. These are: organizational, infrastructure, politics, process reengineering, environment, people management, and cultural issues.

Besides technical issues, we have analyzed here all but the people and cultural issues so far. We have also shown that when preparing for transition from one to multiple sites we have to deal much more with existing processes, environment and infrastructure than solely technological issues.

People. Here we have very interesting situation regarding people management. By transferring less complex work to some other company, engineers will become more motivated since they can focus furthermore on creative development rather than repetitive ports of an existing product without major changes.

Culture. When talking about culture, we just cannot ignore the extreme differences between the culture in the US and India, for example. We do not want to give any personal opinions judging this difference since it is the task of ethnology, but there are probably quite a number companies out there who are confronted with it. Anyhow, besides India there are plenty of other countries that match the USA culturally much closer. So, if this seems to you as an issue, try Slovenia.

5 Solution with Further Research/Work

In the previous section, we identified SCM-related risks that a company faces when preparing for relocation the porting of a product's family. SEI Risk Taxonomy at that point suggests that we estimate the likelihood of an event with losses as negative consequences associated with that event, where risk exposure is the probability times the loss. By calculating the risk exposure on some understandable scale, like dollars it is much easier to justify spending a certain amount of money on risk mitigation. Unfortunately, the estimating of useful probabilities is an extremely difficult task even for an experienced SCM expert. Nevertheless, the figures depend completely on the specifics of the case. Our analysis has shown:

- major SCM risks arise because our SCM solution was planned for single site development exclusively,
- activities were not implemented strictly enough.

What we would like to stress here is the importance of an early enough, proactive behavior. However, things are sometimes unpredictable. Occasionally companies will still face the presented challenge unprepared. At that point, we would like to recommend the methodology described below for addressing SCM risks in such case.

5.1 Evaluate the Implemented SCM Solution

This would include many thins. First, site specifics have to be determined followed by assessment of technological issues and the state of automation. Then the company would have to check available SCM related documentation, the maturity of its processes in order to determine to what extent it are prepared for such a move including the available human resources to support it. Preparing a thorough questionnaire that each involved employee should complete, estimating the current state of SCM, and listing possible problems would be a great thing to do. By doing all that, the company gains an in-depth understanding of the challenge and is ready to proceed to next steps of addressing the SCM risks.

5.2 Evaluate Contract Company

Since both parties matter, we have to determine the suitability of the candidate company. From our experience, we learned that it has to do equally with company's maturity, the CM awareness of its employee, and established communication than just technical issues. Of course, we all know that programming skills of its engineers, familiarity with product's family to be ported, or experience with the CM tool that we are using count even more. However, do not neglect the former criteria.

5.3 Determine Critical Weaknesses

Based on the results from the questionnaire, individual expertise, and past experiences, the most critical weaknesses can be determined. The purpose of doing that is to determine what might go wrong. Moreover, in its optimum, we would like to estimate the probabilities of happening so. When this is known, we can focus on what the reasons are for potential problems, showstoppers or even failures and we can focus on risk mitigation.

5.4 Risk Mitigation

Risk identification, evaluation and awareness means a lot but it just won't solve the problems. Proper risk mitigation is required. Risk mitigation can be considered as the foundation for change. Deciding what has to be changed to make the future virtual enterprise successful (enable parallel distributed development, etc) is as crucial here as the question of how to do it. In a way paper [7] and partially [2] address necessary steps to take. Paper [7] describes a typical life cycle of risk mitigation as follows:

1. Mitigation assignment process
2. Mitigation implementation and risk tracking process
3. Mitigation rejection process
4. Risk completion process

However, it is not enough that only one party is involved in this process. It should concern both parties. They should work together to prepare the best solution for future CM solution of the virtual enterprise. The best way to look at it is to treat it as an opportunity for improvement in general.

6 Conclusions

Although modern SCM tools are very powerful, the presented transition still brings many challenges because technology is not the only thing that matters here. This paper, based on several real-life experiences from Hermes SoftLab, shows that establishing such virtual enterprises from the SCM point of view is not always straightforward especially when it was not planned from the beginning. Major risks arise because of the lack of planning, the absence of defined procedures and especially poor documentation. The more complex a product's family from development/maintenance point of view is, the more carefully you need to identify and evaluate potential risks of failures followed by the mitigation of identified risks.

However, if the tools provide a strong support for shared parallel development across dislocated sites and transition of work is executed step by step with activities carefully planned and performed in a systematic manner, we would recommend it as a good thing to do. Especially, if long-term business relationship is planned.

References

1. Continuus/CM: Change Management for Software Development, Available via the World Wide Web at http://www.continuus.com
2. Susan Dart, "Adopting An Automated Configuration Management Solution", Conference: Software Technology Center '94, Utah, 1994
3. NASA Software Technology Division, NASA Software Configuration Management Guidebook, 1995
4. Brad Appleton, Stephen Berczuk, Ralph Cabrera, and Robert Orenstein, Branching Patterns for Parallel Software Development, PLoP '98 conference, 1998
5. Continuus/CM: Successfully Managing the Rapidly Changing Corporate Intranet, Available via World Wide Web at http://www.continuus.com
6. Martin Cagan, Untangling Configuration Management Mechanism and Methodology in CM Systems, Continuus Software Corporation
7. Susan Dart and Joe Krasnov, Experiences in Risk Mitigation with Configuration Management, Continuus Software Corporation, 4th SEI Risk Conference, Nov, 1995
8. Martin Cagan, An Architecture for Change Management: Mechanisms for the Support of Process-Based Software Configuration Management", Continuus Software Corporation, 1994.
9. Continuus/CM: Managing Corporate Intranet, Available via World Wide Web at http://www.continuus.com
10. MacKey, Stephen A., The State of the Art in Concurrent, Distributed CM, proceeding of the 1995 International Workshop on Computer-Aided Software Engineering, 1995
11. Susan Dart, Concepts in Configuration Management Systems, Software Engineering Institute, Carnegie Mellon University
12. C. Jones, Assessment and Control of Software Risks, Prentice-Hall, 1994.
13. Nadine M. Bounds, Susan A. Dart, Configuration Management (CM) Plans: The Beginning to Your CM Solution, Software Engineering Institute, Carnegie Mellon University, July, 1993
14. International Standard: ISO 10007, Quality management – Guidelines for configuration management
15. IEEE Std. 828 - Standard for Software Configuration Management Plans
16. Capability Maturity Model, Carnegie Mellon University
17. Tausende fehlen, Fachkraftemangel: Informatiker sind dringend gesucht, Suddeutsche Zeitung, Nr. 39 / Seite 27, February 17th, 1999

Why Do Some Mature Organizations Not Use Mature CM Tools?

Ivica Crnkovic

Mälardalen University, Department of Computer Engineering,
S-721 23 Västerås, Sweden
ivica.crnkovic@mdh.se

Abstract: This paper presents a case-study of a Configuration Management (CM) tool evaluation. The evaluation was performed in a company with a long tradition of using CM tools. Although several generations of CM tools have been developed internally, different reasons led to a decision not to use CM tools internally developed but to buy a tool available on the market. A detailed evaluation was performed on the basis of the company's experience. The investigation procedure, the criteria for the evaluation, and the results are presented in the paper. The results of the evaluation, taken to the final selection of a tool, have shown the superiority of one tool, but another tool, considerably inferior to the first has been chosen. Why? This paper analyses the background of the decision and points out the factors, not always of a technical nature, which significantly influence d the decision, and which are sometimes forgotten by the tool suppliers.

1 Introduction

ABB Automation Products, a $340-million company, is responsible for developing automation products within ABB and employs 2000 people. The automation products encompass several families of industrial process-control systems including both software and hardware.

The main characteristics of the products are reliability, high quality and compatibility. These features are results of responses to the main customers requirements: The customers need stable products, running around the clock year after year, which can be easily upgraded without impact on the existing process. The requirements on the high quality and long life of the products have made corresponding demands on Configuration Management. Indeed, the company has a long tradition in using CM. Several CM tools, internally developed, have been used systematically for more than 15 years. Three major CM products have been developed and used on different platforms, VAX/VMS, Unix and Windows NT. The Unix and NT products, SDE (Software Development Environment) and WinSDE (SDE for Windows) are compatible and very similar, yet with certain differences in functions, with GUI and API adjusted to the development platforms [4], [5]. A stable and accurate CM process has been established during the 15 years of using, developing and maintaining the CM tools.

In recent years customers' requirements and development circumstances have changed dramatically. In addition to standard requirements, customers have presented new requirements related to standard products, and demand the possibility of integrating of real-time process systems with office and administration tools. The Web and Internet technology has also placed new demands on the products. These factors and other changes in software and hardware technology [1] have introduced a new paradigm in the development process: From complete proprietary monolithic systems with internally developed hardware and software, the development process has focused on the use of standard and de-facto standard components, outsourcing and COTS (commercial-off-the-shelf). The final products are no longer closed monolith systems, but are instead component-based products which can be integrated with other products available on the market.

The changes in the development process and the importance of the time-to-market factor have particular influence on the CM process and its support. The company has no resources to develop and maintain tools which do not directly belong to the core interest of the development. The outsourcing of development of some parts of the products has introduced new requirements with regard to CM tools. The subcontract-partner companies wish to use the same CM tool as the main company, but wish, at the same time they to use a standard CM tool, established on the market. The internally developed tool may be a very good solution for internal development, but it can be too complicated and too difficult for external developers.

Although the theoretical aspects of CM technology have not been dramatically changed in recent years, CM tools have been significantly improved. They are more user-friendly, more closely integrated with other tools, faster, etc. The general awareness of CM issues has also increases, and a number of new CM tools, or tools related to the CM process have appeared. These reasons have together introduced the management to decide to replace internally developed CM tools with a new CM tool available on the market.

This paper describes the evaluation process, the decision taken and an analysis of the decisions. Chapter 2 describes the evaluation project and the evaluation criteria. Chapter 3 shows the results of the evaluation of certain tools in comparison with the internal tool. Chapter 4 presents the decision, partially based on the results of the evolution, but also based on other factors. The decision and the characteristics of the tools, in relation to the decisions, are discussed. The decision indicates that some other factors, different from the pure CM functions, do play a significant role in the selection of a CM tool.

2 The Evaluation Process

The evaluation of CM tools was a continuous process in the company even during the development of internal CM tools. Existing CM tools and methods have been compared with internal CM tools and processes, especially when new versions of the tools have been developed. When the decision to use of a commercial tool was made, a new evaluation process was started. The activities concerned are managed within the frame of a project.

2.1 The Evaluation Project

Several groups of developers, the management and the quality assurance group, were involved in the process. The goal of the project was to find the most suitable CM and Defect Tracking tool and to propose its deployment. In this paper, only issues related to CM will be presented.

The project members were selected from the CM group, a group which is responsible for the CM process in the company, and which has previously developed the company's CM tools

The tasks of the project groups were:

- Write the requirement specification for the CM tools;
- Investigate the market and find the most appropriate CM tools;
- Collect experiences of using specific CM tools from other companies and other sources;
- Evaluate the most interesting tools;
- Write the evaluation report;
- Recommend a CM tool;
- Recommend the deployment process.

Other groups were also involved in the project. SEPG (Software Engineering Process Group) was instructed to discuss the evaluation report, relate it to other development processes, analyze the economical aspects and correlate the results from the report with the company's development strategy. One development project group has tested the most interesting tools in their environment. Their task was to determine what efforts would be needed to adjust the project environment for the new tool, and how the tool could respond to the project's requirements. Representatives of other ABB companies took part in the evaluation process. Finally, a decision group consisting of the development managers, a representatives of SEPG and the CM group were required to make the final decision.

The project has completed within four months requiring approximately 30 man-weeks work. Certain external help was provided in the form of presentations, courses and consulting help from the suppliers of the tools.

2.2 The Evaluation Criteria

As the company had considerable experience in using CM tools in large development projects, and as the CM process was already well defined, there was no problem in specifying what are the most important requirements. The requirements were classified according to the main CM disciplines, and other requirements relating to integration, flexibility, the possibilities of modification and adding new functions, etc.

- Version Management (VM)
- Configuration (CM)
- Build Management (BM)

- Work Space Management (WM)
- Change Management (ChM)
- Release Management (RM)
- Parallel Development, team support (PD)
- Distributed Development (DD)
- Integration with other tools - first of all on the NT platform (Int)
- Integration of CM tool with internal development environment (Int)
- Conversion structures from WinSDE (Adm)
- Administration of the tool and data (Adm)
- Possibility to migrate from the current tools to the new tools
- Possibility of using the same CM tool in partner companies
- Possibility of delivering the development environment together with the CM tool to the customers
- Training and Maintenance Support
- Costs

An evaluation table with items of the most interest for the company's CM process was created from the requirement list. The evaluation table with points for the evaluated CM tools is shown in chapter 3.

2.3 Market Investigation

A market investigation has begun when the requirement specification was completed and approved. The goal of this phase was to select the most interesting CM tools. The process was relative simple, and was completed in a short period because there are many sources of information related to CM tools. Configuration Management Yellow pages [13] is the best place to start with. A good overview of almost all well-known CM tools is presented in "Ovum Evaluates" report [11]. The project group also received information about the use of CM tools from other companies, such as Ericsson and several ABB companies. One source of valuable information was the project "Distributed Development and CM", organized by Swedish industrial companies (ABB, Ericsson, Volvo, SAAB, etc.). Finally, much of information in form of opinions and experiences with different CM tools was collected from the CM news group.

The result of the investigation was a list of the most interesting CM tools. In the first round, four tools were selected, then three. These three tools were investigated further, in one [3] case by means of a one-day presentation. Finally two tools were selected as major candidates, Rational ClearCase (CC) [7],[8],[10] and Microsoft SourceSafe (VSS). These tools are quite different and the selection of a tool would determine the CM and development strategy in general. CC is a powerful and complex tool, which makes possible a total control over the CM process. VSS is a simple tool, easy to deploy and efficient for use in small projects without requiring the use of sophisticated CM processes.

3 Tool Selection and Results of the Evaluation

The two tools selected have been systematically evaluated. The evaluation was related to the existing company's CM process and the existing CM tools. Different types of evaluation were performed: a test of functional characteristics, the market position of the tools and suppliers, requirements on the company in order to use the tools in the most efficient way, and finally the costs and return on investments.

3.1 Functional Characteristics of the Selected Tools

A number of evaluation items were defined and each item has been assigned by a grade. The items were not defined to measure the "absolute" values of characteristics of the tools, but characteristic interesting to the company. For example, the company was not interested in using tools on several platforms, the Windows NT platform was of the only interest. The tools were also compared with WinSDE, to show the possible advantages and disadvantages of another tool.

The classification of the grades is as follows:

0 - no function, 2 - poor functionality, 5 - should be improved, 7 - acceptable as it is, 10 - excellent

Generally, grade 7 denotes an acceptable function which can be directly used without additional effort.

Evaluation Table:

Item Cat.	CC	VSS	Win SDE	Item Description *Comment on the tools*
1 Adm	8	9	9	Installation (client and server part)
2 Adm	10	5	10	Conversion from WinSDE structures *CC takes the complete information* *VSS can take a snapshot*
3 Adm	10	10	5	Conversion from VSS *CC takes the complete information* *WinSDE can take a snapshot*
4 Adm	10	10	10	Implementation of the WinSDE or a similar structure
5 VM	7	7	7	Check in/check out process
6 VM	7	5	5	History information *CC - missing history information in the files* *VSS- possible to see the history of only one file* *WinSDE- not possible to see history per project*

Item Cat.	CC	VSS	Win SDE	Item Description / *Comment on the tools*
7 VM	7	2	6	Version attributes *CC- two steps in defining attributes (define and set)* *VSS- possible to set only labels in a limited way* *WinSDE-Labels and Status available*
8 CM	8	4	7	Configuration and baselining process *CC- two steps in doing baselines (define and set)* *VSS- not proper support. Managing labels and pins complicated and limited and may easily lead to errors. Files do not have branches. Projects have them instead.* *WinSDE- not possible to see baselines for a project*
9 CM	7	5	4	Possibility of finding differences between two baselines *VSS- problem with managing baselines* *WinSDE- no support for showing the difference in the entire structure*
10 CM	8	5	4	Possibility of merging differences between two baselines (on the entire or on the individual file level). *VSS- problem with merging structures* *WinSDE - problem with merging structures*
11 BM	6	0	0	Generation and usage of ClearCase Make (omake) *VSS and WinSDE do not have special support for make, instead Developer Studio is used for the building.*
12 BM	10	0	0	Configuration Control of derived objects from the binary pool for the build purpose
13 ChM	6	4	6	Change and maintenance process: Finding items belonging to a specific product release. Finding changes ("change requests") implemented in a release. Possibility of propagating of a change (logical changes and physical changes between files) between two releases (baselines). *CC - Change Request (CR) support missing* *VSS - limited possibilities of managing old file versions, no CR support, some problems when checking out files from Developer Studio* *WinSDE - Limited possibilities of change propagation between two releases*
14 ChM	3	2	8	Integration between CM tool and a Change Request tool. How can information be passed between these two tools?
15 ChM	7	3	8	Statistics and metrics - Possible usage of data saved in CM repositories.
16 ChM	7	3	6	Possibility to implement a CM Process *CC- good possibilities to control a CM process* *VSS- additional programming is required* *WinSDE- a CM process is already supported*

Item Cat.	CC	VSS	Win SDE	Item Description / *Comment on the tools*
17 DD	7	2	3	Distributed development
				CC - Multisite features- replication of databases. Possibility of moving data between databases. References to different databases from environment development. There are some limitations in using branches.
				VSS- possible to copy the entire database or send a snapshot
				WinSDE- possible to copy entire or part of a structure or send a snapshot
18 PD	9	5	5	Teamwork- coordination between project members
19 Int	7	9	6	Integration with other tools- in particular Developer Studio and Visual Basic. Possible integration with other tools (VxWorks/Tornado) on the command and COM/API-level.
20 Int	7	5	4	Possible integration of other tools in the CM tool (automatic invocation of other tools with some specific events).
21 Int	7	5	4	Possibility of extracting/importing structures placed outside CM tool. Possibility of updating of data for outsourced software. Coordination with other CM tools
22 GUI	7	8	7	User Interface
				CC - DS and VB as SourceSafe, Additional GUI OK but some features are missing (drag/drop, too many instances of windows, not automatically update in details window). Too many functions connected only to line commands
				VSS- limited possibility to see file versions
				WinSDE- Some features missing in DS and VB integration
23 Gen	9	5	6	Additional functionality
				CC-powerful line commands
				VSS-a lot of functions are missing and must be implemented or integrated with other tools.
				WinSDE- Include CR-management, some metrics, a process support.
24 Gen	8	6	6	Batch processing (automate actions)
25 Gen	6	8	7	Efforts to start using the tool
				CC- Education for CM responsible required, good planning required, powerful servers required
				VSS- easy to start for small projects
				WinSDE- education required, support is available
26 Gen	7	6	7	Reliability
				CC- known as a stable product, but not completely tested
				VSS- a lot of small bugs, some serious reports with larger data bases (according to reports)
				WinSDE- small bugs exist, but there is a direct support

The graphical presentation of the characteristics can be seen in Figure 1.

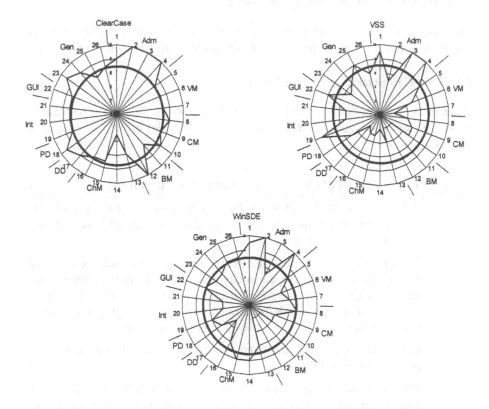

Fig. 1. Tools functional characteristics

The table and figures show the obvious superiority of ClearCase in functional charac-teristics as compared with VSS. Version Management, Configuration and Build Man-agement, and Change Management,i.e. those disciplines that are essential for configuration management, in particular are inadequate in VSS. Parallel and distrib-uted development is not sufficiently supported. Build management is under the control of development tools, such as Visual Studio, and this support is known to be conve-nient for individual programmers and inconvenient for large groups. On the other hand, VSS is very well integrated in the Microsoft development tools (being part of them), and also provides a very good support for integration with other tools where both command lines and OLE Automation interfaces is available.

ClearCase satisfies almost all requirements. A weak point is Change Management, as this does not support the management of changes on a logical level. To achieve better support for Change Management and for a CM process in general, ClearCase is sup-posed to be integrated with ClearGuide [8], or ClearQuest. Unfortunately, integration with ClearQuest did not met the expectations. ClearGuide, in spite of its systematic approach to the CM process, has not reached the dominant position on the market as, for example, ClearCase. The project group felt that it would be difficult to motivate the additional investments required for ClearGuide.

The analysis of the tools technical characteristic has shown that the company can achieve a significant improvement in Configuration Management by using ClearCase.

3.2 Other Characteristics of the Selected Tools

Other parts of the evaluation show the non-technical issues. General characteristics, advantages and disadvantages have been reported. The tables below list some of the characteristics analyzed:

Other characteristics of ClearCase (+ Advantages, - Disadvantages)
+ ClearCase is a very good CM tool for large organizations and especially for those organizations which wish to follow CMM level 2 and 3 and to retain control over the CM process.
+ The tool makes the implementation the defined CM model possible and ensures that the model is used as designed. It is difficult to perform some actions which are not under control of the defined process. Yet, the programmers do not feel the inflexibility fi on the contrary, programmers see very little from the CM in the daily development process.
+ ClearCase support from Rational is very good. Courses, the consultant support, etc. are excellent.
+   - The successful deployment and implementation of ClearCase requires a good organization around CM. A certain level of organization maturity is required for successful implementation.
-   + ClearCase requires considerable resources fi in addition to powerful servers, trained staff with both responsibility and authority are necessary for successful CM support. However, the hidden costs in the projects around CM are minimal.
- Integration with MS Developer Studio is good but there is the risk that Rational will not be able to follow the changes in new releases of MS Developer Studio.
- Integration with ClearQuest is inadequate.
- he ClearCase position on the market is very strong today, but competition from MS Visual SourceSafe will present Rational with a serious challenge in the future (although these tools are not in the same category).

Other characteristics of VSS (+ Advantages, - Disadvantages)

+   VSS is a tool easy to install and deploy.

+   VSS is the integral part of MS Visual Studio Enterprise Edition. No additional efforts are required for the installation, no additional costs are required.

+   VSS is a Microsoft product, which means that is used by a large number of programmers. There is a probability that VSS will become the de facto standard CM tool. The same is valid for VSS API. Even some other CM providers use VSS API.

+   A good product for small projects where maintenance is not very important.

-     It prefers a "bottom-up" approach allowing developers considerable flexibility. It has limited support for keeping an SCM-process under control. Easy to use within small groups.

-     VSS is not sufficient for the CM process defined by CMM. For example, VSS has no support for change management or release management. A Change Management tool must be integrated with VSS to provide this support.

-     VSS is not sufficient for a more complex CM process. Additional functions (commands or applications) must be built upon it or additional program packages must be bought.

-     Support from Microsoft is inadequate, but much help can be obtained from
+   news and other groups.

3.3 Costs and Return on Investment

ClearCase license costs are significantly larger than VSS licenses. This is especially the case when using the Visual Studio Enterprise Edition which includes VSS as a standard part. The initial costs of ClearCase are also larger because of the requirements of powerful servers.

License costs are however not the total costs. An analysis of the total costs has been performed. The following costs have been discussed:

- product/licence cost
- maintenance cost
- general support cost
- training
- deployment
- hardware costs (servers)
- additional internal development
- additional software required.

The costs are of two kinds, external, with costs of external support paid for by the company, and internal, the costs for internal activities. The initial costs and annual costs for each year have also been estimated. Figure 2, shows the initial costs estimated for the company.

Initial Costs

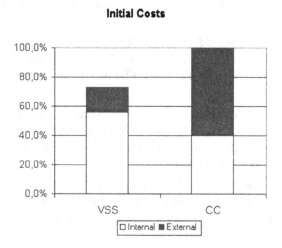

Fig. 2. Initial costs for CC and VSS

Surprisingly, the initial costs for SourceSafe were only approximately 25% less than those for ClearCase. Most of the costs for VSS were internal costs, since additional development was required to achieve at least similar functions which existed in WinSDE. The analysis has shown that the maintenance costs for VSS are about 60% of the maintenance costs for ClearCase.

The initial costs for ClearCase are visibly higher, but return on investment is of greater importance. According to some reports [6], the increase of the development productivity can be up to 20%, assuming that the development time takes 50% of the total time. Of course, this is a very high percentage, and having in mind that the company already has an established and well working CM process, the savings would not be of that order of magnitude. However, even a 10% increase in productivity, the estimate of the project group, would make significant savings.

Unfortunately, no source of such information was not found for VSS. Having no information, the project group has made no estimate for return on investments for VSS.

Figure 3 shows the estimation of the project group the dynamics of the investment, utilized CM functionality and expected return on investment.

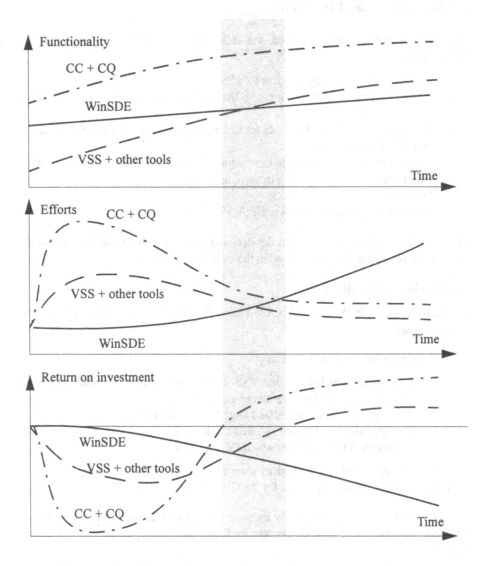

Fig. 3. Estimated investments and return on investments

In the case of internal, WinSDE, development, it is expected that the efforts and functionality will raise, but the return on investments will get down. In a case of using a commercial tool, the expectations are that the functionality will raise faster. The investments will be in the begging higher, and the new functions will not be used optimally, but with time the efforts will be lower an the return on the investments will be considerable higher. ClearCase costs are estimated to be higher, especially in the beginning. The time where ClearCase return on investment reaches the WinSDE curve is estimated to one year.

4 The Decision and Its Analysis

When the evaluation was completed, the following conclusion was reached by the project group:

- ClearCase is technically superior to VSS.
- If the company wishes to improve the CM process considerably, ClearCase should be used.
- The costs, especially initial costs for ClearCase are higher, but a higher return of investment is expected.
- It would be easier to persuade the customers of our products with development environment, to use VSS than to use ClearCase.
- Our subcontractors prefer VSS.
- Our pilot-project participants prefer VSS.

The final decision was made within the decision group, i.e. the management and the representatives of the groups involved in the evaluation process.

The decision was as follows:

1. Visual SourceSafe (VSS) shall be used as a CM tool for development and maintenance purpose.

   The decision was made because:

   - The participants believe that VSS will be improved and a many new tools related to VSS will appear on the market.
   - The organization cannot afford large large initial costs for CC.
   - The organization has not reached the maturity level required to introduce and utilize all the features which CC supports.

2. A new project should be started as soon as possible. The goal of the project is: Implement and deliver a product for the CM process based on VSS.

The decision has shown that not only the pure CM features are important for selection and deployment of a CM tool. In this case the following factors played the most important roles:

- **Deployment Scaleability**

  As the development accelerates and delivery cycles shorten, the pressure to deliver products in short time, leaves no time available for other activities. This is especially the case when an extra time is required for a tool deployment. The tools which could manage a single and simple installation and its use, and could support a smooth growth of usage within small and later larger groups, etc., have greater chances to of acceptance on a large scale.

- **Simple Use**

  Many advanced CM-tools are very CM-oriented. This means that the users of these tools must execute explicitly the CM commands to access objects with which they are work. As CM is not the goal itself in a development process, but a tool which help to achieve a goal, it should be no more visible than necessary and as simple to use as possible in its usage. For this reason simple CM tools, such as RCS, are still widely used. This is to a degree the strength of ClearCase with its virtual file system which allows users to work on the standard file structure which encapsulates the version and configuration functions. However, too much efforts is required to learn the administration part, and to design a CM process. Proper default values in structures and process definitions, not necessarily optimized, would simplify the tool usage.

- **Integration with other tools and the development platform**

  CM tools should be integrated as far as possible with other tools. No additional installations or special actions should be required to achieve the integration. The CM tool should be a "natural" part of development tools and the developers should hardly be aware of the presence of the CM tool. Similarly, the integration with the development platform, "look and feel", must work perfectly. If some standard functions, such as cut and paste, short cuts, drag and drop, or mouse functions, are absent, the developers may feel irritated and the tool may not be accepted. Some CM tools try to keep the same GUI through several platforms, but a more important factor is to have the same "look and feel" of the current platform. Another important factor is the function implementation style. While most Unix users accept and even prefer a line-command interface, Windows users prefer mouse-functions.

- **Costs**

  Although it is generally considered that the real costs, or the total costs, are those which count, among of the most important factors are the initial visible costs - i.e. license and resource costs. Suppliers who begin with low prices, or even with no prices at all, and than gradually increase the prices, have more chances of introducing their products and persuading developers to use them.

- **Requirements on CM functions**

  As the development cycles become shorter, some new CM functions increase in importance while others become less significant. For example, there is a general trend toward faster replacement or updating of software with less requirements on software compatibility. Instead, standard formats of persistent objects, for example documentation, are used to make it possible to use different tools, or incompatible versions of the tools. A consequence of this is that the maintenance factor, and in particular version management, especially identification of older versions, becomes less important. On the other hand, the more frequent updating increases the demands on the configuration management, not only in the development environment, but also in the run-time environment. CM tools which will be able to cover configuration functions in both environments will become more attractive. An increasing trend toward the use of standard components, and thereby, achieving a high degree of composeability in a product line, introduces tremendous challenges in configuration management [2].

5 Conclusion

A case of an evaluation of CM tools, and a decision a decision to use a particular CM tool is described in this paper. The study has shown that a tool, despite its superiority with respect to CM functions, which were actually required, was not selected because of other factors, more of an organizational and psychological nature. The company decided to use a low-level CM tool, which implies that additional software, or internal development will be required. In that sense the new paradigm, to buy instead of to develop, has not been fully realized. The case has also shown that CM functionality is not the only criteria for selecting a tool. Other factors, such as integration with other tools, usability, simple deployment, etc., are as important as the "classic" CM features.

6 References

[1]   M. Aoyama: New Age of Software Development: How Component-Based Software Engineering Changes the Way of Software Development, 1998 International Workshop on CBSE

[2]   Alan W. Brown, Kurt C. Wallnau: An Examination of the Current State of CBSE: A Report on the ICSE Workshop on Component-Based Software Engineering, 1998 International Workshop on CBSE

[3]   Continuus Software Corporation, Task-Based Configuration Management, Version 2.0,http://www.continuus.com/developers/developersACEA.html

[4]   Ivica Crnkovic, Experience with Change Oriented SCM Tools, Software Configuration Management SCM-7, Springer Verlag, ISBN 3-540-63014-7, 1997, pages 222-234

[5]   Ivica Crnkovic, Per Willför, Change Measurements in an SCM process, System Configuration Management SCM-8, Springer Verlag, ISBN 3-540-64733-3 1998, pages 26-32

[6]   Jens-Otto Larsen, Helge M. Roald, Introducing ClearCase as a Process Improvement Experiment, Lecture Notes 1439, Springer Verlag 1998, SCM-8

[7]   David B. Leblang, The CM Challenge: Configuration Management that Works, Configuration Management, edited by Walter F. Tichy, John Wiley & Sons, ISBN 0 471 9424

[8]   David B. Leblang, Managing the Software Development Process with Clear-Guide, Software Configuration Management SCM-7, Springer Verlag, ISBN 3-54063014-7, 1997, pages 66-80

[9]   Steve McConnell, Rapid Development: timing wild software schedules, Microsoft Press, 1996, ISBN 1-55615-900-5

[10] Rational http://www.rational.com/products/clearquest/index.jtmpl, 1998

[11] CliveBurrows, Ian Wesley, Ovum Evaluates Configuration Management, Ovum Ltd, ISBN 1 898972 24 9

[12] Darcy Wiborg Weber, Change Sets versus Change Packages, Software Configuration Management SCM-7, Springer Verlag, ISBN 3-54063014-7, 1997, pages 25-35

[13] André van der Hoek, Configuration Management Yellow Pages, http://www.cs.colorado.edu/~andre/configuration_management.html

An Experience in Configuration Management in SODALIA

M.Banzi, F.Macugli, S.Borion, G. La Commare
Sodalia Spa
Via V. Zambra 1
38100 – Trento
ITALY

Abstract. In this paper we describe how Configuration Management (CM) activities are organized and performed in Sodalia's Network and Application Management Department. Here a group is called to provide cross-department CM activities according to SEI CMM level 3 requirements. Rational ClearCase, as main CM tool, and ClearDDTS, for change request tracking, have been enriched with several additional scripts and customization to suit our needs. In order to facilitate information sharing among software engineers, a CM Web Page has been made available via Sodalia Intranet to allow easy access to constantly up to date information. CM services have reached an excellent quality, providing the department areas with a globally recognized, reliable foundation that supports all phases of the software development life cycle. As a consequence, CM culture is widespread within all the personnel involved in the development process, ensuring a good cooperative environment from which the CM team itself benefits considerably.

1. Introduction

A software firm aimed at delivering high quality products, according to an accepted model, e.g. the Software Engineering Institute Capability Maturity Model (SEI CMM), needs to implement an effective Configuration Management (CM) environment. This is mandatory and can be gained defining procedures detailing the process to be followed in performing standard CM actions such as Identification, Versioning, Status Accounting and Change Management. The main challenge is making this environment more and more efficient and globally accepted.

Once the process is defined, tools adaptable to it have to be chosen, to support Configuration Manager activity. These tools will require a tailoring on the process whose cost will depend on the complexity of the defined process.

Then a constant effort has to be paid to always improve the usability of the CM environment. Core business for developers is to produce code and often whatever possible obstacle to their activity is unpopular. The consciousness that with low effort great benefits can result, creates that CM culture that contributes in increasing efficiency. Moreover if CM environment is sufficiently automated, certain simple actions can be delegated to developers thus reducing possible bottlenecks imposed by CM actions.

Another very important aspect is the supply of a constantly updated accounting on the status of the system under development. As obvious, Configuration Manager has to deliver reports on the status of the configuration, but in case of concurrent development of several products, which is the case of an efficient firm, it is necessary to provide constantly up-to-date information. Facilities implementing this task should capture actions when they are performed, and make them available to everyone in a gathering point, such as a web page.

2. Context

SODALIA is a telecommunication software development company founded in 1993 and part of the Telecom Italia Group (the main Telecom Operator in Italy). The mission of Sodalia is to provide advanced Telecommunications Products, Solutions, and Services to Telecommunications Companies worldwide. Currently the company has a staff of about 300 employees, the majority of them involved in software engineering. Since the beginning, Sodalia has developed a strong commitment to quality, defining a productive software development process SIMEP (Sodalia Integrated Management and Engineering Process), and a complete set of Quality System Procedures that earned it in few years ISO 9001 certification and SEI CMM Level 3. Within SIMEP, Configuration Management has the central role of effectively and efficiently support software development as detailed in Sodalia Software Engineering Process Guidelines (see FiRENVRENVgure 1).

The experience described in this paper regards the Configuration Management activities performed within one of Sodalia's production departments, Network Administration Management (NAM) department, which is in charge of the development of Operation Support Systems (OSS) in the field of telecommunication Network and Service Management. Our solutions are based both on internally developed and third party products that are customized to provide customer specific solutions. We often run into concurrent development of several versions at different development and maintenance stages of core products as well as their customizations

The department is organized in four main areas: one in charge for product line definition, two responsible for product development and one responsible for the implementation of the final solution.

The CM group provides cross project services to the various department areas (see Figure 2).

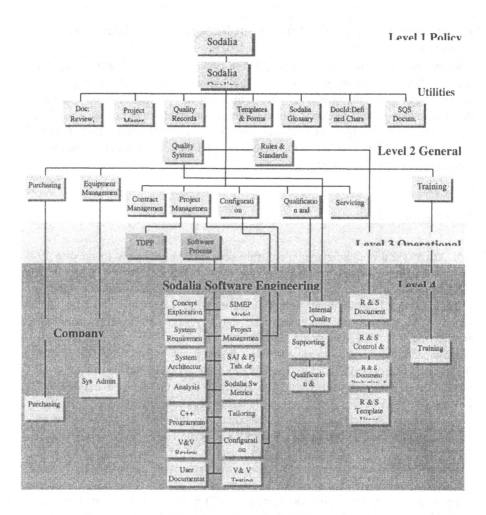

Figure 1.   SEQARABICSEQARABICSodalia Quality System

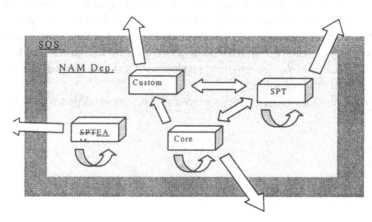

Figure 2.   arrows represent code movements between projects. Each of which is mediated by CM group

3. CM Organization

CM services are crucial for the ordinary activity flow in such a complex environment. Ordinary CM needs of software development projects, are further complicated due to the interrelated dependencies between artifacts belonging to product lines and custom developments.
Efficiency and effectiveness of CM activities have been two major objectives in our experience. CM needs to be effective since it is aimed at reducing complexity both in software development and in process implementation. CM has also to be efficient, and thus achieved in a cost-effective way, since it cannot overload project budgets and require too much effort from software developers.

To achieve both these goals, the CM group has performed three major steps:
- CM environment definition. A standard project repository structure across the various areas in the department and a common tailoring of Sodalia CM policies, enables the use of common CM tools and facilitates cross-area artifact delivery and communication. In addition, tools ensure easier maintenance of existing projects and startup of new ones, and keep software engineers needs of CM training low in case of reallocation.
- The adoption of an adequate set of tools. Sodalia has currently adopted two major tools: ClearCase for configuration management and ClearDDTs for change management. A significant customization effort was invested to integrate the tools and adapt them to the company and department needs. Reaching a significant level of CM and Software Engineering process automation and productivity improvement. The use of these tools is described in better detail in the next sections.
- The implementation of an adequate set of instruments for CM users. As described in the next sections, a relevant set of scripts and Web based information points have been implement to facilitate the use of CM facilities and to provide up to date information to the community of software developers (see RENVFigure 3).

As a result, only two configuration managers support the activity of more than 80 software engineers. CM operations have reached a considerable level of automation and the CM culture is spread among the development teams.

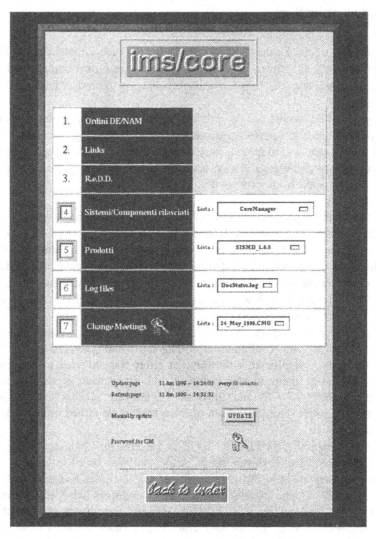

Figure 3.   **Main page of Core Project CM web site**

CM Activities

The CM group performs the following activities
- Repository and Development environment Management
- Status accounting
- Identification of documentation and code artifacts
- Versions management
- Change management
- Build of products released either internally and externally
- Packaging and delivery.

Details on their implementation in our context are given in the following paragraphs.

3.1. Repository and Development Environment Management

When a new project is started, the first activity performed by the CM team is to set up the artifact repository and give the developers controlled access to it.

The most common development environment involves at least two platforms: Unix and Windows NT. This requires concurrent access to the project repository from different run-time environment types. The repository is implemented on Unix volumes, placed on server machines and is made accessible (i.e. mounted) from the different types of development workstations (e.g., NT clients). Project wide UNIX accounts, imported in a common NT domain, are used, to ensure a first level of protection.

The standard set of accounts includes:

- an administrator profile
- a development profile
- a testing profile.

They all share the same configuration files to ensure a common set up of the environment.

Role	Ownership	Account	Conf.files
Administrator	Owner of the repository main structure, of all VOBs and of administrations views	<project>-adm	.profile .kshrc
Development engineer	Owner of all development and product views	<project>-dev	
Test engineer	Owner of test views	<project>-tst	

Figure 4.   SEQARABEaccounts, roles and ownership within a project

The subsequent step in setting up a new project consists in creating the ClearCase Versioned Objects Base (VOB), which is the physical repository of the versioned files. Several personal and product views are then created and shared by UNIX and NT clients. This ensures a further level of security, preventing users (who use common project accounts) from undesired modification of configured artifacts.

Through ClearCase clients, development tools gain transparent distributed access to files physically maintained inside VOB/view (e.g. tools access files under configuration control as regular NFS files). CM is in charge to carefully identifying the correct resource allocation to such common VOB servers, to prevent performance lowering and LAN overload.

Further details on the organization of the code development environment and on documentation management, is given in the following paragraphs.

3.1.1. Code Management

A standardized structure for the code development environment has been adopted, since it provides several advantages, for identification and delivery purposes, build management and for script development and reuse.

A basically recursive structure for the repository of the whole system, its components, and component modules, allows the use of the same general CM policy, and consequently of the same set of scripts and commands, possibly only slightly customized.

Product views on VOB server were created for reference build and personal ones were supplied to developers to ensure independent working environments. However, during the development phase, it was noted that often engineers working on the same component, usually small groups localized in the same room, would distribute their personal views among the various customizations. This avoided frequent switching among the environments on the same view. Substantially they were using product ones. This approach had not initially been adopted fearing conflicts of concurrent development on the same files, however the easy communication among developers, prevented against it.

From here the provisioning of each group with product views instead of personal ones. These can be also supported by local views on personal workstations.

In a very dynamic environment, where developers have to switch frequently among different versions of the product, (recall of the product views, pre-configured to see a specific version of the product), it is necessary to give them not only source code of a specific version, but also all the internal libraries previously built within that version.

These are not configured elements, but just private objects of the build view, usually inaccessible outside it. A solution is necessary to identify and preserve the complete set of libraries and executables built during a build session. This results in the need for sufficient disk space to archive all such information, but ensures a very quick and safe context switching.

The ClearCase derived objects facility and `winkin` command, suitably governed by a set of *ad hoc* scripts, ensure this service at the cost of just one set of libraries per product. Before this, developers used to keep their own version of libraries in their private environment. Apart from disk occupation that was often multiplied by the number of development tasks, this caused uncontrollable misalignment among sets of libraries used by the different tasks.

ClearCase allows to keep the list of all objects build during a common build (better to use ClearCase language saying "created by a common clearaudit process") these are the Derived Objects (DO). DOs are kept inside a particular VOB archive from which they can be extracted by each view using `winkin` command. This is the method used to gather in a common set and then identify all the products of the build of a specific version of the system. The `clearmake` command provided by ClearCase, automatically generates DOs, but it is not currently used because of its incompatibility with UNIX `make` on which our environment is currently based.

3.1.2. Documentation Management

All documents developed within a project are kept under configuration control, so that their files are uniquely identified, localized and protected. These include technical and management documents, but also external contributions, memos, reports and so on.

All technical documents produced undertake the same versioning process as for source code. This allows the use of the same policies adopted for the source code also for documentation, ensuring a consistent tracking of all documents associated to the various versions of a product. Unfortunately, unlike code text files, for which deltas between versions are saved by the CM tool, document binary file versions are handled by the tool as copies, possibly compressed, of the whole file. This causes a considerable use of disk resources and requires periodical cleaning of obsolete versions to prevent exhausting disk space.

Solutions developed in NAM are often made of products and customizations developed by different areas. Thus a solution may contain documents owned by a number of contributors (e.g. architects, development managers, requirement managers, technical writers) belonging to different areas. Further more, it is common practice for product level and solution level documentation to be packaged together. Documents are identified using a unique identification code (DocId) which encodes information about the project it belongs to and the document type (e.g. component design, user manual, ...). Such codes are constructed and managed by the CM (according to the company's documentation management process) so that the proper level of control is assured.

Each document is initially configured, that is, a set of attributes is assigned to the directory containing the document files. Such attributes define the title of the document, its status (draft or final), last delivered version of the same, the product which it belongs to and so on.

Attributes are updated automatically by triggers (actions associated to the execution of commands) at file check in and at document release. The release of a document is performed by the document author through a command which labels and locks the files and copies them into the protected archive directory updating a link to a delivery directory containing the last delivered version. In this delivery directory, all documents belonging to a specific product version, delivered by different projects, are collected and rendered available to everyone even outside the CM environment.

3.2. Status Accounting

Status accounting is a key CM activity which consists in producing periodical reports detailing the status of configuration within a project.

In this section the various accounting activities are described in detail.

3.2.1. Environment and adopted policies accounting

According to Sodalia Quality System (SQS), each project/area delivers a project/area plan containing a CM plan subsection where roles (CM and its staff, Change Management Group, Configuration Control Board) are listed together with audits and major baselines. The plans references the Repository Description Document (ReDD) which describes the project repository structure, the development environment, the equipment and tools adopted, and lists all codes used to identify the products, components, and tasks. Moreover the ReDD contains the tailoring of SQS Procedures and Sodalia guidelines for specific project needs.

The ReDD contains information with different time scope that would potentially force the release of a new version just to capture minor information. Moreover, the presence of a Department CM with cross-department policies and good practices, introduces different applicability scope within the ReDD. To facilitate ReDD maintenance and to avoid duplication of information, each project ReDD has been split into several documents. Each refers to a global document where cross department policies adopted for the project configuration are described. Within each ReDD, describing just specific situations, frequently changing information are extracted in Addenda just referenced by the ReDD itself. These are delivered as required, independently by the ReDD.

3.2.2. Products and components structure accounting

Within a scenario as the one described it is necessary a constantly up to date information on newly released software.

For this reason the same scripts that perform the release of code at whatever level (system, component, module) record the structure of the delivered artifact in several files and notify by e-mail the interested groups. Log files are then processed by scripts supplying a complete description of the new product structure in Configuration Management web page, thus ensuring online accounting.

In this way developers working in a very dynamic scenario are constantly informed on availability of the planned new libraries and modules to be used in their activity as soon as these are released.

3.2.3. Change Request status accounting

ClearDDTS has been chosen to implement Sodalia change management process using suitably customized flow diagrams. CM group uses the information stored in the tool database to report on status of CRs in its periodic report. The necessary information is extracted from the database in text files by cron scripts, which ensure updated information at very low cost.

These files are also made available to everyone in the CM web (see RENVRENVFUSIONFORMATFigure 5). Further improvement would be to integrate this page directly with ClearDDTS Web Interface thus ensuring direct and dynamic access to ClearDDTS repository.

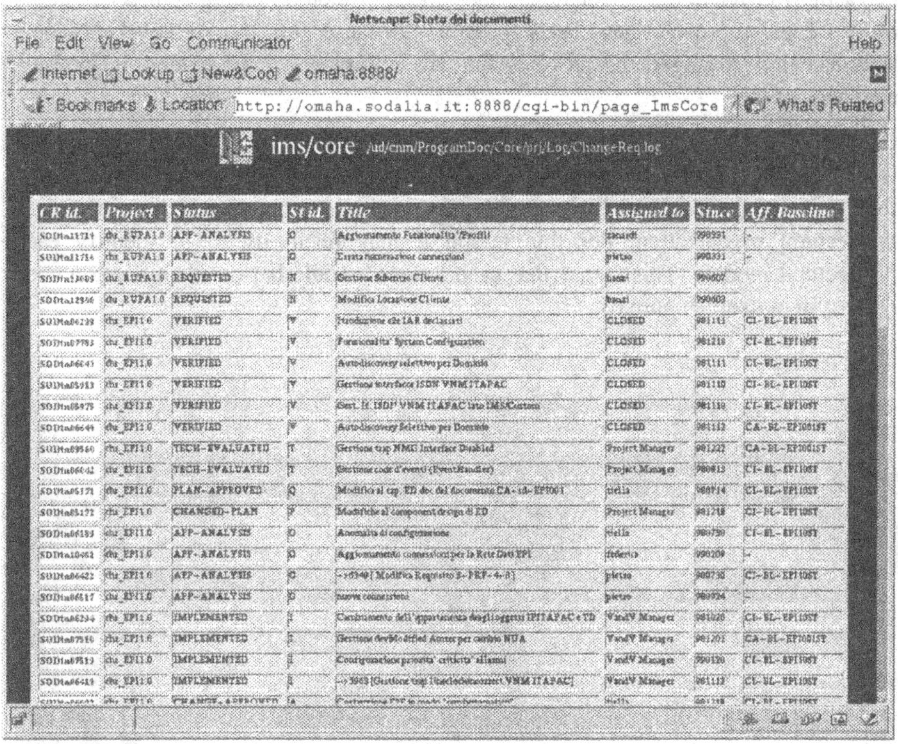

Figure 5.   Change requests status accounting through web interface

3.3. Identification of documentation and code artifacts

Identification, in our case, means associate to artifacts one or more identification labels to aggregate set of files. The higher level of identification is the baseline that identifies that consistent set of artifacts which constitutes the product. These labels contain information such as the name of the artifact or its identification code and its version. The latest is a version code assigned by Configuration Manager according to the artifact history and development phase, nothing to do with versioning associated to the tool, which is a device to keep modification history for each file.

3.3.1.   Documentation

Compared to software, documents are structurally simple artifacts, although their number is considerable when developing complex products: requirements, architecture, designs, manuals. Without an adequate set of tools, documentation management can be an extremely costly activity for CM.

As a consequence, the documentation management process has been synthesized in a set of scripts, partially triggered by ClearCase commands and partially to be executed directly by document owners. This synergy among CM and developers results in an increasingly efficient documentation management, without reducing confidence in the result. This approach has been possible because of the relatively simple documentation management process, but we are planning to extend it to code management too.

3.3.2. Code

Code artifacts are distributed in a multilevel directories structure which reflects their architectural organization. For this reason it may result useful to identify each architectural module. This means that each lowest module has an identification code as the system itself (Figure 6).

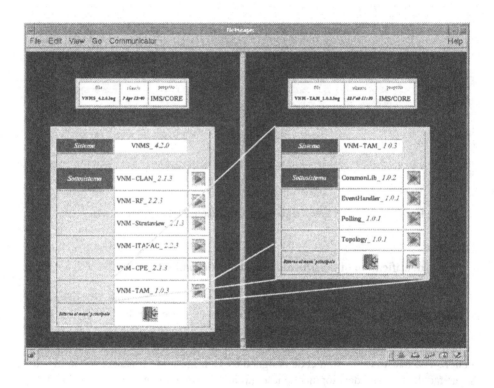

Figure 6.   Hierarchical identification: system VNMS is made of various components among which VNM-TAM, whose modules are identified too.

Clearly this allows the substitution of a single module within an installed product or also the composition of new version of a product by merely modifying some of its modules. The advantage of such an approach when developing customization of a same product is evident. It is also evident that the complexity of the identification process requires great care.

Identification of code artifacts is achieved using ClearCase labels attached recursively to all releasing artifact files. The use of a self-similar tree-structure for the system, components, and modules ensures the use of the same delivery script at every level: Such labels are locked to the identified versions and only the administrator has the rights to remove them.

The labeling process also updates the version files compiled during the build process and used to create hard-coded strings embedded in libraries and executables.

Identification of installed code is thus automatically aligned to its source.

Identification scripts also generates a whole set of log files used for accounting on delivered components and on the structure of each system version. These files, loaded by CM web page as soon as they are produced, are also used for a better integration with ClearDDTS forcing the opening of CR using exactly the identifier of the impacted module.

3.3.3. Baselines

Once a product is to be delivered, the complete set of related code and documentation artifacts is to be identified as a whole with a unique label that ensures its recovery. This is the baseline that collects the exact version of each Configuration Item (CI) composing the product.

Baselining is also achieved using labels. Once identified all artifacts (code and documentation) belonging to a common baseline, a new label is attached by a script using each single artifact identification label as a handle. As usual the scripts also update log files: describing the structure of the newly created baseline but also recording the performed action.

3.4. Version Management

When dealing with many versions of a product developed concurrently, several considerations can play relevant roles in choosing the policy to be adopted to manage the development.

It may be necessary to branch all the files of a product because that specific version is in deployment and patching is to be done exactly on the deployed version awaiting for a new release. This way, bug fixings have to be ported to the concurrently developed versions. We conventionally call this a "maintenance" branch.

During the development phases, when customizations of the product are concurrent, the approach described can be substituted with a more efficient one. Here branches are performed only on files to be really customized among the various versions. This ensures bug fixing just once at least on shared files.

ClearCase allows the creation of branches in each file/directory version tree. Access to branches is governed by a careful use of views whose configuration is set accordingly to the specific use. The case of maintenance branching is very simple:

developers have to simply operate on a branch other than the standard 'main branch'. Also the rules for the view to be used are very simple. In the case of development branching the view may have configuration specification files very complex that developers are not requested to manage. In this case, product views are also used to simplify such access and prevent casualty errors due to hurry switching among versions.

In both cases, on all files in case of maintenance or just on customized ones in the other case, merging is used for porting fixes among versions. This is a very strong feature in the CM tool, but one that requires great care in its application. Nevertheless we found it very useful for porting bug fixing else than editing files on all branches. This because ClearCase recalls this action through merge arrows thus updating what it calls the 'base contributor' of the merge: the version from which the code of the file is diverging. Complex merges will result easier and safer.

3.5. Change Management

Change management involves handling modifications of baselined artifacts. Such modifications can be triggered by external inputs (e.g. servicing calls form a customer) or internal inputs (e.g. refinements of a design document). Different change requests involve different authorities for their management: for instance, changes on functionalities require a Configuration Control Board (CCB), which includes a customer representative; defects, on the other hand, are handled by the Change Management Group (CMG). In order to properly support the change management process, a customization of ClearDDTS has been adopted. This tool provides the concept of class, which is a flow diagram which defines transitions enabled to specified roles identified by personal accounts (e.g. who can open, approve, implement a change request. Three ClearDDTS classes are used for change request management: one for the servicing calls, another for changes to requirements and/or to improved/added functionalities, and a third to track defects. Due to the different authorities involved, and the different process each request goes through, ClearDDTS has been customized to work as a simple work flow tool for change management. The management process has been modeled as a finite state automata with encoded the various stages a request goes; to each state are associated the members that can authorize a state transition; finally, when a state transition occurs, the next personality involved is automatically notified (e.g. via e-mail).

Tracking of the status of change requested is obtained through queries on ClearDDTS database that regularly update log files as explained in the accounting paragraph.

3.6. Build

The build of a final product is performed under configuration control in a view configured to allow access to exactly the needed source code.. The execution of a product level makefile ensures the building of each module with common compile options.

Build views are created on the same build server to ensure optimization of compilation time.

3.6.1. CM charged with build activities

The CM group is responsible for both builds of products to be delivered internally, for instance for Verification and Validation (V&V) and builds of a validated product to be delivered to the end customer. Product builds are executed in a controlled environment using a specifically configured view. This ensures the necessary isolation required to avoid that uncontrollable development temporary settings can reduce the confidence in the final product.

Since code the given to system build has to be identified by CM, the group first knows the configuration of the system as a whole and defines the specifications of the view to be used for the build. For this reason it was decided to task the CM group with system build.

3.6.2. Dependencies

When dealing with highly structured components, the risk of dependencies misalignment is very high. Centralization of dependency information helps its control.

A file, unique for all components, lists the dependencies (all the libraries used, their version and location in the file system); while another defines all the common compiler options and variables to be used for the build of the whole system.

Developers are supplied with makefile templates, including the above files, that they use to give instance to generic definitions, placing them in the final components directory and thus building their modules.

3.7. Packaging and Delivery

Delivery is approached in two ways, depending on the final user. Internal releases (to integration or system test within the project) are performed by simple copy of the executables and their configuration from the build environment to a well defined target set of directories. Deliveries to the end customer, on the other hand, are performed by taking advantage from the standard packaging tools provided by the various vendors (e.g. HP-UX swpackage, Windows NT environment Install Shield.The product is stored on CD-ROMs, DATs or other media on the basis of the customer preferences. Packages are carefully structured in bundles, products, and filesets to allow multilevel and partial installation procedures. Control scripts are also provided so that pre- and post- installation controls are performed.

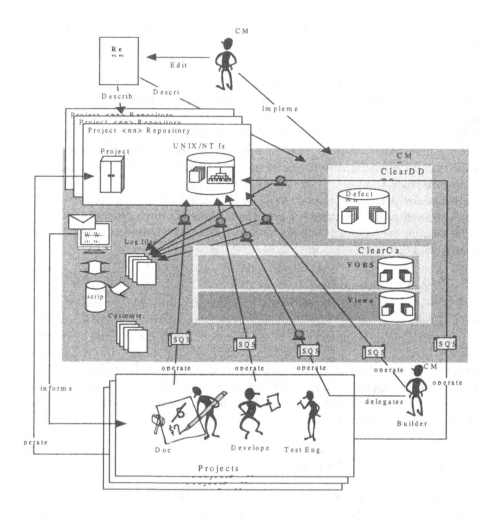

Configuration Management Effort

To assess the impact of the CM organization, a sample tracking of one year of Configuration Management activities is analyzed. CM activity in that period (the first complete year with the current CM organization) has involved the release (internal or external) of about 520 software modules and about 100 document versions. Data provided in picture (reference to Figure 8RENV), reports the effort needed to manage four projects during 1998. Two projects are steady (identified as Core and Custom), one started that year (SPT) and having had its first major release in the last quarter of the year, and a fourth still in the its initial phase (EAM). The diagram seems to reveal that the trend of CM effort required to support a project approaches a common value for all mature projects. An explanation for this behavior can be found in the uniform and stable set of CM procedures and tools which are shared by all projects. It can be noted that SPT did not have the initial startup load, necessary for setting up the environment that one can expect. This is probably due to the fact that it could benefit of an environment already enough steady. CM Effort trend for four projects two already matures (Core and Custom), one in growth (SPT), and a fourth in its initial phase. The second diagram (Figure

8) represents the distribution of effort among the various activities of CM group. It can be noted the cost of CM environment setting up, enough high, but great part of the scripts for baselining, documentation management and for the creation of CM web page have been encoded during the first quarter of that year. Moreover the effort for the number of releases cited above would have been higher if it was not supported by the environment.

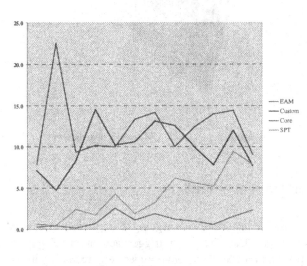

Figure 7. distribution CM Effort trend for four projects two already matures (Core and Custom), one in growth (SPT), and a fourth in its initial phase.

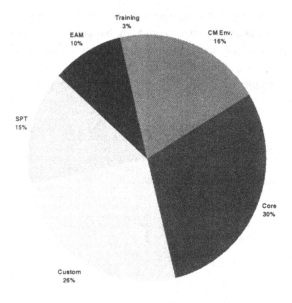

Figure 8.   **CM activity distribution**

4. Further Improvement

The following items are just ideas we are going to implement in our CM environment:

- State transition in ClearDDTS can trigger activation of processes performing directly operation on ClearCase environment e.g. recording in the file descriptor the defect id fixed in a newly created version of a file. This is a way to better use ClearCase-ClearDDTS integration.
- Use of ClearCase attributes to record in files metric information. By applying a simple, intelligent line counter to a file, the results can be frozen in the description of its active version. This way a query on the attributes of files belonging to a specific product can give its size in a repeatable way.
- Performance can be further improved by using distributed built. This is a feature of ClearCase currently not used, that can reduce build times.
- Better tracking of dependencies between libraries: we still have to implement an effective mechanism to produce the list of libraries really linked by executables.
- Improvement in the centralized set of makefile: this useful build environment should be improved to be compliant with ClearCase build tool (`clearmake`) and to implement new requirements arisen during the development currently hard-coded in terminal component `makefiles`.

5. Conclusions

In implementing a CM solution, it has been very useful to use a reference model upon which create a complete set of guidelines. We used SEI CMM where CM is a key process area of level 2. It is important to start with a theoretical framework defining procedures to be followed. In this way we ensure effectiveness. But this framework has to be sufficiently adaptable to all possible situations. This ensures efficiency. However efficiency is a target that can be reached progressively, through experience and trials. In the following paragraphs some lessons we learned while trying to reach this target are described.

5.1. CM Tools

CM activity has to be supported by one or more tools and on the market several ones can be found to fulfill CM requirements. However, in defining a CM solution, it has to be chosen whether to adapt a solution to the tool or to acquire a customized tool and tailor it to the company process.

The second approach, which is the one adopted in Sodalia, is clearly more flexible, but certainly it requires considerable effort to ensure a CM solution user friendly, efficient, and accepted by the final user.

The commands supplied by whatever tool, are many, certainly complex, and not easily usable by developers who cannot be requested to know details of CM tool. This is a task for the Configuration Manager. Customization has to reduce the skill requested to final users, in this way they will found the real value of CM solution without feeling too much its constraints.

Another aspect to be considered is the cost of the tool. Whatever you choose, its cost-per-license is certainly high and a compromise is to be found between safety and burden for the project. From here, in our approach, the use of project accounts and of personal and product views. The first reduces the security re-gained by a careful use of the seconds that also contribute to the success of the chosen CM solution by answering to a specific developers need, as previously seen.

In any case the effort spent in the implementation of this Configuration Management environment can be earned in the reduction of time required to perform CM actions and in ensuring, contemporarily, an higher degree of confidence in them.

5.2. Department CM

CM activity requires considerable specific skill especially if a complex tool is used in support of it. Moreover CM activity is not uniformly distributed along project life-cycle. After an initial peak of effort required to set up the environment, produce all necessary documentation and train developers on it, a low-load activity period follows, up to first deliveries. Our statistics show that CM activity costs to project about half a person per month. And the other half? Of course a Configuration Manager can also develop code or collect requirements, but skill optimization and the task of

Configuration Manager that pursues a control over development, suggest to keep these roles disjoined. Hence the Department Configuration Management Group which revealed itself to be a good solution.

5.3. CM / developers synergy

To enhance project efficiency, CM must be felt as a support to development, not as a constraint. Developers should be enabled to cooperate with CM activity thus creating a widespread CM culture. This can be gained only if CM environment is friendly and everyone completely understands that effort spent in these activities results in a safer development and in higher quality product. Conversely badly implemented CM results in an unpleased overhead for development. Additional advantage of this approach is that routine activities can be delegated to developers without reducing confidence in the product. This produces the side-effect of training developers in simple CM actions, so that, if necessary, personnel can be easily temporarily staffed to CM activity.

5.4. Development versus CM

Development environment structure and CM solution are strictly correlated. Almost every CM action shall operate on the environment and a modification in its overall structure may require a modification on the scripts. Thus, great care has to be paid in designing both the development environment structure and CM scripts interfaces to it.
CM activity has always to fit project needs, but has also to lead to solutions always more effective in the interest of the project itself. So project's own solutions, even if temporarily implemented to answer to contingency, must be generalized and made available to every other project: standardization remains a key target.
Product view else than project or personal ones, seems to be the correct approach in every CM action and setting. This in customizing the CM tools, in organizing the Archive and in CM metrics.
In developing several version of a product concurrently, customization ones and maintenance ones, branching code rather than duplicating it, is effective approach, but great care has to be used in its managing as well as in merging of changes among the various versions.
Personal workstations can efficiently support servers for development purposes: reduce server and LAN load and improves compilation time, but this achievement can be easily lost if no reciprocal alignment is constantly ensured.

5.5. Up to date accounting

In complex and very dynamic environments, the time scope of reports is usually tool long to draw from them useful information. The use of automatic mechanism for information deployment is a must. When designing macros to perform actions either directly through CM tool or by customized scripts, the action itself should record its result in a file open to everyone. In this way up-to-date information is always available not only internally to a project, but also outside development groups, to all other roles directly interested such as other projects with dependencies or Quality System area. Better is if all the information is gathered in a single reference point well organized and where it is simple to navigate through only essential information.

6. Acknowledgments

We wish to thank Patricia Chiasera, for her precious comments and suggestions; and Annalisa Mattuzzi for her help and contributions.
Special thanks to Michele Marini for his revision and his consense to the effort necessary in the writing of the paper.

A Branching/Merging Strategy for Parallel Software Development

Jim Buffenbarger[1] and Kirk Gruell[2]

[1] Boise State University
and
Hewlett-Packard Company
buff@cs.boisestate.edu
[2] Hewlett-Packard Company
gruell@boi.hp.com

Abstract. In many software configuration management (SCM) systems, branching and merging are fundamental operations, supporting isolation and integration (respectively). Unfortunately, the obvious branching and merging strategies have unpleasant consequences. This paper presents a less obvious branching and merging strategy, for parallel software development, which does not suffer these consequences. In particular, it presents a way of updating an active branch from a new baseline. The strategy can be described as "merging at a label." It has been successful at managing unnecessary branch proliferation and change isolation in an industrial SCM environment.

1 Introduction

Software configuration management (SCM) systems can be partitioned into version-oriented and change-oriented systems [3]. Version-oriented systems are represented by Sccs [9], Rcs [11], Cvs [7], and CLEARCASE [2]. Change-oriented systems are less popular; one such system is AIDEDECAMP [10]. This paper focuses on version-oriented SCM systems.

In a version-oriented SCM system, branching and merging are fundamental operations. A software system is typically created and maintained by multiple developers working simultaneously, often modifying the same file at the same time. Branching provides isolation, while merging provides subsequent integration. The idea seems simple, and the literature promotes this simplicity, but the obvious strategies have unpleasant consequences. Some of these side-effects are well known [13]. Others are described here, along with a less obvious strategy that is free from the side-effects. This new strategy has been successful in an industrial SCM environment.

The strategy described here is applicable to SCM systems supporting versions, branches, and merging. This set includes many popular systems (e.g., Sccs, Rcs, Cvs, and CLEARCASE). The strategy is particularly suitable for projects composed of many tasks, where each task adds a feature to the product or fixes a bug. Many projects fit this profile.

The problem with the obvious strategies is that they conflict with the reasonable philosophy of isolating independent changes on separate branches. It is a somewhat subtle problem, but there are two symptoms: independent work that cannot be merged, removed, or analyzed independently; and too many files with a particular branch. The former symptom might produce the complaint "I couldn't just merge. I had to cut-and-paste some of my previous changes onto my new branch." The latter symptom might provoke the invective "Hey! When I updated my branch from the new baseline, the merge tool checked-out a zillion files on my branch."

A successful strategy for branching and merging is important to a software-development project. At one level, it accomplishes the Project Plan, supporting multiple serial and parallel subprojects and their integration milestones. At another level, it mirrors the genealogy of product families [4].

A multiple-developer project is considered here, but the strategy scales easily to a multiple-team project.

Section 2 reviews terminology, Section 3 discusses a developer's requirements for a branching/merging strategy, Section 4 describes obvious strategies, Section 5 presents a less obvious strategy with several advantages, Section 6 considers implementation with two popular SCM tools, and Section 7 concludes the paper.

2 Terminology

Since SCM is a relatively new field, its terminology is still developing. Nevertheless, precise definition of terms is beneficial. These definitions are consistent with those of CLEARCASE, but should be familiar to users of other tools.

Version An SCM data structure, representing the value of a file or directory at a particular time. In some systems, a new version is created by a check-out operation; in others, by a check-in. In all systems, a new version's content is finalized by a check-in operation. Once a version is checked-in, its value does not change.

Element An SCM data structure, representing all versions of a particular file or directory. In its simplest form, an element is a tree, with one node per version. The predecessor/successor relationship of versions is represented by arcs. An arguably better name for this concept is *version group* [12].

Branch One of an element's many subtrees. Starting at the root, or a node with multiple successors, a branch is all nodes and arcs on a path between the start node and a leaf (inclusive).

Label An identifier associated with one version of an element.

Merge The process of creating a new version of an element from a predecessor version and at least one other contributor version. The contributor/result relationship can be represented, in the element tree, by special arcs.

Configuration A set of versions: one for each member of a set of elements. A configuration is typically thought of a as a "version" of an entire system.

Baseline A labeled configuration, often the result of integrating other configurations, and often with desirable characteristics (e.g., "tested" or "released").

3 Requirements

This section describes the portion of a typical software-development lifecycle relevant to a strategy for branching and merging. The sub-lifecycle induces a set of requirements for any branching/merging strategy.

A developer begins a task by selecting a labeled configuration upon which to work. The configuration may be a baseline, or it may be another developer's labeled configuration. For different elements, a label may select versions on different branches.

For example, given the elements in Figure 1, a developer may begin working with a configuration labeled Mem1. Mem1 is evidently baseline Rel1 plus some memory enhancements (i.e., Mem1 is a descendant of Rel1).

The notation in Figure 1 is like that of CLEARCASE. The element name is on top (e.g., main.c). A circle represents a version. The integer in a circle is the version number. A string near a circle represents a label. A rectangle represents the start of a branch. The string in a rectangle is the branch name. The selected configuration is bold circled.

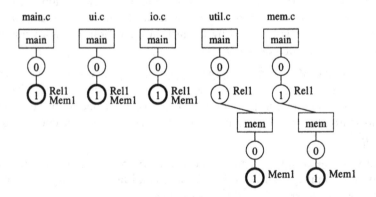

Fig. 1. A developer begins a task.

These five elements are used in examples throughout the paper. Initially, their version trees fall into two structural categories, but they diverge in later examples. Furthermore, the development on each branch is artificially simple, to compress the figures. A reader should imagine a longer sequence of versions on each branch.

While a developer performs a task, changes are isolated from other tasks and other developers [15] . This requires a task's changes to occur on a *task branch*.

A developer changes an element by creating a new version of the element. A new version is created at the lower tip of a task branch. If the task branch does not yet exist, it is created. A task branch is created at the version whose label made it part of the starting configuration.

For example, Figure 2 shows the elements from Figure 1, after ui.c and util.c have been changed as part of as task named gui, which might add a graphical user interface. As before, the selected configuration is bold circled.

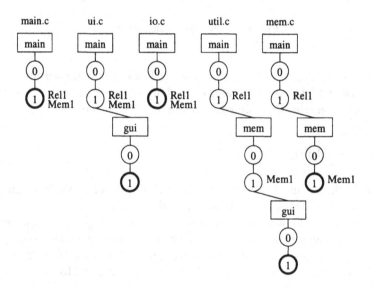

Fig. 2. A developer changes elements.

After a developer has finished a task, or reached a milestone, the selected configuration may be labeled. As before, for different elements, a label may select versions on different branches.

For example, Figure 3 shows the elements from Figure 2, after labeling as Gui1. As before, the selected configuration is bold circled.

Some tasks are "simply" integrations of other tasks. In particular, the task of making a baseline may consist of merging labeled configurations from multiple task branches. An integration task may use an existing branch (e.g., main) as its task branch.

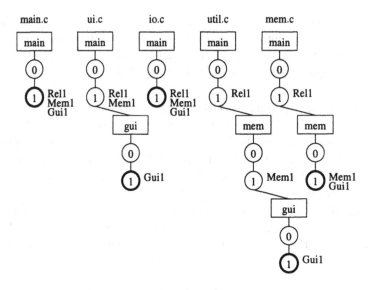

Fig. 3. A developer finishes a task.

For example, Figure 4 shows the elements from Figure 3, after integration to branch main and labeling as Rel2. A dashed arc represents a merge contribution. The selected configuration, after the merge, is bold circled.

4   The Problem

Now, go back in time to Figure 2. The gui developer is working on a task, creating new versions of elements on her task branch.

Suppose someone produces a configuration, and the gui developer wants to "update" her configuration from the other configuration. The other configuration may be a recent baseline, or it may be the result of someone's work on another task branch. This is a very common scenario (e.g., pages 113, 379, and 386 of [2]).

For example, in Figure 5, another baseline Rel2 has become available, and the gui developer would like to incorporate its changes.

An obvious way for the gui task to incorporate Rel2 changes is for the gui developer to merge from versions labeled Rel2. For example, such a merge would transform Figure 5 into Figure 6.

Unfortunately, this merge causes every element changed between Rel1 and Rel2 to have an gui task branch, regardless of whether the element is actually changed as part of the gui task (e.g., io.c and mem.c in Figure 6).

The io.c case represents the vast majority of elements, and is especially distressing. Typically, the number of elements changed for a task is relatively small, compared to the number of elements changed between baselines. Therefore, a merge like that of Figure 6 typically creates an overwhelming number

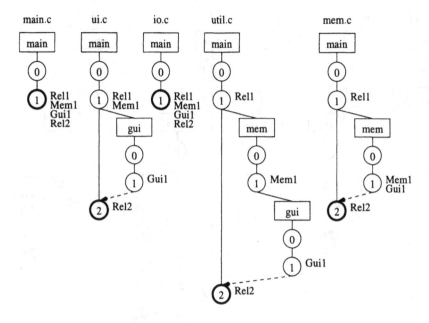

Fig. 4. A developer makes a baseline.

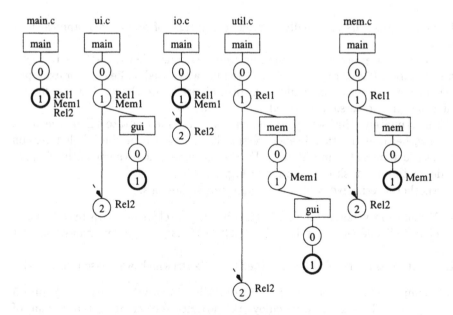

Fig. 5. A developer wants to update her configuration.

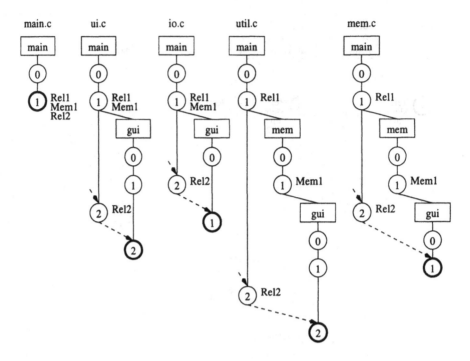

Fig. 6. An obvious merge to update a configuration.

of branches that are not really related to the task of adding a graphical user interface.

An obvious alternative to merging from versions labeled Rel2, is to select versions labeled Rel2 rather than Mem1 (which was based on Rel1). For example, such a change in selection would transform Figure 5 into Figure 7. These figures differ only in the versions selected for io.c and mem.c.

Unfortunately, this selection change does not incorporate all of the Rel2 changes, because the task-branch version is preferred over the labeled version (e.g., ui.c and util.c in Figure 7). Furthermore, it removes some of the changes made for the mem task (e.g., mem.c in Figure 7).

Another alternative, which is perhaps not so obvious, is to:

1. Merge from versions labeled Rel2, but only for elements with branches mem or gui. While this sounds difficult, CLEARCASE merge commands support it.
2. Select versions labeled Rel2 rather than Mem1 (which was based on Rel1).

For example, such a merge and change in selection would transform Figure 5 into Figure 8. This alternative enjoys the advantage of creating a minimum of new branches, but it suffers from the disadvantage of adding some of the Rel2 changes to the gui branch. Such an addition is a disadvantage because once changes are added they are difficult to remove. Removal could be required if a serious defect is subsequently discovered in the Rel2 changes. Similarly, the

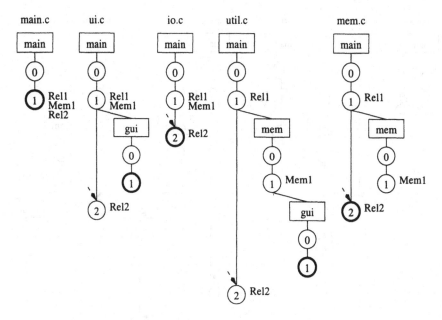

Fig. 7. An obvious selection change to update a configuration.

gui changes might be needed elsewhere, without (some of) the Rel2 changes. Fundamentally, the gui task is separate from the task of integrating the gui and Rel2 changes, so they should be performed on separate branches.

Thus, the obvious solutions have unpleasant consequences.

5 A Solution

Consider Figure 5 again, where a developer has created a task branch named gui, from a configuration labeled Mem1, which is based on baseline Rel1. As before, when another baseline Rel2 becomes available, the gui developer would like to incorporate its changes. A better way to add the Rel2 changes to the gui changes is to:

1. Choose a new task branch upon which to work, say gui2.
2. Select versions labeled Rel2 rather than Mem1 (which was based on Rel1).
3. Merge from the old task branch gui, creating the new task branch gui2, at the version labeled Rel2. In addition to the gui changes, this merge adds some of the mem changes to gui2 (e.g., util.c in Figure 5).
4. Merge from the label Mem1, perhaps creating the new task branch gui2, at the version labeled Rel2. This merge adds the rest of the mem changes to gui2 (e.g., mem.c in Figure 5).

This process is colloquially called "merging at a label" and is shown in Figure 9.

Creating a new branch is reasonable, because it is for a new task. Branch gui2 contains the integration of the Mem1 configuration, the gui changes, and the

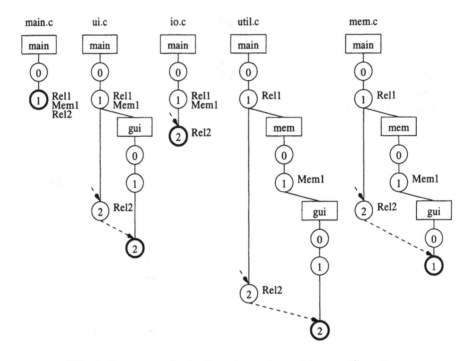

Fig. 8. A merge and selection change to update a configuration.

Rel2 baseline. Furthermore, it is the starting point for additional gui2 changes. If a defect is detected during work on the gui2 branch, the pre-integration configuration can be easily tested for the defect, because no post-integration work occurs on the gui branch. In other words, it is easy to reselect the configuration of Figure 5.

Creating a branch for each element changed for a task is much better than creating a branch for each element changed for a baseline. This is because a task typically changes far fewer elements than a baseline. Comparing Figure 9 to Figures 6, 7, and 8:

- There is no difference for stable elements, like main.c.
- A new task branch is created for elements changed in the old task, like ui.c and util.c. This is acceptable, because there should be few such elements.
- A new task branch is not created for elements changed only in the new baseline, like io.c. This is good, because there should be many such elements.
- Either way, a new task branch is created for elements that did not select the old baseline, like mem.c.

On the surface, this strategy appears similar to the strategy of Template Regulated Alternative Development (TRAD) [5]. TRAD is merge protocol that determines if a merge from a "private" branch to a "public" branch can be performed safely. If so, it is. Otherwise, the merge automatically makes a new private branch, which is merged to instead. After the new private branch has

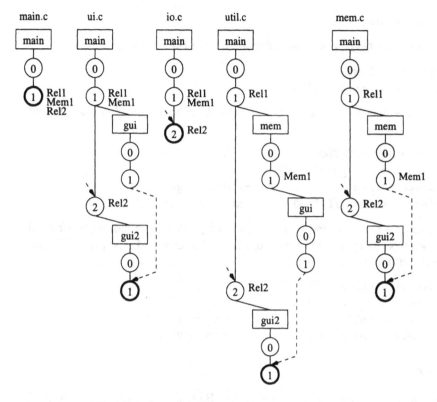

Fig. 9. An better way to update a configuration.

been reviewed and tested, it can then be merged to the public branch. The difference, then, is that merging at a label simplifies integration from a public branch to a private branch, while TRAD regulates integration from a private branch to a public branch.

Merging at a label is a low-level integration mechanism, but it is well-suited to today's version-oriented SCM systems. While the strategy can certainly be employed directly, one can imagine a tool layer based upon RCS or CLEARCASE (for example), which implements the strategy. Such a tool would present a more abstract environment to a user, who typically thinks in terms of "my changes" and "their changes," and has a vague desire to combine them. The tool would accept arguments naming tasks and labels and transform a user's environment appropriately. In this way, an SCM system could offer some of the benefits of "change sets" or "change packages" [10] [6] [14], without too much overhead.

6   Implementation

The merge-at-a-label strategy is easy to implement with CLEARCASE, but it can also be implemented with RCS (or one of its variants).

6.1 ClearCase

A developer can begin work, as in Figure 1, with the config spec:

```
element * Mem1
element * /main/LATEST
```

Then, a developer can work on a task branch, as in Figure 2, with the config spec:

```
element * CHECKEDOUT
element * .../gui/LATEST
element * Mem1              -mkbranch gui
element * /main/LATEST      -mkbranch gui
```

Finally, after a new baseline becomes available, a developer can incorporate the new baseline's changes by merging from the old branch and label, as in Figure 9, to a view with the new config spec:

```
element * CHECKEDOUT
element * .../gui2/LATEST
element * Rel2             -mkbranch gui2
element * /main/LATEST     -mkbranch gui2
```

6.2 RCS

The following commands assume a shell like BASH [8] and reasonable values for the shell variables AllFiles, FilesToChange, and FilesToMerge.

A developer can begin work, as in Figure 1, with the command:

```
co -uMem1 $AllFiles
```

Then, a developer can work on a task branch, as in Figure 2, with the commands:

```
for f in $FilesToChange ; do
    ci -f -u$(version $f).1 $f    #make branch
    rcs -ngui:$(branch $f) $f     #name branch
    co -lgui. $f                  #check out
done
```

where version determines a working file's version:

```
ident $1 | awk 'NF==8 {print $3;}'
```

and branch determines a working file's branch:

```
version $1 | awk '{sub(/\.[^.]+$/,""); print;}'
```

Finally, after a new baseline becomes available, a developer can incorporate the new baseline's changes by merging from the old branch and label, as in Figure 9:

```
co -uRel2 $AllFiles
for f in $FilesToMerge ; do
    ci -f -u$(version $f).1 $f   #make branch
    rcs -ngui2:$(branch $f) $f   #name branch
    co -lgui2. $f                #check out
    rcsmerge ...                 #merge
done
```

7 Summary and Conclusion

Branching and merging are rather simple operations, when viewed from a low-level perspective, but the high-level problems of task and integration management can be more difficult to solve. The obvious techniques for updating a task branch with a new baseline —merging from the new label or selecting the new label— are unsatisfactory. Instead, the technique of merging at the new label, thus creating a new task branch, is more effective.

This strategy has been successfully employed at Hewlett-Packard's (HP) Workgroup Color Division (WCD) in Boise, which develops firmware for HP's color laser printers. WCD is a CLEARCASE and MULTISITE [1] shop, with about one hundred developers. The following narrative, from WCD's integration engineer, describes their initial recognition of the problem.

> At the beginning of our project, we were changing about 600 to 900 versions per release, with release intervals being typically a week. Most of the changes were due to drops of code from different partners. Usually, the developers in our lab were just consumers of the drops of code and had no intention of changing, let alone looking at, the drops of code. With our first strategy, we quickly found problems of, what appeared to be, branching files for no reason, basically creating duplicate versions for most of the elements. These problems were coupled with the confusion of having files on the development branch that were not related to the developers' tasks. One such case, I recall, was a team of about 4 developers trying to update their team's development branch with a new baseline. They had been working on their branch in isolation for the course of about three releases. When it came time to update, they were amazed to find out that about 800 files ended up being merged to their branch, especially since there were only about 35 files on their branch before the merge.

Initially, WCD was using the first obvious strategy described in Section 4. After a couple of months, to alleviate the problem, the second obvious strategy described in Section 4 was tried. Gradually, after another couple of months, the merge-at-a-label strategy was adopted. None of these strategies were enforced processes. Rather, they were simply recommended methods of integration. Integration is a difficult process, and most developers are more than willing to listen to suggestions for improvement.

The strategy has likewise been employed at HP Boise's Workgroup LaserJet Division (WLD), which also uses CLEARCASE and MULTISITE. WLD develops firmware for some of HP's monochrome laser printers. An experiment was performed about a week before the camera-ready version of this paper was submitted. The experiment involved a task requiring changes to one source file. The task began from the latest release of the firmware, corresponding to label Rel1 of Figure 5. Before the task was finished, the task branch was updated from a new release, corresponding to label Rel2 of the same figure. The first obvious strategy created 449 branches, whereas the merge-at-a-label strategy created only one branch. The other strategies discussed in Section 4 would have created zero branches and one branch (respectively), but would have suffered from the problems described in that section.

The merge-at-a-label strategy is particularly applicable to a project whose product is constructed by performing a set of many tasks, where a typical task adds a feature to the product. This is related to the idea of change sets and change packages. By isolating tasks on separate branches, a developer can integrate at the task level. This is important, because once multiple tasks are integrated to a branch, it is very difficult to separate them. In a multiple-product code base, a feature may not be valid in all products, so it is not very wise to mix the development of a product-specific feature with the development of a feature destined for all products.

References

1. Atria Software, Inc. *ClearCase MultiSite Manual*, 1996.
2. Atria Software, Inc. *ClearCase User's Manual (Unix/Release 3.0)*, 1996.
3. P. Feiler. Configuration management models in commercial environments. Technical Report CMU/SEI-91-TR-7, Software Engineering Institute, Carnegie Mellon University, 1991.
4. C. Ghezzi, M. Jazayeri, and D. Mandrioli. *Fundamentals of Software Engineering*. Prentice Hall, 1991.
5. J. Hunt, F. Lamers, J. Reuter, and W. Tichy. Distributed configuration management via Java and the World Wide Web. In *Proceedings of the International Conference on Software Engineering, 7th Workshop on Software Configuration Management*, pages 161–174. Springer-Verlag, 1997. Also: *Lecture Notes in Computer Science #1235*.
6. D. Leblang. Managing the software development process with ClearGuide. In *Proceedings of the International Conference on Software Engineering, 7th Workshop on Software Configuration Management*, pages 66–80. Springer-Verlag, 1997. Also: *Lecture Notes in Computer Science #1235*.
7. R. Pesch. *CVS — Concurrent Versions System*. http://www.delorie.com/gnu/docs/cvs/cvs_toc.html.
8. C. Ramey and B. Fox. *Bash Reference Manual*. ftp://prep.ai.mit.edu/pub/gnu/bash.
9. M. Rochkind. The source code control system. *IEEE Transactions on Software Engineering*, pages 364–370, December 1975.

10. Software Maintenance and Development Systems, Inc. *Aide-de-Camp Product Overview*, 1995.
11. W. Tichy. RCS: A system for version control. *Software: Practice and Experience*, 15(7):637–654, July 1985.
12. W. Tichy. Tools for software configuration management. In *Proceedings of the International Workshop on Software Version and Configuration Control*, pages 1–20. Teubner-Verlag, 1988.
13. S. Vance. Advanced SCM branching strategies. In *1998 Perforce Users Conference*, 1998. http://www.vance.com/steve/perforce/Branching_Strategies.html.
14. D. Weber. Change sets versus change packages: Comparing implementations of change-based SCM. In *Proceedings of the International Conference on Software Engineering, 7th Workshop on Software Configuration Management*, pages 25–35. Springer-Verlag, 1997. Also: *Lecture Notes in Computer Science #1235*.
15. L. Wingerd and C. Seiwald. High-level best practices in software configuration management. In *Proceedings of the 8th International Workshop on Software on Configuration Management*. Springer-Verlag, 1998. http://www.perforce.com/perforce/bestpractices.html.

The Unified Extensional Versioning Model

Ulf Asklund[1], Lars Bendix[2],
Henrik B. Christensen[3], and Boris Magnusson[1]

[1] Department of Computer Science, Lund University, Sweden. {ulf I boris}@cs.lth.se
[2] Department of Computer Science, Aalborg University, Denmark. bendix@cs.auc.dk
[3] Department of Computer Science, University of Aarhus, Denmark. hbc@daimi.au.dk

Abstract. Versioning of components in a system is a well-researched field where various adequate techniques have already been established. In this paper, we look at how versioning can be extended to cover also the structural aspects of a system. There exist two basic techniques for versioning - intentional and extensional - and we propose a unified extensional versioning model for versioning of both components and structure in the same way. The unified model is described in detail and three different policies that can be implemented on top of the general model are exemplified/illustrated by three prototype tools constructed by the authors. The model is analysed with respect to the number of versions and configurations it generates and has to manage. Finally, the unified extensional model is compared to more traditional intentional models on some important parameters. The conclusions are that the unified model is indeed viable. It not only provides the functionality offered by the intentional model with respect to flexibility during development and management of combinatoric complexity, but also offers a framework for management of configurations that enables systems to provide much more advanced support than is commonly available.

1 Introduction

Many models for configuration management [Tic88, CW98], as well as available tools, e.g. ClearCase [Clear] and CVS [Ced93], make a clear separation between how they handle atomic entities (versioned objects, modules, etc.) and composites (configurations, libraries, systems). In these models, atomic entities are version controlled individually while configurations are formed by applying *selection mechanisms*. When considering all atomic entities at the same time the number of possible combinations of their versions and variants is overwhelming. Using rules (such as the 'latest') is an attempt to automate this selection process.

We present experience from using another model, the *Unified Extensional Versioning Model*, where both atomic entities and configurations are version controlled extensionally. This model relies on a mechanism, *version concentration*, to reduce the number of combinations that need to be considered. These combinations, i.e. versions of configurations, that arise are the subset of versions that the user actually explore and are thus the ones that are, or have been, interesting and meaningful for the user.

The unified extensional versioning model has several interesting features compared to models that combine extensional versioning of atomic entities and intentional selection of configurations:

- Simple conceptual framework: Basically developers/users have to learn only one single concept namely "a version of an entity".
- Modularization principle: As any version of an entity embodies the bound sub-configuration that is rooted in it, it allows the well-known principle of encapsulation and abstraction to be applied at the SCM level.
- Scaleability: It is general in the sense that it can be used recursively - configurations can form parts of new configurations.
- Consistency: The versions of configurations that are encountered are the ones explicitly created, and thus likely to be interesting; in contrast to a combination generated by a (potentially flawed) ruleset.
- Architectural traceability: A configuration in a particular version uniquely defines the version of all its constituent parts; thereby not only the evolution of atomic data (like source-code or document text) is traced, but just as important also the evolution of the very structure and architecture of the system, that is, changed, added, and deleted relations between entities.

Elements of the unified extensional versioning model has independently been developed and explored by the authors while building three different systems with different aims and motivations.

COOP/Orm is a configuration management prototype system that has been designed explicitly to support development in distributed groups, people that work tightly together, but are geographically distributed [Ask99, AMP99]. Some of the demands from this situation - collaborative awareness and supporting both synchronous and asynchronous interaction - have been reflected in the design: a very explicit version control system, support for fine-grained version control and support for hierarchical structures.

CoEd is a research prototype for supporting collaborative writing of hierarchically structured documents. It was designed to solve the specific problems students had when writing their semester reports. In particular, focus is put on providing overview of the document and communicating information through version histories. Furthermore, it is possible to directly modify the structure of the document under full version control.

Ragnarok is an architecture based software development environment prototype. The logical architecture of a software project is used as framework for version- and configuration management; this leads to an SCM model that minimizes the gap between the architecture oriented design domain and the SCM domain. Furthermore, it provides strong traceability of the architectural evolution.

In all three systems we have arrived at models that share a common foundation. In some cases, the prototypes we build do not support all the same functionality. This is because we have focused on different aspects but in each case the systems can (at least in principle) be extended to support the full unified extensional versioning model. We thus argue, that the model has proved useful in these different situations and has a value also in its generality, and simplicity.

In the rest of this paper, we first characterize the traditional models and identify some of their drawbacks. Then we present a *unified extensional versioning model*, both in its general version and the particulars of its three different instantiations. In chapter 4, we discuss the implications of the model and compare it with the intentional model. Finally, we draw our conclusions.

2 Existing Versioning and Configuration Models

One of the fundamental problems when dealing with configurations is that with already a small number of components - each in a number of versions and variants - the number of possible combinations get very large. Mathematically, the number of combinations grow exponentially with the number of components and versions and any attempt to deal manually with **all** of them is unmanageable. This problem of combinatorical explosion has to be dealt with in every model. First we survey and evaluate existing solutions before presenting our model in the next chapter.

At this point we also need to be precise about how we use the term 'configuration'. *A configuration is a named collection of atomic entities and other configurations.* Two versions of the same configuration may differ in that they include different entities and/ or the same entity in different versions. Other authors would see what we call 'versions of configurations' as different configurations. We see a set of selection rules as a *specification of a configuration* while others would identify the specification with the configuration it might result in. In our terminology a configuration is always bound, while a configuration specification can be bound or generic. Our use of the terms is consistent with the common CM-view on atomic entities where a file has identity and might exist in several versions (which is in contrast to non-version-aware tools that see different versions as different files).

2.1 Dealing with configurations - Intentional versioning

Many existing CM-systems (ClearCase, CVS, etc.) and models use what is sometimes called 'intentional versioning' of configurations in order to handle the problem of combinatorical explosion. The approach builds on formulating selection rules which are then used to choose the particular variant and version of an atomic entity. Often these rules are evaluated on demand when the atomic entity, a file, is needed - for viewing, editing or translation. Although this approach is one way to limit the selection problem, it has some drawbacks.

- The representation of a configuration is indirect, embedded in the formulation of the rules (e.g. in a small script file), and in the build information (often in a 'makefile'). Given such a rule-based specification, the only way to find out what the configuration really is, in terms of what files are included and in what versions, is to actually build it and register the result.
- Differences between configurations in terms of what files are included in what versions are hard to find out since that can not be deduced from comparing the sets of rules. The only way to find out is to evaluate the different sets, register them and then compare the results.

- Consistency is hard to guarantee since incompleteness or 'errors' in the rules may go unnoticed for a long time, and only show when a new version of some file is created and then result in an unintentional (wrong) configuration. As a consequence there is never a guarantee that a given rule will result in the same set of files in the same versions when evaluated at a later time. For important configurations, such as releases, it is often paramount to be sure that all included files can be found and recreated in exactly the relevant version. As a safeguard all files included in such configurations are often copied and stored separately.

- Tagging is a way to label versions of individual files and when used methodically can be used to pin the files and their versions as included in a configuration. Unfortunately this is a rather primitive mechanism since there is not always a guarantee that such lables are not changed afterwards. There is no support for relating configurations registered in this way to each other or to calculate the difference between them.

- The rules can include generic facilities such as selecting the 'Latest' version of a file which change over time, resulting in so called 'generic' configuration specifications. The same rule-based specification of a configuration can thus over time result in many different resulting configurations. This mechanism can thus be seen as a further way to limit the effects of the combinatorical explosion problem, but it creates a new problem since it defeats traceability. It is impossible to guarantee that the same system will be build from the same generic rules at a later time. In the extreme case one can not be sure that the versions of the files just compiled are the same as the ones viewed in an editor.

Intentional versioning of configurations is used by most traditional, state-based CM systems as well as by change-based systems. Based on the analysis above and the obvious lack of support for rather common situations we have found it motivated to explore other ways to solve the problem of combinatorical explosion. Before outlining the solution presented in this paper we will first review how versioning of atomic entities, files, are handled.

2.2 Dealing with atomic entities - Extensional versus Intentional versioning

Change-based systems, e.g. Aide-de-Camp [Crn92, AdC90], COV [GKY91, MLG+93], name deltas between versions of atomic entities rather than the versions themselves. An advantage of this mechanism is that the deltas can be combined in many more ways than there are typically versions in a state-based systems and also in ways not foreseen by the creators of the deltas. The possible combinations are somewhat limited by restrictions among some of the deltas that might exclude or presume each other, but the difference is still big. For example all versions that in a state-based system can be created through a trivial merge can here be created directly. A needed version of an atomic entity (a file) is put together on demand when needed (for viewing, editing, translating). In existing changed based systems this task is handled through rules and selection, thus using intentional versioning also for atomic entities.

In a change-based system the number of potential versions of each atomic entity is larger. The number of possible combinations is thus also larger. The combinatorical explosion problem of configurations thus gets even worse in change-based systems. In existing systems this problem is again handled through use of selection rules. 'Intentional versioning' is thus used consistently for atomic entities as well as for configurations.The criticism we formulated above for handling configurations with intentional versioning thus applies both when dealing with configurations and atomic entities. The change based approach might have other advantages, but when combined with intentional versioning as commonly done it does not improve on the situation described above.

In contrast to change-based systems, *state-based systems* use 'extensional versioning' when dealing with atomic entities, e.g. files. Extensional versioning means that all the versions of the entity are explicitly represented. They can for example be presented as a version graph and a given version can be retrieved by identity at a later time in exactly the form it was created. Versions of entities can be compared and related to each other, e.g. by the partial relation 'derived from'.The problems we listed above for configurations when using intentional versioning are thus not present when dealing with atomic entities using extensional versioning.

A fundamental criticism of traditional state-based systems is that they offer very different mechanisms for dealing with atomic entities and with configurations. Unfortunately this leads not only to proliferation of concepts, but also to a weak support for managing configurations.

New approach: The Unified Extensional Versioning Model

Traditional state-based systems and change-based systems are similar in that they use intentional versioning for handling configurations. In this paper we put forward a radically different approach - using explicit versioning also for configurations. We will show how we with this approach counter the problem of combinatorical explosion both in general, and further with different mechanisms in the three prototype systems we have built. The model we present also avoids the problems discussed above in connection with intentional versioning of configurations. Finally it has the advantage of offering one unified version model for atomic entities as well as for configurations.

	Atomic entities (files)	*Configurations*
Intentional versioning (rules)	Change-based systems	Change-based systems Traditional, state-based systems
Extensional versioning (explicit versions)	Traditional, state-based systems UNIFIED MODEL	UNIFIED MODEL

3   The Unified Extensional Versioning Model

In this chapter we first present the unified model, both from a somewhat formal perspective and illustrate with examples. We then describe how the model has been used in three systems we have built.

3.1   The model

Document model

A 'document' in this model is structured and the structure can be expressed in a grammar as shown in Figure 1. Relations between documents is also part of the model through the notion of links. 'Document' is here used in a general sense of a file, dataset, that can contain any form of information, e.g. program source, English text, graphics, etc.

```
D ::= T                       D - document (abstract node, non-terminal
T ::= C|L|N                   T - tree (abstract node, non-terminal)
C ::= T* ['local data']       C - composite node (concrete node, production
L ::= 'name' 'version'        L - link node (concrete node, production)
N ::= 'local data'            N - atomic node (concrete node, production)
```

Fig. 1.   Grammar specifying the document structure

- N-nodes support storing data. It can be text, source code, graphics or any other information which is thus of no concern to the model. Different N-nodes can contain different types of data, so the model supports documents with mixed data.
- C-nodes support Composition, whole-part relations. This is introduced in recognition of the need for support of hierarchies commonly used to structure text documents (chapters, sections, paragraphs), programs (modules, classes routines) and many other kinds of information.
- L-nodes support Reference semantics, arbitrary relations between documents. This is introduced in recognition of a need to share common parts between configurations (libraries, modules, classes in programs, and illustrations, appendix, quotations etc. in textual documents). The 'name' attribute stored in an L-node is the information needed to link to another document. The 'version' attribute is the information needed to denote a specific version of the document which will be explained in the next section.

The model supports structure in two ways, through C-nodes and L-nodes. There is thus some redundancy in the model since composition, tree-structures, can be built out of a restricted use of L-nodes. The motivation to include C-nodes and explicit support for composition in the model is that tree-structures is a fairly common case and that we view composition and reference semantics as distinct cases.

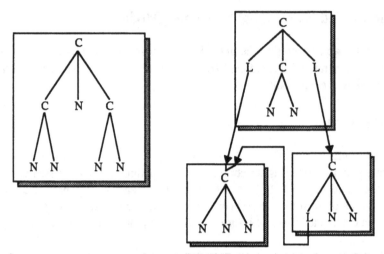

Fig. 2. Composite document and configuration represented in the Unified Extensional Versioning Model.

Traditional document models can be understood in our model as documents which only contain one N-node. Such models does not support internally structured documents and do not support relations between documents.

Examples of structured documents

Figure 2 depicts examples of document structures. The left hand example shows a single tree-structured document. The right hand example shows three structured documents linked together. Lines indicate composition in a document while arrows are references between documents.

A more concrete example of a tree structure is a book. The left hand example in Figure 3 depicts such a book consisting of three chapters, where chapter one and three both have two sections respectively. The relation between the book, the chapters, and the sections are 'consists of' or 'contains' and the total structure represents one entity - the book.

A concrete example of a structure also using L nodes is Java source code for an application consisting of classes and packages. The small right hand application in Figure 3 consists of one class and it imports two classes, A and B. The class-to-operation relation is of the same type as the relations used in the book, i.e. 'consists of' or 'contains'. The relations import-to-class and su.cl-to-class (super class) is, however, references i.e. links. It would e.g. be wrong to say that class B consists of class A. Moreover, both class A and B might be included in many other applications. The semantic difference between composition and reference semantics will also show up in versioning of documents discussed below.

Versioning

Both structure and contents of a Document will evolve over time. In the extensional model all node types (N, L, or C in the grammar) are explicitly versioned. Creation of a new version of a node is triggered by any of the following conditions:

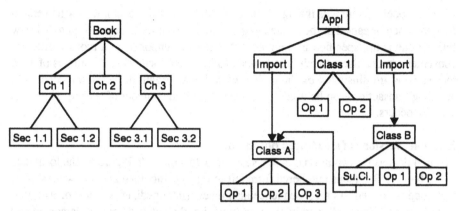

Fig. 3. Example of structured documents: A book and Java source code.

- N,C-nodes - a new version is created when its 'local data' is changed
- L-nodes - when name, or version is changed
- C-nodes - also when any of its sons is added, deleted, or changed

Changes to a document occurs during a 'session', a long transaction. The extent of a session is defined by the user who explicitly or implicitly controls when a session starts and ends. During one session there is created at most one new version of each node if needed according to the rules above. Repeated edits to local data in one node are thus part of the same change to that node. Several additions, deletions and changes to the sons of a C-node also result in only one new version of the node. The length of a session, and thus the amount of changes that go into the same version, can be used to control the granularity of the versioning. When a session is ended the created versions of the nodes can no longer be modified.

Versions are related through the derived-from relation and can form arbitrary DAG structures. The version mechanism thus can represent concurrent development and merge of Documents, atomic entities as well as configurations.

For a document a session means that a new version of the document is created. For each node changed during the session a new version of the node is created (but only one). The rule that C-nodes are considered changed also when only their sons are changed results in an effect know as 'change propagation' [Kat90]. Any change will result in new versions of all father nodes of the changed node up to the top node (if not already changed in the same session). The effect that there is only one new version of a father-node during a session can be seen as a *version concentration* mechanism.

This automatic change propagation mechanism for documents is consistent with how changes of compositions are perceived. For example a change to a paragraph in this paper means the whole paper is changed. It also means that a version of a document uniquely determines which internal nodes to include and for these which version.

For relations between documents the version attribute of an L-node determines the version of the referenced document. If another version of the referenced document is wanted the version attribute of the L-node needs to be changed (and thus the L-node itself, all enclosing C-nodes, and ultimately the document where it resides).

The model thus implies that updating a link to another (for example newer) version of a document means that the referencing document must be changed. When and how this is done is not specified in the model, but can be supported in a tool by different convenient mechanisms to administer updates between documents. Examples of such mechanisms are illustrated by the tools present below. Again the session mechanisms and long transactions can be used by the user to limit the number of such versions that actually occurs.

Example, versions of structured document

Figure 4 depicts the evolution of a tree structured document. In Figure 4b the local data in the N-node '3.1' (sons numbered from left to right) is modified and a new version of that node is created. As a consequence also a new (intermediate) version of its father node is created (node '3') and of the root node, i.e. the entire document is considered changed. In Figure 4c the user has continued the session by also modifying node '2', thus creating a new version of it. Since a new version of its father node already exists change propagation has no effect in this case. It is thus possible to make many related modifications to the document, all included in one and the same version of the document. The user controls when a session is ended and thus when and what versions are actually created.

An example where the structure shown in Figure 4 might arise is a book with three chapters, see Figure 3. A change in one of its paragraphs results in a new version of the book and so does several modifications during the same session. This situation is consistent with the situation that would arise if the versioning model would not acknowledge structure and the three chapters would be maintained as one single file. Versioning of compositions using change propagation coincide with the situation when more primitive composition mechanisms are used. A document can also be seen as a bound configuration of its nodes. Given a version of the document - the version of all its nodes are directly determined.

Example, versions of configurations of documents

In this example we consider a situation with three documents, one (D1) importing the other two (D2, D3) as shown in Figure 5. Modifications to D2 and D3 results in new versions of these, one for each session depending on how the user chooses to organize his work. In Figure 5 we show the situation after one edit session with D2 and two ses-

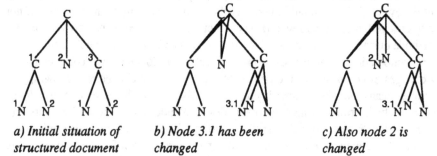

a) Initial situation of structured document   *b) Node 3.1 has been changed*   *c) Also node 2 is changed*

Fig. 4.   Many changes within the same version.

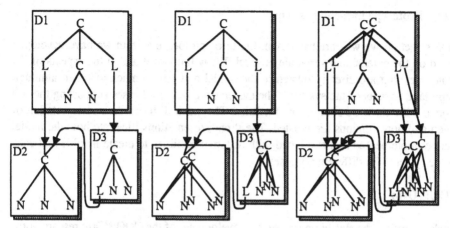

Fig. 5. Editing an L-node often means rebinding to a new version.

sions with D3. In order to use the newer versions of D2 and D3 also a new version of D1 needs to be created where its link nodes are changed. The user can here decide to move to the latest version of D2 and D3 (as shown in the Figure) or to use any other combinations of versions of D2 and D3. The structure is in this case a small graph, but links can be used to build higher trees and indeed arbitrary directed acyclic graphs and the same mechanisms applies. Situations where structures as the one presented in Figure 5 can occur is for example in software development where the documents are source modules, depending on each other such as in the situation illustrated in Figure 3.

Summary
We have presented the unified extensional versioning model and explained how it handles structured information, versioned relations between documents, and how the extensional versioning work for these documents. We have also shown how the combinatorical explosion problem is countered, by the use of long transactions, called sessions, and the effect that hierarchies limits the number of combinations of its components, version concentration.

It still remains to show how this model can be used in tools and to see if it is viable in practice. One can immediately foresee two potential problems. If, for example, sessions in practice are very short the number of versions created can still be very large and this would defeat the version concentration mechanism. Our experience presented below shows that this is not the case. Another possible problem would occur if the overhead to update a link to use a new version of a referenced document would be large, since this will be a fairly common operation. Again the presentation of our tools below show that this is not the case. Mechanisms to swiftly perform such updates over sets of files have been designed and tried out in practice.

3.2 Prototype implementations

In this section we will briefly present the three prototype system we have developed based on the extensional versioning model. We will concentrate on the aspects of the prototypes that are directly related to the model and ignore much of other, although important, aspects of the systems. The systems are not in all cases supporting the full model, but only need some of its facilities. They also differ in their interpretation of when and how versions are created. The three presentations illustrate how the model can be implemented and combined with different facilities to create flexible and easy to use systems for different purposes.

COOP/Orm

Background   The starting point for the development of the COOP/Orm research prototype [MA93, MAM93, MA95, MA96] has been the aim to support teams of programmers working together, providing a collaborative editing environment, an area that combines problems from both CSCW (Computer Supported Cooperative Work) and SE (Software Engineering). From the CSCW perspective the requirements collaborative awareness and support for concurrent work have resulted in fine grained versioning (both spatial and temporal), optimistic check-out and strong support for merge. COOP/Orm is built as an on-line system with a built in editor. Everything is thus stored in the repository rather than in separate workspaces. SE issues have lead to better support of hierarchical structures, and sharing of common parts between applications.

Document model   The COOP/Orm environment implements the grammar as defined in Figure 1. The size of a document is user defined. Typically the granularity of a document could be an article, a class, a package, etc. Within the document the granularity of atomic N-nodes can for example be a section, a method, or even the body of a method (e.g. dividing a method into head, body and documentation), as desired by the user.

Versioning of one document   All changes to a document are made during a session, which involves three steps, (1) selecting an originating version of the document and creating a new version from it, (2) making a sequence of edits to, changing/adding/deleting, one or several nodes within the document, and finally (3) terminating the session by 'freezing' the new version. Both the creation and 'freezing' of versions are explicit operations by the user who thus determines the length of a session.

Versioning of configurations of documents   Relations between documents are implemented through link-nodes, which are nodes within the internal structure of a document and can thus only be changed during a session. In a structure of documents each document has its own sessions, during which its link-nodes can be modified.

A user can choose to modify documents in short sessions thus giving detailed control and traceability, but new versions of configurations for each edit. It is also possible to use long sessions and let versions of documents remain open allowing many changes of their (link) nodes. If this model is mixed with the manual (more frequently freezing versions) a balance of strong version concentration and traceability can be obtained.

CoEd

CoEd [BLNP97, BLNP98] is a prototype environment that supports collaborative writing through the use of advanced version control policies. CoEd manages hierarchically structured textual documents only, where the relation between the parts is that of composition. This means that CoEd does not support the L-nodes of the general model. In the specifying grammar the L-production is removed and the T-production simplified accordingly: T::=C|N. When changes have to be propagated, new versions are created of all nodes on the path from the node that was changed to the root of the document.

CoEd works as a repository only, which means that the user cannot directly edit the bound configurations of the document, as they are immutable. So a traditional checkout-edit-checkin way of working has to be followed. A session starts when a structure is checked out from CoEd. It is possible to check out just a part of the document by indicating the C-node that forms the root of the subpart. When the (sub)structure has been checked out, a single file containing all the LaTex text for the (sub)structure will exist in the users file system. This file is mutable and the user can edit it as he wishes, changing even the structure of the document. After the editing, the file representing the (sub)structure is checked back into CoEd. The file is parsed and if it represents a valid LaTex structure, CoEd discovers what has changed. Changes are propagated all the way up to the root of the document. When the document is in the user's file system, its structure is not explicit anymore, but only indicated by the respective LaTex commands. However, whenever the document is inside the repository, its structure is explicit and it is kept as a series of versions of bound configurations that can be browsed and retrieved.

Even though CoEd has no explicit notion of a workspace, it does implement the possibility to work directly on the structure of a document inside the repository. If we want to 'promote' section 3.2 of this paper to become chapter 4, this can easily be done by dragging the section to the new chapter's place. This creates a new bound configuration of the document, where section 3.2 is deleted from its original place in the structure and inserted at the new place. Presently, there is no explicit session concept when working inside CoEd's repository even though all changes are versioned. This means that if we make several modifications to the structure this will result in several new bound configurations being created, even if they might conceptually be considered as one change.

Ragnarok

Ragnarok [Chr99c, Chr99b, Chr99a, Chr98b, Char98a] is a software development environment with focus on software architecture and architectural evolution. In Ragnarok, a document represents a software abstraction in a software system. A document may have one C-node only, and multiple N- and L-nodes. N-nodes store the implementation of the abstraction (source code), and L-nodes architectural relations (like composition, depend-on (import) or subclass-of) between abstractions. Ragnarok simulates

composition using reference semantics (L-node links) and the tree-structure requirement is ensured by checking at the user interface level.

Ragnarok uses a traditional repository/workspace model. A session takes place
locally in a workspace, and ended (changes are committed back to repository) by a
check-in operation. Ragnarok has transitive change propagation over L-nodes. Thus, if
a document, A, is changed then any document that includes A in its transitive, reflex-
ive, closure of L-links is considered changed; but only locally in the workspace where
the change was made. Ragnarok creates new, local, copies of all affected nodes and
rebinds L-nodes to reflect the changed architecture.[1]

The session concept is highly flexible; essentially each document has its own session. A document's session is started by the first change to the document, directly (edit
of N- or L-nodes) or indirectly (something in its transitive closure changed). A document's session is terminated by a check-in; and the check-in is propagated to all documents in its transitive closure. Thus, changes are committed to the repository and all
sessions closed in the sub-configuration that is rooted in the document. However, document sessions higher in the hierarchy (documents not in the closure of the document,
but related to the document) remains open, which is how version concentration is made
in Ragnarok. As a concrete example, less than 30 versions of the root document in the
ConSys system (see data below) was made over a two year period where the system's
size more than tripled in terms of KLOC.

Finally, Ragnarok allows new configurations to be constructed intensionally in a
workspace, as it provides a rule-based check-out. An example is given in section (4.4
Supporting concurrent work)

Ragnarok is currently used in three real development projects, outlined in the table
below and detailed in [Chr98a]:

	ConSys	*BETA Compiler*	*Ragnarok*
Used since	Mar. 96	Feb. 97	Feb. 96
No. developers	3	4	1
No. files	1340	290	160
No. lines (KLOC)	240+binary	120	45

3.3   Summary

In this chapter we have presented the Unified Extensional Versioning model and three
systems that use the model. The model improves on the observations regarding traditional models that we mentioned above.

---

[1] This propagation and rebinding mechanism simulates ordinary development where
module relations are inherently generic: "A imports B" and thus any change in B indirectly affects A.

- Representation of configurations is direct. A configuration can be represented with a document that contains links to the other documents included in the configuration.
- Configurations are versioned. As any other document a configuration exists in versions. Versions of configurations are explicit, they can be named and organized.
- Versions of configurations are related to each other so their development can be traced. They can be compared and differences can be presented as components being added, deleted or changed. There is no need for auxiliary support such as 'Tagging'.
- Consistency is provided in the versioning sense. A version of a configuration can always be reproduced in exactly the same form. There is no need to copy systems in order to provide reproducibility.

In the presentation of the three systems we have highlighted how the model can be used and tailored to three common, but rather different situations: in a CM tool supporting software development in a traditional Unix tool-based setup, in an integrated tool for authoring papers, and in an integrated environment providing synchronous and asynchronous interaction for development in a geographically distributed setting. The Unified model go beyond traditional models in that it provide more support in a number of important situations.

- Version concentration. The number of versions of a configuration that has to be considered is greatly reduced compared to the possible combinations given by mathematics.
- Architectural traceability. From any level of configurations the exact changes that has been made over time, can be traced down to the individual file.
- Modularization. Configurations can be handled as modules where the internals and its detailed development is separated from its interface and its development from external point of view.
- Scaleability. Configurations can be included as elements in larger configurations thus forming hierarchies is directly supported. This is an essential property when managing any complex system.

These and other aspects of the model will be further discussed in the next chapter.

4   Discussion and Comparison

In this chapter we will discuss some effects and consequences of the unified extensional versioning model and its use and compare with the intentional model.

4.1   The Unified Extensional Versioning Model from the users perspective

A consequence of the unified extensional model is that the concepts 'versioned component' and 'bound configuration' are unified. Extensional versioning is used in both cases which means that the user can use the same model for versioning components as well as for versioning configurations. In the same way as a user can decide what changes go into a new version of a component s\he can control through the session mechanism what goes into a new version of a configuration. In both cases the version represents what the user regards as a meaningful state. The versions of configurations, including content and structure, are explicitly represented in the version database. This allows the user to identify, inspect, compare and reason about the properties of the configurations both in terms of content and structure: How and when new sections or chapters have been added or removed, how the dependency structure between software modules have evolved, etc. The hierarchical formulation of the model allows the user to organize the system in layers of libraries, sub-systems and systems all explicitly represented and versioned.

In a software engineering context, the extensional model implies that a version of a module not only embodies the source of that module but also contains information about the modules that it depends upon, which can be characterized as the SCM equivalent of the modularization principle. The developer creates what s\he thinks are meaningful and consistent combinations of versions of the included documents. The user of such a configuration (a library, module etc.), who have less insight in its internals, are thus confronted with choosing among a small number of meaningful versions of its configuration.

Builds of a system is always made from a bound configuration which in the extensional model is explicitly available as a version of the system configuration. Likewise, bill-of-material facilities are directly supported since the structure of the system and version of all components are given from a version of the system. What remains to capture is external aspects such as versions of used tools, options, etc.

In comparison the intentional versioning scheme is more complex from a user point of view. In order to specify configurations the user needs to master a separate selection mechanism for versions of configurations, often a small, specialized, language. (Languages that are often error-prone to use and does not deal gracefully with structural changes.) Encapsulation is weak since selection is performed over entire systems, also over parts not known in detail by the developer. Resulting, bound, configurations can be labled, but there is no support for comparing or relating such configurations to each other. As a result users are directed to produce and store listings of components and their versions in order to support bill-of-material facilities.

4.2 Managing the combinatorical explosion of configurations

The problem of combinatorical explosion is one of the fundamental problems which has to be countered in every model. In the extensional model this is achieved through the effect called 'version concentration'. Consider first the tiny example in Figure 5c. On the document level, in D3 there are $2**3=8$ possible configurations of versioned nodes of which only 3 have been created. On the relation level there are $2*3=6$ possible configurations of the existing versions of D2 and D3, but here only 2 have been created. The fact that mathematical combinatorics give that there are in all 32 possible combinations of the versions of the leaf nodes in this small example is thus of no interest since the user have control over which combinations to explore and only these, for him/her interesting configurations, are created. Furthermore, the two-session update of D3 is only reflected as one new version of the configuration, D1. The hierarchical structuring in combination with the session mechanism is thus helpful in reducing the number of versions of configurations - version concentration also on the configuration level. For the rest of the system, using D1, the number of combinations of the files in this sub-system that needs to be considered is thus decreased from 32 to 2. Should, however, a user want to use another configuration of D1, say using the middle version of D3, the model makes it easy to represent such a configuration as another version of D1.

In realistic situations the numbers are much higher, 100 files in 10 versions each result in $10*100$ mathematically possible combinations which are concentrated to perhaps 100 interesting versions of the configuration. Of these only a small number are relevant at any given time, often the last in each sequence of versions resulting from concurrent work (branch).The version concentration mechanism works in the same way at each level of configuring sub-systems into larger sub-systems and so on. At the system level there are comparatively few versions of the configuration corresponding to interesting versions of the system as a whole; releases, test-versions and so on.

In the intentional model the problem of combinatorical explosion is countered by using selection rules, ideally choosing the intended version of each file. Such rules are not directly depending on the number of revisions of files (i.e. the age of the system) which makes this approach scale up over time. The rules do, however, depend on the size of the system since the number of modules, each with its branches and labled configurations, will grow with the system. Selection rules are global and need to reflect all the modules at the same time. In contrast the hierarchical composition used in the extensional system scales well as illustrated with the Ragnarok experience. A system with 1340 files resulted in only 30 versions on the system level during a period of 2 years. A period when the system was heavily modified and trippled in size and the number of possible configurations would be uncountable.

4.3   Supporting and managing changes

A CM system must support simple and low-overhead facilities for developers to change and extend a system. Ideally such support should be possible to offer staying within the used versioning model. The main mechanism in the intentional model for this is generic selection rules, such as 'Latest', selecting the latest created revision of a modified file, which often is what the user intends to use. A configuration specification using generic rules will not need to be changed in order to include a new revision of yet another updated file and is thus convenient to use for a developer.

The corresponding mechanism in the extensional model is the session mechanism which allows several changes to a component as well as to a configuration to be included in one revision. Using this mechanism the developer will create a new revision of a component (or configuration) indicating that this part of the system is under revision. All changes the user makes to the component in this revision will be accumulated. When the user so decides the session is concluded and the version of the component is closed and can no longer be modified. When dealing with components, the situation in the extensional and intentional models for the developer comes fairly close. Check-out and check-in corresponds to creating and closing a revision of a component.

When dealing with configurations the situation is, however, different. In the extensional model the user needs to create revisions also of configurations in order to include revisions of its components, thus also if the component itself is not explicitly revised. Thanks to the session mechanism, the user can leave a revision of a configuration open and thus accumulate revisions of several of its components and also several revisions of the same component. Again, when the user so decides, the session is concluded and the user can thus control the granularity of the revision, for example to let a revision of a configuration represent a logical change. The experience from the use of Ragnarok shows that sessions tend to be longer the higher up the hierarchy the component is, and thus very long on the system level.

There are situations where a number of revisions needs to be created or closed at the same time. When the user decides to finish a session and close a revision of a configuration, all open revisions of its components that it uses must also be closed in order to form a bound configuration. This could be a tedious operation, involving many components. The Ragnarok system has demonstrated how it can find and close the relevant revisions of the components leaving to the user only to close a revision of the configuration acting as the root in a sub-graph. The users of Ragnarok has been interviewed [Chr98a] and they state that the 'intermediate' versions created were not problematic. 'It is the job of the tool' to handle the internal, possibly complicated, bindings, but the tool was reported to handle this adequately, and they did not find the presence of intermediate versions a problem. The 'intermediate' versions are, however, essential in order to facilitate full traceability in all situations. In the intentional model this operation corresponds to checking in components, labeling the configuration, and updating the selection rules (making sure generic rules are replaced), seemingly a heavier operation.

The extensional model trivially supports reconstruction of a version of a configuration that has been closed since it can no longer be modified. In the intentional model this takes a correctly formulated, and stored, set of selection rules, which is hard to guarantee in particular in presence of heavy restructuring of the system. Alternatively one has to store the full list of components and versions for the entire system. On top of this the extensional model offers full traceability among the explicitly stored versions of configurations. It supports relations between such versions of configurations and a tool can show how they are derived from each other, compare them, show the differences down to every included component.

4.4 Supporting concurrent work

In projects involving many developers it is often a necessity that work can be done concurrently by several developers, including revising the same documents and configurations. To make this a practical possibility, it must be simple and swift to merge the result of concurrent work affecting both the component and configuration level. Merging concurrently developed revisions, temporary variants, of a component is an established technique. Here tools make use of the known content of the two temporary variants and their common ancestor to perform a three-way-merge, suggesting the resulting merge and detecting lexically interfering changes in the two variants. Dealing with configurations the work is often structured so development starts from a common alternative, but done in a separate alternative. When such a task is concluded the revisions are made available by updating the common alterative. In case of concurrent work, any changes in the common alterative must first be merged with the new changes in the separate alterative, tested etc., and then used to update the common alternative. Thus the last developer to conclude his concurrent work will have to deal with merging with earlier work.

In the intentional model concurrent work is often aided by workspace areas where the revisions of changed files are stored and visible for the local developer. The tool then aides in updating the common alterative as well as merging parallel work, i.e. updating the workspace with files changed in the common alterative and initiating merge of files that has been changed in both places.

In the extensional model configurations are explicitly versioned and concurrent work is represented as variants in its versiongraph. Merge is thus achieved in the same way as for components - a new version is created with the variants as predecessors. With the same rules as in the intentional system a tool will select the latest revision of a component changed in only one of the alternatives and initiate a merge of a component that has been modified in both alteratives. Since the model is recursive a component might be a new configuration and the process repeated until all components have been merged (the same ones as in the intentional model), and the affected configurations have been facilitated with a new version representing the merge. The difference between the models thus lies in the last point. The explicit versioning of configurations makes it simple to explore the history of configurations which is particularly useful in the context of concurrent work and merges.

In the merge-case above we notice that all the versions of the involved configurations are a consequence of the model and can be automatically managed by a tool. A similar situation occurs when one want to integrate with changes to the system unrelated to the concurrent development. In the intentional model this is provided through the generic rules (e.g. the 'latest' rule of ClearCase, and the CVS command 'cvs update'). As an example of similar functionality in the extensional model, the Ragnarok prototype provides a command, 'gettip', that specifies that the latest version of any component should be used in the users workspace. This command retrieves the latest revision of all components from the version database, updates the bindings between the components and configurations in the workspace, creating new versions of configurations as needed. This is a proven and often used technique to merge parallel work of different parts of a software system.

4.5   Implementation aspects and some usage experience

Storage space overhead is an important aspect when managing large systems. When storing components, standard delta storage techniques can be used as usual for compact storage of revisions. On top of that, the model presented in this paper can represent internal structure in a document, which can be used to share common nodes and subtrees between variants facilitating compact storage and fast retrieval of variants. The representation of bindings between documents, L-nodes, is comparable to what is already present in form of external declarations (or comparable mechanisms) in source-files. The representation of explicit versions of these bindings is an additional, but very small cost and to store differences of these bindings is very compact. It should be compared to label all files in a system using the traditional approach. Although we have not made a careful study of this we are confident that our approach will come out favorable in a comparison due to the hierarchical structure (even if the labels are chosen very short).

In all long-lived systems the version history becomes long-winded and partially uninteresting. In particular long sequences of successive updates tend to be of little interest after a while. This is a general problem that can be observed already with common tools for versioning components. In the extensional model the effect of 'intermediate' versions may contribute to make such sequences for configurations even longer. In any case the problem is general and in a graphical interface (such the one used by some of the systems described earlier) may have to consider techniques where such sequences are collapsed, but still accessible, in the presentation.

In this paper we have argued that the 'version concentration' effect will eliminate the potential overhead created by the intermediate versions of configurations. This effect is created by the session mechanism (collecting revisions over time) and the version propagation mechanism (collecting revisions over a sub-tree/sub-graph of the system). The last mechanism will work better with a certain fan out at each configuration and will clearly not help in the unlikely situation of a system built as a linear list of components. In order to see how 'version concentration' worked in practice, the Ragnarok prototype was in early February 1997 equipped with two additional house-keeping attributes, that allows the actual amount of proliferation in the version database to be assessed quantitatively. During check-in each new version stores two boolean values: 1) if this version has a change in the 'local data' attribute compared to the ancestor version, and 2) if this version was created as a result of a directly issued check-in command. In Figure 6 below, data for these attributes is shown for every quarter of the year in the period 1997 to 1998. Column T shows the total number of versions entered into the version database during the indicated period. S is the percentage of T where attribute 1) is true, i.e. the percentage of versions where 'local data' was changed. Similarly, O is the percentage of T where attribute 2) is true, i.e. the percentage of versions created by a direct command. Thus 100%-S is the percentage of intermediate version, versions that would not have been created in an intentional model.

The important point is the stability over time of the percentages O and S. The number of version nodes in the repository is proportional to the number of check-ins and to the number of changes; thus there is no combinatorial explosion. Furthermore, the numbers tells us that there is roughly one 'intermediate' version for each 'essential' version. For each explicit check-in there is 3-8 files checked in (which means 1.5-4 'essential' versions). Thus rather than creating more work for the user having to check

	ConSys			BETA Compiler			Ragnarok		
Quarter	T	O	S	T	O	S	T	O	S
1997 I	-	-	-	-	-	-	13%	12%	44%
1997 II	405	20%	29%	255	34%	53%	447	13%	36%
1997 III	332	43%	58%	505	30%	55%	457	12%	39%
1997 IV	290	24%	33%	366	23%	62%	138	11%	32%
1998 I	289	31%	43%	253	34%	66%	111	11%	54%
1998 II	499	25%	32%	624	29%	64%	106	12%	36%
1998 III	478	44%	51%	385	26%	52%	207	10%	35%
1998 IV	349	19%	46%	147	32%	60%	73	13%	57%
Sum	2438	32%	45%	2518	30%	60%	1648	13%	40%

Fig. 6. Data from use of Ragnarok

in 'intermediate' versions the situation is that in Ragnarok a user have to handle fewer explicit check-ins than in a traditional system.

4.6 Support for variant selection

The presentation of the Unified Extensional Versioning Model in this paper has focused on its support for versioning, including temporary variants for concurrent work. The presentation has not considered support for permanent variants. The intentional model has an advantage here in that its selection rules can be used both to select among revisions and variants. The extensional model thus needs to be extended in order to support representation and selection of variants. The authors do, however, feel that an interesting approach would be to include facilities in the tradition of 'conditional compilation' and thus provide conditional parts of a document. This would make it possible to keep variant parts close together, often preferred by developers, rather than enforcing them to be separate files (or separate variants of a file). Integrating support for variants in the model is for the time being left as future work.

5 Conclusions

In this paper we have described a new model for versioning of both components and structure of a system. In our analysis of existing approaches we came to the conclusion that in general it is better to use the same concept for the versioning of structures as for the versioning of components. Furthermore, we identified some weak points in the intentional model for versioning of structures and that it had some weaknesses compared to the extensional model used for atomic entities. This led us to propose our unified extensional versioning model using extensional versioning for both atomic entities and configurations. We have shown that the good aspects of the intentional model, flexibility in development and reducing the problems of combinatorical explosion, can also be achieved in the extensional model. On top of that we also have shown that it facilitates a number of other essential aspects. The applicability and use of the model have been demonstrated by presenting three different systems built using the model.

We have also shown that the unified model is superior in several important aspects.

- It offers the Version Concentration mechanism to counter the combinatorical explosion of versions.
- The explicit representation of Configurations makes it possible to organize configurations hierarchical, and to modularized configuration management,
- The explicit versioning of configurations makes it possible to guarantee repeatability, a version of a configuration is well defined and can always be recreated. This makes it unnecessary to make dedicated copies of important configurations - such as releases. It support architectural traceability which is achieved through comparing versions of configurations, and it also directly support grouping related changes together into logical changes.
- The model is general since it does not restrict the tool-implementor and the model in itself does not impose any specific policy or process on the user.

The use of the model in three systems for rather different situations support the claims on generality and of cause also of the usefulness of the model. Experience and data from in particular one of the implementations support the claim that version concentration works also in practice.

On a more subjective level we think it is a benefit that the problem of managing configurations and atomic entities can be handled through one set of concepts and mechanisms rather than two. Rather obviously we find the concepts we have developed natural and simple, but more importantly we have found them easy to explain and to adapt by users. This makes us believe that the model we have presented is to some extent 'natural' and since it also powerful, as argued above, we like to suggest it as an alterative for others building CM systems.

References

[AdC90]   Software Maintenance and Development Systems. Aide-de-Camp Product Overview. Software Maintenance and Development Systems, Concord, MA 1990.

[Ask94]   Ulf Asklund. Identifying Conflicts During Structural Merge. In Magnusson et al. MHM94.

[Ask99]   Ulf Asklund. Configuration Management for Distributed Development - Practice and Needs. Licentiate thesis, Dept. of Computer Science, Lund University, Sweden. 1999.

[AM97]   U. Asklund and B. Magnusson. A Case-Study of Configuration Management
           with ClearCase in an Industrial Environment. In Proceedings from SCM7 -
           International Workshop on Software Configuration Management, R. Conradi
           (Ed.), Boston, May 1997, LNCS, Springer Verlag.

[AMP99]   U. Asklund, B. Magnusson, and A. Persson. Experiences; Distributed
           Development and Software Configuration Management. In *Proceedings from
           SCM9 - International Symposium on System Configuration Management*,
           J. Estublier (Ed.), Toulousem France, Sept. 1999, LNCS, Springer Verlag. To
           appear.

[BLNP97]   Lars Bendix, Per N. Larsen, Anders I. Nielsen, Jesper L. S. Petersen: CoEd -
           A Tool for Cooperative Development of Hierarchical Documents, Technical
           Report R-97-5012, Department of Computer Science, Aalborg University,
           Denmark, September 1997.

[BLNP98]   Lars Bendix, Per N. Larsen, Anders I. Nielsen, and Jesper L. S. Petersen. CoEd
           - A Tool for Versioning of Hierarchical Documents. In Magnusson [Mag98].

[Ced93]   Per Cederqvist. Version Management with CVS. Available from
           infosignum.se, 1993.

[Chr98a]   Henrik Bærbak Christensen. Experiences with Architectural Software
           Configuration Management in Ragnarok. In Magnusson [Mag98].

[Chr98b]   Henrik Bærbak Christensen. Utilising a Geographic Space Metaphor in a
           Software Development Environment. In Prasun Dewan, editor, *Proceedings of
           EHCI'98, IFIP Working Conference on Engineering for Human-Computer
           Interaction*, Crete, Greece, September 1998. Kluwer. To appear.

[Chr99a]   Henrik Bærbak Christensen. The Ragnarok Architectural Software
           Configuration Management Model. In Jr. Ralph H. Sprague, editor,
           *Proceedings of the 32nd Annual Hawaii International Conference on System
           Sciences*, Maui, Hawaii, January 1999.

[Chr99b]   Henrik Bærbak Christensen. The Ragnarok Software Development
           Environment. *Nordic Journal of Computing*, 6(1), Jan 1999.

[Chr99c]   Henrik Bærbak Christensen. RAGNAROK: An Architecture Based Software
           Development Environment. PhD thesis, Department of Computer Science,
           University of Aarhus, Denmark. 1999.

[Clear]   http://www.rational.com/products/clearcase

[Crn92]   R. D. Cronk. Tributaries and deltas. BYTE, pages 177-186, January 1992.

[CW98]   Reidar Conradi and Bernhard Westfechtel. Version Models for Software
           Configuration Management. *ACM Computing Surveys*, 30(2):232--282, June
           1998.

[GKY91]   B. Gulla, E.-A. Karlsson, and D. Yeh. Change-oriented version descriptions in
           EPOS. Soft. Eng. J. 6, 6 (Nov.), 378-386. 1991.

[HM88]   G. Hedin and B. Magnusson. The Mjölner environment: Direct interaction
           with abstractions. In S. Gjessing and K. Nygaard, editors, Proceedings of the
           2nd European Conference on Object-Oriented Programming (ECOOP'88),
           volume 322 of Lecture Notes in Computer Science, pages 41-54, Oslo, August
           1988. Springer-Verlag.

[Kat90]   Randy H. Katz. Toward a Unified Framework for Version Modeling in
           Engineering Databases. ACM Computing Surveys, 22(4), December 1990.

[MA95]   Boris Magnusson and Ulf Asklund: Collaborative Editing - Distributed and
           replication of shared versioned objects. Presented at the Workshop on

Mobility and Replication, held with ECOOP 95, Aarhus, August 1995. Available as: LU-CS-TR:96-162, Dept. of Computer Science, Lund, Sweden.

[MA96]   Boris Magnusson and Ulf Asklund. Fine Grained Version Control of Configurations in COOP/Orm. In Sommerville, I., editor, Proceedings of the 6th International Workshop on Software Configuration Management, LNCS, Springer Verlag, Berlin. 1996

[Mag98]   Boris Magnusson, editor. *System Configuration Management*, Lecture Notes in Computer Science 1439. ECOOP'98 SCM-8 Symposium, Springer Verlag, 1998.

[MAM93]   Boris Magnusson, Ulf Asklund, and Sten Minör. Fine-Grained Revision Control for Collaborative Software Development. In Proceedings of ACM SIGSOFT'93 - Symposium on the Foundations of Software Engineering, Los Angeles, California, 7-10 December 1993.

[MHM94]   Magnusson, Hedin, and Minör (eds). Proceedings of Noridc Workshop on Programming Environment Research. Lund, June, 1994.

[MLG+93]   B.P. Munch, J.-O. Larsen, B. Gulla, et. al.. Uniform versioning: The change-oriented model. In Proceedings of the 4th International Workshop on Software Configuratino Management. Baltimore, MD, May 1993.

[MM93]   Sten Minör and Boris Magnusson. A Model for Semi-(a)Synchronous Collaborative Editing. In Proceedings of the Third European Conference on Computer Supported Cooperative Work, Milano, Italy, 1993. Kluwer Academic Publishers.

[MMAxx]   Boris Magnusson, Sten Minör and Ulf Asklund: A Model for Semi-(a)Synchronous Collaborative Editing. To appear in Journal of Computer Supported Collaborative Work.

[Ols94]   Torsten Olsson. Group Awareness Using Fine-Grained Revision Control. In Magnusson et al. MHM94.

[Tic88]   Walter F. Tichy. Tools for software configuration management. In Proceedings from International Workshop on Software Version and Configuration Control, Grassau, Germany, February 1988.

Deployment Descriptions in a World of COTS and Open Source

Wilfred J. Hansen

Software Engineering Institute, Carnegie Mellon University,
Pittsburgh, PA 15213-3890, USA
wjh@sei.cmu.edu

Abstract. Deploying software to a user environment now involves much more than copying a few files. The deployer—software or human—must test for needed COTS components and modify various system files to establish the conditions needed for the new package. With the advent of "open source" distributions, deployment expands to encompass building the system as well as installing it. Describing this process for automated execution entails writing statements in languages for describing the environment, dependencies thereon, and requisite actions. We consider requirements for these three languages in light of our experience with developing an open source distribution at the Software Engineering Institute.

Keywords. COTS, deployment, system build, software build, Makefile, make, imake, open source, system construction scripts, system modeling, module interconnection language

1 Introduction

"Open source" software available in source form now augments the burgeoning set of COTS (Commercial-off-the-shelf) software products already available. Both introduce new complexities to configuration management. Other projects such as Adele [2] and PCL [9] have concerned themselves with the problems of modeling and managing the complexity arising from externally initiated, asynchronous upgrades; this paper explores the impacts on the task of describing system construction and deployment. Occasionally, deployment can be done with a simple file transfer, but usually it also requires updates to system information, emplacement of icons, initiation of background processes, and the like. We will consider all these deployment difficulties here in the light of some experience with creating scripts for GEE, a pedagogical prototype at the Software Engineering Institute. In particular, this paper will focus on three languages needed to express aspects of the deployment task—languages for expressing environmental conditions, dependencies, and actions.

The main "theme" of the effort to create the construction/deployment system for GEE was Avoidance of Duplication. The goal was that each piece of information be specified in one of a few central definition files and derived from there wherever it was needed. All of the following and more were centralized:

- GEE version number
- directory and file locations
- URLs, host names, and port numbers
- Java CLASSPATH
- command sequences for compilation and testing
- platform dependent flags for system commands

While there is certainly some saving in not repeating lengthy command sequences, the real benefit of Avoiding Duplication is that changes can be made in the definition files and will be consistently reflected throughout the system.

The bulk of the utilization of centralized information was for the generation of the construction/deployment scripts in the form of Makefiles. Most configuration managers offer some mechanism for automatic generation of Makefiles, but descriptions of these systems do not make clear how this occurs. From our experience, no simple scheme where processing is dependent strictly on file extensions is likely to be satisfactory; indeed, seven of the nine Makefiles for GEE components required GEE-specific processing above and beyond compilation and installation. COTS software was accommodated in the system sources by additional directories with idiosyncratic Makefile provisions for

- installation
- addition of libraries to the Java CLASSPATH
- server initiation
- connection between GEE and the COTS product

In what follows, the deployment problems will be largely expressed in terms of deployment of GEE, although the same considerations will apply to any COTS or open source system.

This paper will use the term *transmittal* for an incoming package containing software to be deployed. A transmittal includes the files to be deployed, instructions for their deployment, and various user documentation such as a description of the features and improvements in the new software.

To simplify the recipient's task, the instructions for deployment should be automated by software which we will call a *deployment processor*. Its input is the newly released transmittal; its result is an operational system on the target computer. Use of the deployment processor avoids manual command entry, a process which is tedious, time consuming, error-prone and difficult to document due to the abundance of options and the diversity of possible target environments. Indeed, we suspect that creating deployment processor instructions may be easier than writing accurate and comprehensive, easily-followed instructions for manual deployment.

A critical part of a transmittal is the control files to instruct the deployment processor. Hall, Heimbigner, and Wolf [6] (hereafter, "HHW") identify five categories of such information—*assert constraints, dependency constraints, artifacts, configuration, and activities*—and have implemented a system supporting them [5]. Assert constraints describe dependencies on pre-existing COTS software at the site;

dependency constraints do the same but additionally specify actions that can be taken to ameliorate unresolved constraints. The artifacts describe the files in the distribution. The configuration defines system file changes needed to describe the installation. Finally the activities category is a catchall for arbitrary additional activities.

The HHW categories are mainly descriptive/declarative rather than executable. As such they offer opportunities for automatic processing to aid extensively in building and understanding the installation of the transmittal. However, a purely descriptive interface is insufficient for distribution of software in open source form; there must be greater resort to the executable specifications in the "activities" category. Examining the five HHW categories more closely we can find three sublanguages in which portions are written:

Environment Description Sublanguage - A statement in this language is part of the environment and describes what facilities pre-exist. At the end of a deployment, this statement will be modified to include the changes wrought by the newly installed transmittal. This is also the language of the "artifacts" category.

Dependency Description Sublanguage - Statements in this language specify how the transmittal depends on the environment. What other COTS software must be present? What conditions require the dependency processor to invoke specific actions? This is the language of the "assert constraints" and the preconditions on the "dependency constraints."

Action Description Sublanguage - When a dependency detects that some adjustment is needed--whether a change to the environment or an alteration of the files in the transmittal--the action is specified by statements in this sublanguage. This language is clearly the language of the "activities" category and some subset is needed for the "configuration" category.

Requirements for these sublanguages form the last section of this paper.

Environment Description Sublanguage definitions have been the recent work of two initiatives, Software MIF (now superseded by CIM[1]) and OSD [11]. HHW paints an unpromising picture of these, demonstrating that both are inadequate, even without the added complexity of open source distributions. For the vast majority of users, the issue is moot; they will continue to receive transmittals in object file format and the considerations of HHW will continue to dominate the problem. However, some recipients—we can call them *adjunct developers*--will receive the package in source form, modify it if necessary, build it, and install the result. The source form of the package must carry with it all the information to enable building and testing the system in addition to deploying it.

2 The Deployment Process

Deployment of a COTS product is described by HHW as a life cycle with eight activities:

- *Release* - The transmittal is assembled by the vendor, typically as an archived collection of files.
- *Install* - The files are unpacked from the archive and inserted into appropriate directories on the destination system.
- *Activate* - System files are modified as necessary to allow the user to utilize the product. Icons are added to menus. Initiation of background processes may be arranged.
- *Deactivate* - Remove the modifications made by Activation.
- *Deinstall* - Remove files inserted by Installation.
- *Derelease* - The world is notified of the withdrawal of the product, although sites may continue to use it.
- *Update* - The transmittal is a set of revised files. Appropriate subsets of Install and Activate are performed to incorporate the new files into the system.
- *Adapt* – Definition files are modified to tailor the product to local needs and desires. Files such as document boilerplate may be modified or added.

Open source distributions still require all the above activities, but three new ones must be added: source modification, system build, and test. Rather than try to describe these in a life cycle, I have expressed them in the flow diagram of Figure 1, where the data being operated on are named explicitly.

In this Figure, ovals are sets of files, round rectangles are manual processes, and rectangles are activities carried out by the deployment processor under control of its instructions (which are part of the Source Files). Corresponding to each rectangle is another activity which undoes the action of the rectangle: Build is undone by Clean, Install by Deinstall, Test by Exit, Activate by Deactivate, and Update by Revert. These additional activities are omitted here to reduce complexity.

The most comprehensive viewpoint on Figure 1 is that of a vendor developer who has been asked to add a feature to the system. He or she begins by extracting from a source manager the sources for the subsystem to be changed. The steps continue thus:

The *Modify* step is the manual process of changing the source files as desired. The result is a different version of the source files: some changed, some added, some deleted.

The *Build* step compiles the source files to produce the object files. This may use a specialized deployment processor like *make*. Note that the programmer may build only a single component instead of the entire system.

Adapt, as with HHW, modifies definition files to tailor the package to the needs and desires of the deployment site. For testing, our developer may add temporary control file entries. Ideally, for neither tester nor deployer will these modifications include specifying the locations of existing COTS products; this information should come from statements in the Environment Description Sublanguage.

To conduct a *Test*, the deployment processor initiates the product's execution, but in such a way that the newly built object files supplant those of the same component in the released system. This permits testing to proceed even while the currently released version is in use.

Under control of dependency-action description files, the *Install* and *Activate* steps put the files in suitable locations and initiate any necessary background processes.

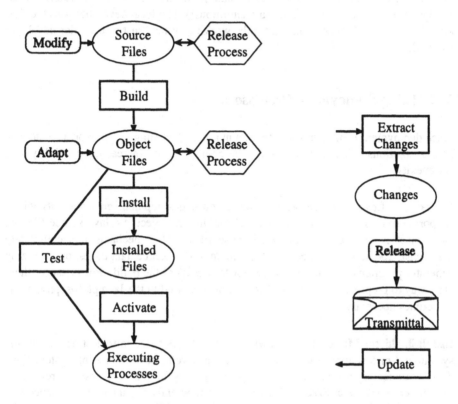

Fig. 1. Deployment Process. The two "release process" hexagons are instances of the process shown on the right.

Figure 1 shows separate instances of *"Release Process"* for source and object files; both proceed through the steps shown on the right in the Figure. The *ExtractChanges* activity determines what files have changed. The *Release* activity takes those files, adds human readable explanations, and creates the transmittal, most likely as a web site or CD-ROM. Finally, the *Update* activity modifies the collection of sources or objects at the destination.

A second viewpoint on Figure 1 is that of a typical destination site. Here there are no Source Files, no Changes, and no activities are performed for Modify, Build, Test, Extract Changes, or Release. The Release Process reduces to receiving the Transmittal and Updating (or initially creating) the Object Files. The administrator then goes through the activities of Adaptation, Installation, and Activation to arrive at a working system. Subsequent Updates are triggered by the arrival of a transmittal package containing either a new system or replacement files.

The last viewpoint is that of destination sites having one or more local adjunct developers who modify the Source Files to improve the package or adapt it for local requirements. At such sites all the blocks of Figures 1 are active. The developer may even Extract Changes from the sources and create a Transmittal for return to the vendor. (The version control issues are enormous!) The local developer uses the Test activity to do tests independently from the working system, just as a vendor developer would do.

3 Existing Deployment Processors

Since deployment is not a new problem, a number of existing systems provide at least partial solutions. We consider them here in order of increasing capability and complexity.

Projects. Least complex are the various code development environments which support *"projects."* In Java versions, each file in the project is a Java source file and the project is built by compiling all those files. This mechanism is completely inadequate for serious projects written in multiple source languages or utilizing generator programs to produce sources for later parts of the build. For instance, there is no way to preprocess Java files. This is not supported in the Java philosophy, but is sometimes necessary.

InstallShield for Microsoft Windows [7] copies files to various destinations in the system and makes appropriate changes to certain well known operating system files. This is satisfactory for object file releases, but useless for source releases. Creation of the delivery package utilized by InstallShield is inherently a manual process since it is driven by a GUI user interface. This renders the InstallShield generator unsuitable for the most general case since it cannot be driven from a script or Makefile

Software Dock [5] provides a complete architecture for deployment. A "field dock" at each deployment site keeps track of all software installed thereon. A "release dock" is created for each deployable system. When a user wishes to deploy a piece of software advertised by a release dock, he or she initiates an agent which negotiates between the local field dock and the desired release dock. The two collaborate to install the software and arrange for notification of future update availability. The current implementation has no provision for building from an open source distribution.

Scripting languages. IBM systems have long had the *REXX* macro language which provides very expressive string handling; Unix systems have various scripting/macro languages like TCL and Perl. All these systems lack an explicit notion of dependencies, but can simulate dependencies with if-then-else. These systems have the same power to solve the deployment problems as any other programming language; their one advantage is in close ties to the shell so program initiation can readily be incorporated in script execution.

Make. The granddaddy of all dependency processor is *make* [3] and its variants like *gnumake* and *nmake*. In these systems, a dependency and its actions are expressed in a `Makefile` with the syntax

```
target-file: source-file(s)
            actions to build target from source-file(s)
```

When the *make* process is invoked, the target-file is checked to see if it is older than one or more of the listed source-file(s). If so, the actions are executed and are assumed to produce a newer version of target-file. Since the actions are passed to a shell, absolutely any action can be taken, so *make* is very general in this respect and has been used for many tasks other than compilation initiation. For instance in a deployment process based on *make* would there would be a target for each of the activities shown in Figure 1.

Despite its power, *make* suffers a number of shortcomings:

(a) At least one process and often two are initiated for each action. This overhead becomes non-trivial when many actions are needed.
(b) The supported dependency mechanism is ill-equipped to deal with the large variety of dependencies required in practice.
(c) It may be necessary to specify different variants of the actions depending on the host platform.
(d) Makefiles can be tediously repetitious due to its limited mechanisms for avoiding repeated actions for multiple target files.

We will see below that various alternative systems solve one or more of these problems, but there is no comprehensive solution to them all.

Autoconf/Configure. *Make's* shortcoming (c), platform dependencies, is addressed by the Free Software Foundation's *autoconf* tool [8], which read a specification of required system capabilities and generates a *configure* script. This script is distributed with the source and executed to initiate a build; its output is a `Makefile`. With this approach, a developer need not create a new system definition file for each of a large number of platforms. Instead, the *configure* script automatically tests for the presence and semantics of libraries in order to create the system definition file and also a definitions file to be included into each C or C++ source file. (Cleverly, *configure* itself uses this definitions file in each of a series of executions which test for one or more capabilities. Thus the file being generated is simultaneously serving as input to the generation process.) Anyone who has tried porting C or C++ programs, without benefit of *autoconf* or some alternative, understands completely the passion of Java proponents for write-once-run-anywhere compatibility.

Imake. Make's shortcoming (d), repetition, is addressed by the X Consortium's *imake* [4]. At heart, the *imake* command itself does nothing more than invoke the C preprocessor on a specified template file. This template #includes first a macro definition file and then a directory-specific file called Imakefile. For each source file or collection of similar source files, the Imakefile calls one of the defined macros which expands to an entire *make* rule including target-file, source-file(s), and actions. In general, an Imakefile is less than 5% of the size of the corresponding Makefile. With imake, shortcoming (c), platform dependencies, is solved by having alternate versions of the definition files for each platform. A combination of *imake* and *autoconf* would have made life much simpler for C developers.

Qed/qef. The most general alternative to *make* is the qed/qef system [10]. As with *imake*, *make's* shortcoming (d), repetition, is solved with macro expansion of a tiny control file in each source directory. A further capability of qed/qef is the provision of several small languages for text processing. These are all interpreted by one process, eliminating much of the system call overhead for actions in *make's* shortcoming (a).

4 The GEE Project

The GEE project—the name stands for Generic Enterprise Ensemble—is an ensemble of COTS products and application code that implements a model enterprise-level information system. Customers are expected to study GEE to understand how the COTS products can be used together and may then subsume some generic portions of GEE into their own systems. Accordingly, GEE is distributed in open source form. In a sense, GEE provides a sort of fill-in-the-blanks enterprise information system; we called it a "genotype" because in addition to the functions of a prototype it also serves as a framework for building a real-life system. COTS products used GEE include Java, Netscape servers and browsers, the Visibroker CORBA tool, an Oracle data base, and Live Software's Jrun tool for Java servlets.

As part of GEE, we implemented a system for build and install that supports both local development and eventual distribution. It addresses many needs:

- Multiple versions. Old versions must remain buildable and installed in order to maintain our history and resolve issues raised by users of those versions.
- Partial build. Permit independent builds of components so we can test local changes without rebuilding the entire system.
- Independent testing. Allow each developer to test a newly revised component without installing it into a full-blown version of the system.
- Developer full build. Let each developer have a separate full installation of the system, if desired.

- Full build and install. Rebuild the system every night to ensure that the released version is current.
- Multiple platforms. Support building on different hardware and operating systems.
- Build at foreign site. Enable a distribution recipient to build and install the system.

In the *make* tradition, build and install are driven from a single control file. The install operation checks first that all object files are up-to-date and, if not, does any necessary compilations

To be able to build GEE on multiple platforms and at foreign sites, our policy of Avoidance of Duplication was employed. Environmental dependencies are segregated into a small number of files that are referenced from everywhere else in the system. The first of these, gee.properties, is a typical Java properties file. However, some of its information is needed also by the build commands and by program modules written in other languages, such as HTML or C. To cope, a small tool was written to read gee.properties and produce gee.h and gee.sed suitable for use as, respectively, a C includes file and a sed control file. With their aid, any file can be converted from a generic version to one tailored by gee.properties. The *imake* dependency processor was chosen as the basis for the build command mechanisms. Its template file, as written for GEE, utilizes the gee.properties definitions via the C includes file.

To support both full builds and component builds, the source tree was split by component, which we defined as roughly the amount of code a developer would create in a week. There is an Imakefile in each component directory and each super-directory contains its own Imakefile with instructions for recursive builds. Distinct *make* targets in all Imakefiles provide separate operations for building, testing, and installation.

Alongside the tree of source components is another tree called external/ and containing installation instructions for each of the COTS products utilized. Performing *imake* and *make* in these directories does whatever is necessary to install that product and utilize it for GEE.

5   Requirements for the Three Description Sublanguages

On the basis of our experience with GEE and other projects we can suggest a number of attributes that the three Description Sublanguages must have. In support of each suggestion, we recount some of our experiences with constructing the GEE build/deployment system.

5.1 Environment Description Sublanguage

Most of what is needed for the Environment Description Sublanguage is covered by CIM [1]. It provides a rich set of attributes and an object oriented structure. Version numbers, for example, are described as three integers separated with decimal points. For GEE itself we support multiple versions and need multiple versions of Java, so CIM provides attributes that could be tested if GEE and Java were described in CIM.

Treating the environment description as solely a tool for deployment processing means that additional mechanisms are necessary if values from the environment are to be utilized in deployed systems. In GEE, for instance, the gee.sed file is utilized to tailor HTML files and shell scripts. This means that the system *must* be built and installed from sources unless it is to be installed into directory paths chosen by the original developers. Various techniques are available for deferral of this value fetching, including server-side-includes for HTML files, but all such techniques add complexity. Moreover, each must be able to fetch values at run-time from the Environment Description.

A single system-wide description of the environment will not suffice. The GEE testing regime attempts to allow each developer a separate environment so there can be independent testing. When two developers are using different versions of Java, their environments are best described in separate environment descriptions. Other tester specific environment information that should be (but sometimes isn't) allowed in GEE include distinct Visibroker ports, web page areas, Java class paths, servlet collections, and data bases.

New Java distributions were not painless for GEE. Package name changes meant that Java source files using those packages had to be revised. The vendor omitted sending an automated tool for this task and it was small enough for us to do by hand. These changes, however, require us to retain the several Java distributions used by various GEE versions.

In order to be able to utilize environment descriptions, there must be well-known sets of attributes names and for each an expected range of values so dependency descriptions can know what information will be available and the precise meaning for each value. It would be too bad if a deployment looked for Netscape and the environment description said that Mozilla (Netscape's internal name for its browser) was available. The definitions of attributes, expected values, and hierarchies must be ever evolving as new technologies and products appear. Since this evolution must be recorded and maintained by some standards organization, it will be interesting to see how this activity is financed and how that financing affects its stability.

5.2 Dependency Description Sublanguage

In *make*, dependencies are expressed in terms of the relative timestamps of source and target files. Clearly the dependency language must also allow expressions referring to attributes and their values from the Environment Description. In addition to the usual arithmetic expressions, the Dependency Description Sublanguage should also offer tests of set membership and numeric range inclusion. Some additional requirements follow.

Better timestamps. When the GEE Imakefiles were first used to unpack distributions of Jrun, JDBC, etc., timestamps failed to prevent repetition of this step because the unpacked files had timestamps preceding that of the archive. From this we suggest that there must also be some form of note that a particular action, say unpacking, has been done to a particular file, in this case the archive. With *make* this is typically done by creating an empty marker file, say .unpacked. This fails, however, when a new archive is installed and the marker file is inadvertently left in place; an easy error since files named .xxx are not normally listed among the files of a Unix directory.

Call signature dependencies. In C++, a class #includes the definitions file for any other class it references. This makes it possible to automatically determine which object files need to be recompiled when the definition of a class has changed. In Java, there are two uncertainties: it is unclear if a change to a source file has changed the class's definition and it is unclear what classes a source file depends upon. There is provision for declaring what classes are utilized, but this can be side-stepped by using fully qualified names or names from classes in the same package--which may be a large number of source files and need not be qualified or imported at all. These conditions make it much more difficult to determine accurately whether a given source file needs to be recompiled due to a change in another source file; it cannot be done with the simple timestamp processing of *make*.

Multi-file compilation. Java supports simultaneous compilation of any number of source files, which is essential to resolve circularities that cannot be resolved with one-at-a-time compilation. This does not mesh well with the standard *make* approach which assumes single-source-file compilation. For GEE, we implemented a little program which checks a list of Java class files and determines that the corresponding source file needs to be recompiled if it is more recent. If a change alters a class definition any client class which is not recompiled will encounter a run-time error. Fortunately, this is infrequent because developers usually remember to change all clients when a class definition changes and changes to those source files will ensure their recompilation.

Platform description. It may be necessary to specify different variants of the actions depending on the host platform. This is not the case with Java, but is an important consideration for systems including components written in C or C++.

Recursive component processing dependencies. Java provides a *javadoc* function to produce a set of web pages describing the interfaces to packages. In preparation for running this command, a list of all source files to be processed is needed. Running *javadoc* for a single directory is fairly easy, but to get full documentation of all packages, a single invocation of *javadoc* over the entire set of sources is needed. The full documentation for GEE had to be produced from the build system, and it was also necessary to be able to create the web pages for a single component or subtree of components. Providing all these capabilities under *make's* limited dependency language proved to be a challenge. It required five rules in the template file, another rule for each Java package, a separate *make* target to build a list of Java source files, and two variables defined in each recursive invocation of *make*.

One large challenge in design of the Dependency Description Sublanguage is to arrange to permit the sort of precedence ordering done by *make*. As far as possible, the user should not have to sequence the instructions in the description file so as to produce an appropriate order of execution for builds and installs. This and other processing are simplified if the Dependency Description Sublanguage is declarative rather than procedural.

5.3 Action Description Sublanguage

Doubtless, the Action Description Sublanguage can be as trivial as that in *make* wherein every action is the invocation of a program; indeed, this capability must be made available as the ultimate fallback. We consider this option below after first describing a number of other less general, but more useful facilities.

Built-in Actions. Rather than initiate a process for every action—as is done in *make*— it seems preferable that the deployment processor provide some set of actions that can be performed directly. These would be available in any environment and would always have the same semantics. A prime example of a desirable built-in action is that of installing a file into a directory. Not only is this capability lacking from *make*, but it is provided in Unix by two programs both called *install* but having different command line syntaxes. Thus *install* had to become one of the GEE properties; it is specified the *imake* template file. Other useful specialized commands would modify system configuration information as for specifying icons, specifying MIME types, and updating the Environment Description.

Installation of COTS components for GEE could have been more easily implemented if each used a standard install built-in command. As it was, they differed. Oracle's distribution of its JDBC interface was accompanied with a list of thirteen steps necessary for installation. Jrun installation initiated an interactive program which further required that the web server be shutdown and restarted. Visibroker and Java had conflicting ORBS which—after much fiddling—was solved by specifying the Java `bootclasspath` switch. Each COTS product also had idiosyncratic setup steps that were necessary in order to connect between itself and GEE.

Macro processing Despite the macro processing done by imake to create `Makefiles` from `Imakefiles`, many problems remained in GEE that could have been solved with a more powerful text processing language available as an integral part of the Action Description Sublanguage. In addition to the uses of `gee.sed` for macro expansion, GEE even needs to preprocess a Java source file:

`GeeProperties.java` is preprocessed so its source code contains the default location for `gee.properties`.

Trying to utilize an external macro processor was especially difficult for generating commands to process Java files. Trickiest was the fact that some Java file names contain dollar signs, which have special, and different, meanings to both *make* and the shell. These files had to be listed for processing by the Java *jar* utility. Moreover, another list with the same files but different directory prefixes had to be created as an additional input. Ultimately, a small program had to be written to massage the *jar* argument list, but despite this every dollar sign in a file name must be represented with four(!) dollar signs in the `Imakefile`.

Since the C preprocessor, *make*, the shell, and *awk* have overlapping quote characters, some tasks were tricky to code. For example, to set the ownership and group of a file it was necessary to write:

```
(df=dest/file; \
cmd=`${LSLD} dest | ${AWK} '/^d/\
  {print "${CHOWN} " $$3 " '"$$df"'";";\
   print "${CHGRP} " $$4 " '"$$df"'"}'`;\
${SH} -c "$$cmd")
```

In this fragment, 'dest' and 'file' are macro expanded into a destination directory and the name of a file therein. The `${LSLD}` command runs *ls* on the destination directory and the output is processed through *awk* to generate a shell command which is executed by the last line. Maddeningly, it is essential to have each and every dollar sign and the quote marks in all three flavors. (The example can be written more naturally if *awk* is invoked twice. But I wanted to use only the most efficient method for a pedagogical example.)

`Makefiles` can be tediously repetitive due to *make*'s limited mechanisms for avoiding repeated actions for multiple target files. In a situation where a Java compilation is a six step process, those same six steps must be repeated for every compilation request. This problem was of course solved by using *imake*, but would have been better solved if *make* itself better supported macros.

Deferred Actions. The `external/` directories in GEE each contain a target `SystemInstall` which is to be executed by the system administrator account. Under this target are those installation steps which cannot normally be done by developers. Commands under this target install other COTS products, arrange initiation of background processes, and so on. They proved their worth when new versions of Jrun and Visibroker were installed, integrated into the environment and connected to GEE via the facilities of their respective subtrees of `external/`. However, since ordinary installers and developers should not utilize administrator privileges as a matter of course, the best way to implement these sorts of actions would be some sort of deferred action queue that the system administrator could review and act on appropriately.

Arbitrary programs. As an ultimate fallback, execution of arbitrary programs is necessary in any build/install language, but there are disadvantages. The program must be found and executed, usually requiring more system resources of memory and processes. There is also a heavy reliance on details of the deployment environment, which may be altered even by such peculiarities as individual deployer's idiosyncratic definitions of system commands. In GEE it proved necessary to use the full path name of every system command in order to avoid such definitions. Having no tools except arbitrary programs leads to tiny helper programs which must themselves be source-managed, built, and made executable for at least the duration of the deployment. Each such tool increases the risk of conflict with some such tool introduced for another product.

Smart Executor. Our problems in GEE with interference from developer definitions leads to the notion that a deployment system, or even the full system, can offer a "smart executor." This tool would be cognizant of the environment description and would chose the appropriate version of a tool for each requestor. Among the other GEE problems that this would solve are that one tool, the Visibroker idl2java, needs to execute under Java 1.1 while the rest of GEE is designed for Java 1.2. The smart executor would notice this from the description of idl2java. As another instance, GEE introduced special commands gj, gjc, and vbstart for running Java, compiling Java, and starting Visibroker, respectively. These were necessary to incorporate all the environment information from gee.properties into the execution; environment information which should have been in an Environment Description were one available.

6 Conclusion

COTS and the advent of open source distributions place new requirements on the deployment processor and its sublanguages for describing the environment, dependencies, and actions. The paper has illustrated these problems with examples from the GEE project undertaken at the Software Engineering Institute.

We have shown that the deployment process itself must be extended to include building and testing the software. These must be provided for by either the deployment processor or an adjunct which serves the role of *make*. Alternatively, the entire deployment may be conducted by the latter, as it is in GEE. In any case, the processor will permit deployment with a minimum of manual processing, leading to less effort, fewer errors, and more seamless operations.

The main theme of the GEE scripts effort was to Avoid Duplication; as far as possible specifications and data were moved to a few central definition files from which all other instances of these values are derived. This produced a flexible construction system, but one in which names are bound too early. Based on the GEE script effort the paper has pointed out a number of characteristics that would be of value in the description sublanguages for environments, dependencies, and actions.

Among other factors, we discovered a great diversity in the requirements imposed by COTS systems: They differed in their mechanisms for installation and interconnection to the application and other COTS products and all added Java libraries that had to be in the CLASSPATH. This complexity would be reduced if all were deployed by a common mechanism.

Do all these experiences suggest that it is time to abandon *make*? It certainly would be pleasant to avoid some of *make*'s quoting nightmares. However, *make* is well known and widely available and still provides enormous flexibility, so it is difficult to see what advantages a new system can offer to wean-away *make*'s existing users.

Acknowledgements I am indebted to the other members of the GEE team: Scott Hissom, Fred Long, and Robert Seacord under the leadership of Kurt Wallnau.

References

1. Desktop Management Task Force, "Common Information Model (CIM); Core model white paper", Version 1, August 5th, 1998 (http://www.dmtf.org/spec/-cims.html)
2. Estublier, J., R. Casallas, "The Adele Configuration Manager," in Configuration Management, Ed. W. Tichy, J. Wiley and Sons, 1994 (ftp://ftp.imag.fr/pub/-ADELE/Conf-Manager.Book.ps.gz)
3. Feldman, S. I., "Make – a program for maintaining computer programs," UNIX Programmer's Supplementary Documents Vol. 1 (PS1), USENIX Assn. (1986), pp. PS1:12-1--PS1:12-9.
4. Fulton, Jim, "Configuration Management in the X Window System," X Consortium, MIT Laboratory for Computer Science, (Cambridge, MA, 1989) pp. 12. (http://www.primate.wisc.edu/software/imake-stuff/fulton.txt)
5. Hall, Richard S., D. Heimbigner, A. van der Hoek, A. Wolf, "An architecture for postdevelopment configuration management in a wide area network," Proc. 1997 Intl. Conf. on Distributed Configurable Systems, IEEE Computing Society, (May, 1997) pp. 269-278
6. Hall, Richard S., Dennis Heimbigner, Alexander L. Wolf, "Software deployment languages and schema", Dept. of Computer Science, U. of Colorado, CU-SERL-203-97, December 18, 1997 (http://www.cs.colorado.edu/users/rickhall/-deployment/SchemaPaper/Schema.html)
7. InstallShield, "InstallShield Software Corporation of Schaumberg, IL", April, 1999 (http://www.installshield.com)
8. MacKenzie, David, Ben Elliston, Autoconf: Creating Automatic Configuration Scripts, Edition 2.13, Cygnus Solutions, 1998 (http://sourceware.cygnus.com/-autoconf/autoconf_toc.html)

9. Sommerville, I. G. Dean, PCL: A configuration language for modeling evolving software architectures, Computing Department, Lancaster University, 1995 (ftp://ftp.comp.lancs.ac.uk/pub/proteus/PCL/PCL_overview.ps)

10. Tibrook, D., "An architecture for a construction system," Software Configuration Management, ECOOP'96 SCM-6 Workshop, Berlin, Germany, March, 1996, Springer, Lecture Notes in Computer Science # 1167, pp. 76-87 (http://www.iptweb.com/tools/stdprod/qef/qef.html) (Although the paper lists "Tibrook" as author, it was written by Dave Tilbrook.)

11. van Hoff, H. Partovi, and T. Thai. "The Open Software Description format (OSD)," Microsoft Corp. and Marimba, Inc., Aug. 13, 1997(http://www.w3.org/-TR/NOTE-OSD.html)

VTML for Fine-Grained Change Tracking in Editing Structured Documents

Lars Bendix[1] and Fabio Vitali[2]

[1] Department of Computer Science, Aalborg University, Fredrik Bajers Vej 7E,
DK-9220 Aalborg Øst, Denmark
bendix@cs.auc.dk
[2] Computer Science Department, University of Bologna, Mura Anteo Zamboni 7,
I-40121 Bologna, Italy
fabio@cs.unibo.it

Abstract. The task of creating documents collaboratively is complex and it requires sophisticated tools. Structured documents provide a semi-organised writing environment where collaboration may assume more controlled forms than with other document types. CoEd is a writing environment that provides integrated structure support, content overview and version management for complex and hierarchical documents (e.g. technical documentation). The present implementation has, however, limitations in the efficient management of disk usage and in providing more sophisticated collaboration functionality. This led us to consider the VTML change tracking language as a backend for improving the performance and feature set of CoEd. This paper explores the advantages of using a sophisticated change-tracking language in a versioning system for collaborative writing.

1 Introduction

Collaborative writing of documents requires great care and discipline from the participants to avoid coordination problems. On the other hand extreme flexibility must still be possible in what can be a highly creative and unpredictable process. This poses great demands on tools that have to support such work. Organising the document in a hierarchical way provides enough structure to control how the collaboration develops. Under such conditions environments can make assumptions that make the task easier.

The CoEd system [BLNP98] was born to provide support for collaborative writing to teams of students at the University of Aalborg needing to prepare Latex reports for software projects connected with their courses. The available tools were felt lacking in facilities for global overview, co-ordination, version control and communication among writers.

The first prototypes [BNLP97] built at the University of Aalborg provided overview of the structure of the texts and version management of the basic text units of the students' reports. Thus, CoEd was able to solve many problems connected to the mentioned tasks. Students could carry out satisfactorily the processes connected to writing their reports and the availability of a sophisticated tool such as CoEd reduced the efforts for creating and correcting them.

On the other hand, CoEd implements an unsatisfactory management of persistent data, by storing whole versions and ignoring the inherent structure of the documents handled. Furthermore, many useful features are not implementable given the current underlying data model, such as support for managing and visualising differences in the structure, querying of attributes or comparison of parallel versions. Evolving the CoEd system to handle this kind of information and to provide the functionality requires deciding on a mechanism for improved internal data management.

VTML (Versioned Text Markup Language, [VD95]) is a markup language for describing changes occurred to arbitrary sequential data types. It allows to specify arbitrary attributes to each change, such as authors and dates, and to build arbitrarily complex version graphs detailing the development of a document. A VTML-based system rely on the VTML format to provide support for efficient data management, version branching, lock-free concurrent access to shared documents [SVWD98], version identification, easy comparison of versions, and reliable addressing space for the document's content.

VTML seems adequate for providing intelligent data management to CoEd, and to provide support for much of the sophisticated functionality mentioned. Other engines were judged inadequate because they are not capable of dealing with structured texts as easily as VTML can. Additionally, the generality of VTML with regard to versioning policies allows an easy adaptation to CoEd's specific policies and collaboration styles among the team members contributing to a document. Finally, additional information, in the form of attributes, is handled in a straightforward way by VTML.

We will create a new prototype for handling change tracking in collaborative writing efforts. It will rely on the old CoEd to provide the user interface and the versioning model, behaving as the front-end of the system, and use VTML to provide the versioning engine and work as the back-end. The new prototype is supposed to give better change tracking than previous systems and better change tracking helps improve the co-ordination and communication in collaborative writing efforts.

In this paper, we describe the goals of our current research project aimed at:

- specifying the requirements for a collaborative writing environment
- specifying the interface between CoEd and VTML
- designing the new integrated prototype
- implementing the services that were not implemented with the old back-end
- testing the flexibility and generality of VTML through the implementation of specific versioning policies

The rest of the paper is structured as follows: In section 2, we describe the problem area and the existing CoEd system and the results that were obtained by using it. In section 3, the VTML language is described and a simple session is analysed to provide insight into the actual working of the language. Section 4 describes the analysis of the problems in implementing CoEd policies using VTML mechanisms and sketches the design of the integrated system. In section 5 we draw some conclusions, draft our plans for future work in the project and state some preliminary results.

2 Collaborative Writing

CoEd is a collaborative tool aimed at supporting teams in writing shared structured documents. For years the students at the Department of Computer Science at Aalborg University have encountered numerous problems when they had to work together to write reports. Each semester these students spend the major part of their time developing a system, enabling them to put the theory they are taught during the courses into practice. They work in groups of 3-8 people over a period of four months. The theory and the process, as well as the final product, have to be documented in a report, which is usually between 80 and 120 pages long. The major part of this report is written during the last three weeks of the project period.

The students experienced problems, not so much during the programming process where existing tools seem to be of sufficient help, as during the writing process which is usually short and hectic and characterised by a very dynamic organisation of tasks and responsibilities. They especially had problems in keeping an overview of the document and how its structure develops through new versions. This caused them to have problems in establishing baselines of the document, to track structural changes and to find proper use of version histories. Finally, communication of information about the development is important as these students often work in a distributed way. Some students in a group may work from home, while others work from the room that each group has at the university, and others yet work from the computer labs at the department. This fact led to creating an environment called CoEd [BLNP97].

The problems of these students are typical examples of the problems present in collaborative writing efforts. Instead of buying a new tool or trying to solve the general problem, our strategy was to try to solve the specific problems of the students in their given context, and to gain experience from the students actually using a prototype of our tool.

All groups of students use Latex for producing their project reports. Some groups have so far used self-imposed group discipline to be able to manage the development, dividing the document up into disjoint parts with respect to responsibility. They have, however, usually encountered serious problems, both because parts of the report are inherently interdependent and because of the complete absence of versioning of the compound document. Most groups have used either RCS [Tichy85] or CVS [Berliner90] as their tool of choice to manage the development, usually based on whether they liked a strict locking mechanism or not. This enabled them to version the development of the single parts of the document, but they still had problems in keeping an overview of the entire document and in manipulating its structure.

2.1 The Problems in Collaboration

The work on CoEd [BLNP98] took its origin in the problems that students had reported from their co-operative work on developing textual documents. The problems experienced were many and varied, but can roughly be grouped into three categories. One that has to do with the lack of overview and co-ordination, both of the document and of what everyone else is doing. Another category that has to do with problems doing version control and change tracking the way that they want and need. And, finally, there are problems that have to do with the communication of information.

Problems that have to do with the lack of overview and co-ordination manifest themselves in several ways. It is very difficult to organise the structure of the report and to have the structure visualised while working in front of the screen. As a result, indices or entire reports are printed on paper to gain overview and much work is lost in manually changing Latex commands (and/or file names) to reflect a reorganisation of the report. This also implies that groups rarely change their way of working. If they work in a top-down fashion, the structure of the paper remains fixed right from the start. Groups working in a bottom-up way remain in a limbo until the very last moment where finally all the pieces can be put together.

These problems are, in part, due to the fact that if we divide the document up into several files, reflecting its hierarchical structure, then the version control tool is treating those just as single pieces and not as a whole too. In part, the problems are due to the lack of a proper GUI that can visualise the structure of the document. Version control tools permit us to divide the document in logic entities, like chapters and sections, reflecting also the division of responsibilities. However, without a proper GUI it is difficult to get a quick overview of the entire document. Furthermore, the fact that the structure is only implied by a directory structure, means that we must manually change this structure every time the organisation of the document is to be changed.

To remedy this problem the CoEd system has knowledge of Latex, so it can automatically create (and maintain) the storage organisation from that implied by the Latex code. Furthermore, the GUI is capable of visualising documents using the Latex structures. Finally, it is possible to visualise - and work with – both the document as a whole and its individual parts.

In the second category of problems we find misfits between the version control needs of the students and the functionality provided by the tools they use. Their needs for version control are not very sophisticated. They do not develop variants and do not have to maintain old versions, as it is usual in software development. Still they have troubles in finding help from traditional version control tools. They have problems identifying and retrieving old versions. Often confusion arises when the supervisor comments on a document and the students find out that it is not the version they printed out just before the meeting. When a section or a chapter is split into two, the version history for one of the parts is lost. These problems are similar to the problems in version selection, baselining and change tracking pointed out in [Tichy88].

Again the problems are, in part, due to the lack of a GUI, and, in part, to problems with the data model that the version tools build on. An adequate GUI makes version selection far easier because one immediately sees what one selects, at least with versions of the individual parts. Baselining the entire document is a cumbersome and sometimes error prone process. This is due to the fact that it is a manual task where the document is viewed as a collection of versioned parts. As such, there is no explicit versioning of the collection as a whole. Furthermore, as the tools are unaware of operations like splitting a unit, this becomes something that is unsupported and has to be carried out outside of the tool's control.

To avoid these problems we made the versioning of a document's structure an integral part of the tool, treated on equal footing with the versioning of the individual parts. Furthermore, we supported splitting of units as a basic functionality. Finally, the GUI facilitates identification and selection, and visualises the result immediately.

2.2 The Architecture of CoEd

The architecture of CoEd is built around the principle that a Latex document has a hierarchical structure and as such consists of a set of leaves and internal nodes, each of which can contain text. Leaves and nodes are the smallest granularity of the system and are called *units*. For the versioning of a unit we use the traditional approach of creating a version group for the unit and let the development of versions be reflected by a version graph. The root node has a special status as it represents the whole document. The root node is versioned just like all other nodes and this provides us with versioning of the document as a whole. A given version of the whole document is called a bound configuration in accordance with the terminology used in software configuration management.

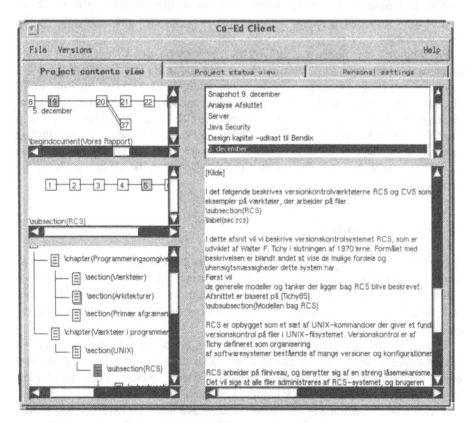

Figure 1. How CoEd presents itself to the user.

CoEd has four browsers which each shows a different aspect of the internal data structure. This makes it possible to look at the data structure (i.e. the document) at varying levels of details allowing for a flexible granularity. Figure 1 shows the GUI of the CoEd system.

The *hierarchy browser* is found at the bottom left. It shows the hierarchical structure of the document as it is implied by the Latex commands. Icons can be expanded and compressed by double-clicking them. This makes it easy to get a quick overview of the document at the desired level of detail. We find the *text browser* at the bottom right. Here is shown a contiguous piece of text that corresponds to the icon selected in the hierarchy browser and the text that immediately precedes or follows the selection.

At the top left, we find the *version browser*, which consists of two windows. The top window shows all the versions of the bound configuration, which is equivalent to showing the version group of the root. In the bottom window is shown the version graph for the unit that is selected in the hierarchy browser.

At the top right, we find the *baseline browser*. This browser was introduced in order to solve the lack of overview caused by the high number of bound configurations. As can be seen in the version browser window, bound configurations can be named to distinguish important ones. These named bound configurations are the ones that appear in the baseline browser. The selection of one of these baselines will cause the icon of the corresponding bound configuration to be selected and highlighted in the version browser.

From figure 1, we can see that initially the user selected the "5. December" baseline in the baseline browser. This caused CoEd to find and select that version of the document (version 19) and highlight it in the upper window of the version browser. CoEd also finds and displays the structure of this bound configuration version in the hierarchy browser. Then the user selected "\subsection{RCS}" as the unit he is interested in and CoEd found and displayed the text of this unit (and of immediately surrounding units to fill out the text window) in the text browser, highlighting it. CoEd also displayed the version group for the selected unit (version 5) in the lower window of the version browser.

2.3 How CoEd Is Used

A typical scenario for the use of CoEd will find us starting with (a piece of) a document which we now want to continue to develop using CoEd. Using the file menu, we will ask CoEd to check in the file containing the document. CoEd parses the Latex code and, if successful, constructs the implied hierarchical structure, otherwise it refuses the text.

Using the version browser, we now select the bound configuration we want to change (usually the latest). We can now use either the hierarchy browser or the text browser to select the contiguous piece of text we want to change (it can span several logic units) and ask CoEd to check it out to a single file.

This file we can edit using our favourite editor and when we have finished editing the text, we ask CoEd to check it in again. CoEd automatically discovers which units have been changed - creating new versions - and which have not - leaving them untouched. It will even discover if units have been added or deleted and react correspondingly.

2.4 Advanced Functionality in CoEd

CoEd also has some more advanced functions that work at the structural level of the document. These are split of a unit, creation of meta-versions and direct manipulation of the structure.

The students create many versions of their documents during the writing phase. Because we consider the document as a whole, each change to one of its parts means that a new version of the whole document is created. The baseline browser reduces this high number of bound configurations, such that it becomes manageable. If changes to more than one unit is carried out in the same edit session, this will create more than one version of the document. This is not a consequence of the extensional versioning used at the document level, but due to the lack of a session concept in CoEd. Meta-versions were introduced to automatically group together all the versions created in one single edit session. Meta-versions can be opened such that the single versions in the meta-version can be accessed.

Let us assume that we have chapters A, B and C, and want to split chapter A into two chapters A1 and A2. When we check in the result - A1, A2, B and C - CoEd will discover that there is one more chapter than was checked out. It will, however, also recognise that A1 and A2 were parts of the original chapter A and create two new version groups and connect them with the version group of the original A in a seamless way, in order not to loose continuity in the compound version history.

It is also possible to directly manipulate the structure and in this way permute units. It is possible to move both single units and parts of the structure. We simply select what has to be moved and then drag it to the place where it has to be inserted. In this way, we can change a chapter to a section (including its sub-structure) or vice versa, and CoEd will make the necessary changes to the Latex code for us.

2.5 Experience with CoEd

We have implemented a working prototype of CoEd and students at Aalborg University have used it for developing their project reports. The results from these experiments are rather promising. The average number of pages handled by CoEd was about 80 pages per project. Some groups just used it to play around because they did not trust the stability of CoEd and were afraid of loosing their data. These groups had relatively little text (about 50 pages), while a few groups used it seriously and had about 120 pages under the control of CoEd. In the end, CoEd turned out to be amazingly stable and very little data was lost the few times it crashed.

The average number of units per project was 147, again with serious user going higher. The number of bound configurations was 2 to 6 times the number of units. That the students were able to maintain an overview anyway, proves the value of the baseline browser and the meta-version concept. There were about 9 versions in meta-versions, but up to 20-30 versions were seen. Especially for groups that brought larger pre-written pieces of text into CoEd rather than using CoEd from the very beginning.

Development was mostly linear with very few branches and merges. Split of units was used but not extensively. The direct manipulation of the structure, on the other hand, was used very extensively and was rated by the students as one of the strongest points about CoEd. And, above all, the fact that direct manipulation could be carried out under full version control and therefore could be undone very easily.

Students also felt that this kind of version control and change tracking lowered the need for face-to-face meetings for exchanging information. This indicates that in the past many such meetings were held mainly for communicating information and for co-ordination purposes, and that by using CoEd they were able to reduce the needs for co-ordination.

The improved support for handling entire documents led to the discovery of new functionality that was desired. The students asked for better visualisation of differences in structure between versions of documents. They wanted to be able to compare parallel versions, both at the structural and the textual level. And, finally, they wanted to be able to attach more information to versions of documents and units. These extensions were difficult to carry out in the current implementation of CoEd. This, and the fact that fine granularity and versioning of structures is not well supported by traditional version engines like RCS, caused us to look for a version engine that was better suited to the requirements of CoEd for supporting change tracking.

3 Change Tracking

VTML is a descriptive data format for fine-grained change tracking. It is not a versioning *system*, but a flexible data format that can be used by systems that implement a wide range of versioning styles. It was born from the tentative of determining an adequate versioning style for hypermedia documents in a collaborative environment ([DHHV94] and [HHDV95]). The versioning styles allowed by VTML can vary from extremely informal and unstructured asynchronous collaboration patterns among creative writers, to the formalised and controlled sequential actions of a team of programmers, to the synchronous access to a shared blueprint by a team of architects and designers. It can be flexibly used with a large number of system architectures, varying from flexible editing clients and dumb storage servers, to extremely dumb clients interacting with a sophisticated versioning server.

The format is designed to be consumed by programs, and so it is relatively terse and simple to parse. Although we are currently applying VTML to the management of text, any text or binary format can be directly represented in a VTML document. In particular, VTML was designed initially to handle the management of versions for HTML documents [VD95], and in general for managing versions of all kinds of markup languages (such as SGML, XML and all other derived languages).

VTML-based systems may make use of the features of VTML to obtain a few interesting features, such as:

- the version history may branch, creating a tree of variants. The version history may also converge, creating a master version that inherits from several different variants by some form of user-guided or automatic merge.
- locks to control accesses to authors are not necessary. This is a consequence of allowing branching versions: conflicting check-in operations can always be allowed, automatically creating new branches of the version tree if necessary. The versions can then be "harmonised" with a merge operation.
- a check out operation is not necessary: users may use copies without synchronisation control by a server or a distributed consistency algorithm, for instance by using a local copy on the client's file space.
- full sequential undo can be easily provided. Since each operation is logged and identified, it is easy to rebuild the state of the document at any point in time. In Palimpsest [Durand93], VTML is even used to allow arbitrary undo: by explicitly expressing the existence context of each change, one can accept or reject arbitrary past operation regardless of their sequence in time.
- automatic version identification is supported, according to a series of numbering schemata. Four numbering schemata can be used, each having equivalent expressive power.
- VTML versions provide a consistent and reliable addressing mechanism for document spans, that requires no modification to the document and can survive unmonitored changes to the document itself. One important service that a VTML-based versioning system can provide is to precisely locate the position of data designated by an offset into a previous version of the document. This is an important operation for the support of external link bases that refer to changing data. The same mechanism can also be used to provide flexible document fragment re-use, with little additional machinery.

VTML stores information about all single modifications to the shared document. It is able to report that something as simple as an insertion has taken place, or something as complex as a sort. Since the list of possible operations is open, VTML describes every complex change as a list of simple operations: insertions, deletions and modifications. Thus the basic purpose of the language (i.e., to be able to build a given version of a document according to the changes it has incurred into since its creation) is preserved even if the meaning of the actual operations is unknown.

Attributes are associated to single changes. This allows an extreme flexibility in describing them. In order to avoid overloading of repeated data, shorthand facilities are provided. The list of data items that can be associated to every change is also open, and possibly very large. Thus, instead of listing extensively the kind of attributes, only a few necessary ones are determined, and a way to add new ones is provided. The necessary attributes are basically used to univocally determine the whereabouts and the correct grouping of the changes. Everything else, from the author or the date of the change to the comments about a given change, or to the author's shoe size, for that matters, is an additional attribute that is not part of the language.

VTML comes in two equivalent formats: the internal format stores side by side the modifications in the positions they have happened. The external format stores them in the chronological order they have happened. A VTML document is composed of one or more VTML blocks, contained within a {VTML} {/VTML} set of tags. VTML blocks are composed either of internal markup (using the elements ATT, USROP, INS, and DEL) or external markup (using the elements ATT, USROP, EXTINS, EXTDEL). The same document may contain VTML blocks of both types.

All change commands that are described with internal tags are stored within a single VTML block, while external tags may be stored in as many blocks as needed. Applications that require support for both internal and external changes in a single file may concatenate multiple blocks together.

VTML is meant to provide change tracking support to markup languages such as HTML and XML. HTML 4.0 [RLJ98] includes two new tags, INS and DEL, that are meant to express changes from previous versions of the same document (e.g., in legal texts); On the contrary, VTML lies on a completely different layer, having the markup as content of its tags. This is due to several reasons:

Different handling of tags and content: users don't simply add content during edits, but may modify tags and attributes. If versioning tags are at the same level as content tags, and parsed at the same time, it is impossible for them to keep information about modifications of content tags. The duplication of tags, and the need for the versioning tags and the document tags to create a legal (extended) HTML document also creates problems with ensuring proper nesting of tags.

Potential for misuses, hacking, and manual modifications: if the document is edited by a versioning-unaware editor, or, even worse, manually, versioning information will inevitably become outdated, inconsistent and possibly will generate a corrupt HTML document.

Complexity of resulting document: HTML is an SGML DTD thought for simple content markup, hypertext links and the like. Versioning tags do *not* modify the appearance or role of the parts of the document but perform a more pragmatic and low-level chore: helping determine whether a piece of the document belongs to a specific version or not. Mixing semantic and rendering markup with content-determination tags creates extremely complex and unreadable documents.

In summary, adding special tags to a markup language does not help change-tracking: being part of the markup language, these tags cannot express changes in the markup itself or changes that disrupt the correct nesting of the markup (e.g., two paragraphs that have been joined, or a link destination that has been changed). The only solution we find acceptable is to foresee two independent parsing steps, the first of which considers and activates just the change-tracking information, building a complete marked-up document, and the second that parses the specific document markup and creates its visual representation.

3.1 A Complete Example Using VTML

Basically, VTML tags are meant to describe the editing operation performed on the document, and describe operations that are not the result of changes in the document data, but rather the selection of some existing changes. Let us suppose we have the following situation: David and Lars are collaborating on writing a document.

First version: Lars inserts the string: "The quick brown fox jumps over the lazy dog."

Second version: David substitutes "quick" with "speedy", and removes "lazy": "The speedy brown fox jumps over the dog."

Third version: Lars substitutes "brown" with "red" and inserts "sleepy" before "dog": The speedy red fox jumps over the sleepy dog".

For reasons known to the VTML engine, version 1 and 2 are stored together with the internal markup, while version 3 is stored externally (maybe the engine hasn't had the time yet to import the new version). Versions 1 and 2 correspond to the following VTML block:

```
{VTML NAME="Hunting" CVERS=2 _AUTHORS="Lars, David"}
{ATTR ID=1 vers=1 _author="Lars"}
{ATTR ID=2 vers=2 _author="David"}

{INS ATT=1} The {INS ATT=2} speedy {/INS} {DEL ATT=2}
quick {/DEL} brown fox jumps over the {DEL ATT=2} lazy
{/DEL} dog. {/INS}{/VTML}
```

Each VTML tag describes the shared context given, at least, by the document name, and the current version, and, in this case, also by the group of legal authors. The ATTR tag stores a few attributes that should be repeated several times in the document tags, and that are associated with the ATT attribute of the actual tags. Therefore, writing

```
{ATTR ID=1 vers=1 _author="Lars"}
{ATTR ID=2 vers=2 _author="David"}
{INS ATT=1} The {INS ATT=2} speedy {/INS} {DEL ATT=2}
quick {/DEL} brown fox jumps over the {DEL ATT=2} lazy
{/DEL} dog. {/INS}
```

is equivalent to writing:

```
{INS vers=1 _author="Lars"} The {INS vers=2
_author="David"} speedy {/INS} {DEL vers=2
_author="David"} quick {/DEL} brown fox jumps over the
{DEL vers=2 _author="David"} lazy {/DEL} dog. {/INS}
```

INS and DEL represent the actual changes that were performed on the text. Since the text is a linear sequential format, there is no need for modification operations, but we can safely restrict to insertions (INS tags) and deletions (DEL tags).

On the other hand, this is an external representation of version 3:

```
{VTML NAME="Hunting" CVERS=3 _AUTHORS="Lars, David"}
{ATTR ID=1 SOURCE="Hunting" VERS=3 _author="Lars"}
  {EXTDEL ATT=1 POS=15 LENGTH=5}
  {EXTINS ATT=1 POS=15}red{/EXTINS}
  {EXTINS ATT=1 POS=42}sleepy {/EXTINS}{/VTML}
```

This VTML block contains an external description of the changes leading to version 3. In this case, insertions (stored as EXTINS tags) specify their position, while deletions (EXTDEL tags) specify both their position and the number of removed characters.

Separately, Fabio opened version 2 of the "Hunting" document and made some other modifications: he substituted "jumps over" with "is not caught by" and inserts "Today" at the beginning of the sentence: "Today the speedy brown fox is not caught by the dog." Therefore, the following is the result of his modifications:

```
{VTML NAME="Hunting" CVERS=3 _author="Fabio,Lars,David"}
{ATTR ID=1 SOURCE="Hunting" VERS=3 _author="Fabio"}
{USROP ATT=1 REF=2 NAME="SUBSTITUTION"}
 {EXTDEL POS=29 LENGTH=10}jumps over{/EXTDEL}
 {EXTINS POS=29}is not caught by{/EXTINS}{/USROP}
{EXTINS ATT=1 POS=1}oday t{/EXTINS}{/VTML}
```

This version, besides making use of the external representation of changes, uses the USROP command, which collects into a single operation a sequence of basic editing commands (insertions, deletions, modifications). In the external format, the USROP tag groups together the basic operations it is composed of, and labels them with a human-understandable name.

The first problem with accepting this version is that both versions claim to be version 3, since both were created from version 2 in absence of other derived versions. Lars decides that his own version will remain in the main branch of the version tree. This affects the numbering of the versions, as Fabio's version is renumbered and becomes 3.1. Then Lars merges Fabio's contributions into a new version: he accepts the substitution of the verb, but NOT the insertion of "Today".

This is a structure of the version tree:

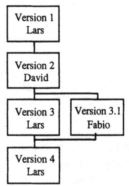

Figure 2. The version tree of the VTML example.

The engine easily generates the following internal representation:

```
{VTML NAME="Hunting" CVERS=CURRENT AUTHORS="Lars,David,
Fabio"}
{ATTR ID=1 ref=1 vers=1 _author="Lars"}
{ATTR ID=2 ref=2 vers=2 _author="David"}
```

```
{ATTR ID=3 ref=3 vers=3 _author="Lars"}
{ATTR ID=4 ref=4 vers=3.1 _author="Fabio"}
{ATTR ID=5 vers=CURRENT _author="Lars"}
{USROP ATT=4 NAME="Substitution" REF=6 INCLUDES="5"}
{USROP ATT=5 NAME="Merge" EXCLUDES="7"}
{INS ATT=1} T{INS ATT=4 REF=7}oday t{/INS}he {INS ATT=2}
speedy {/INS} {DEL ATT=2} quick {/DEL} {DEL ATT=3} brown
{/DEL} {INS ATT=3} red {/INS} fox {DEL REF=5} jumps over
the {/DEL} {INS REF=5}is not caught by {/INS} {INS ATT=3}
sleepy {/INS} {DEL ATT=2} lazy {/DEL} dog. {/INS}{/VTML}
```

The main features of this version are that the internal form of USROP has been used and that a merge has been performed. The internal format of the USROP tag specifies the basic operations it is composed of by listing their REF number in an INCLUDES attribute or listing the other ones in an EXCLUDES attribute. A merge is just another USROP operation where the relevant operations are either accepted or ignored in the merged version. Thus, in this case, version 4 is composed of a single operation that merges all previous operations except for the one with REF = 7.

This new block can either be stored as such by the VTML engine or divided again into elements and stored separately. When the engine saves the document, it will substitute the CURRENT value with the appropriate version number (in this case, 4).

4   Integrating CoEd and VTML

In this section we briefly describe the reasons for integrating CoEd and VTML, the interface between the two systems, and a few example scenarios where using VTML can provide additional functionality to the CoEd collaborative system.

CoEd has proven itself a strong and flexible tool to use for supporting collaborative writing through change tracking, versioning of whole documents and management of document structure. We have, however, found some things to improve through our experiments with the prototype. While CoEd's interface and model layers (see figure 3) work rather well, the engine layer is far too simple, since it does basically nothing but system calls to the file system. CoEd stores each version of a unit in its entirety and does not even try to use space-saving delta mechanisms. This means that using CoEd becomes prohibitive in a larger scale as it really burns up disc space. We made this initial choice because we wanted to put emphasis on the concepts and development of an experimental prototype rather than on an efficient implementation.

In order to further develop the functionality of CoEd and to make it a more efficient tool that can be used for real projects, a more powerful and flexible engine is needed. We have looked into traditional tools for version control, like RCS [Tichy85], and we found that they are simply not powerful enough. Such tools are very efficient in representing version groups in as little space as possible, but they are limited in that they do not go beyond version groups. This still leaves the versioning model of CoEd the task of managing the structure of the document and of versioning this structure.

VTML efficiently represents changes in a versioned text, so that VTML-aware applications may make use of the change-tracking facilities of the language to provide sophisticated versioning support to its users: version selection, branching, comparison, and merge. VTML therefore seems like an optimal choice for the engine component of the next CoEd prototype since it can handle and version both contents and structure. VTML is a language, not a tool, so we had to decide what kind of VTML-enabled application we were looking for. A VTML engine can provide basic parsing and storage functionality. By adding a simple interface layer for the CoEd applications, we can easily provide sophisticated versioning functionality.

In figure 3, we show the overall architecture of the foreseen application.

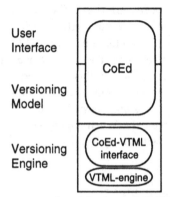

Figure 3. The conceptual architecture of CoEd with VTML.

The interface layer provides the operational interface between CoEd and the VTML engine, and consists of the following operations:

```
Put_version(data:Data_structure,
        depends_on:Version_name) ->
        Version_name;
```

The Put_version operation appends a new version to an existing document. This corresponds to a check-in operation for the VTML engine that generates a diff between the specified version name and the new one submitted. Based on that, the engine determines the VTML coding and the version number corresponding to the new version. The VTML engine will then decide autonomously whether to store the new version using the external format in an autonomous file, or to insert it as internal coding in the existing one. Finally, it will return the new version name for CoEd to update its internal database.

```
Get_version(version:Version_name) -> Data_structure;
```

The Get_version operation creates the required version. This corresponds to a check-out operation for the VTML engine. The engine will retrieve all the versions leading up to the requested one, and will perform the change operations stored in them necessary to build the requested version. It will then return the data corresponding to the requested version.

```
Compare_versions(versions:Version_group_list,
      deleted_data: Boolean) ->
      Comparison_data_structure;
```

A comparison structure is simply a text document that contains some colour coding information. The CoEd model will request a list of versions to be displayed together to ease the comparison. For each version, it will suggest a colour. In the deleted_data parameter, it will then specify whether deleted data should be displayed or not. This corresponds for the VTML to a multiple check-out operation where instead of simply building the requested versions, each version is assigned a colour coding that will be used to specify the display of each document bit. If deleted data are requested, the deletion operations are not performed, but the corresponding data are left in the document with an additional special colour coding.

To clarify the working of the CoEd+VTML system, we examine four possible scenarios where the system is used and provides sophisticated collaborative functionality:

I - Creating a new document

Student A places a sharable and existing document under the wings of CoEd.

In this case CoEd will parse the text of the document and create the hierarchical structure implied by the Latex commands. For each of the leaves and internal nodes in this tree, it will create a new version group and insert the text of the unit as a first version in this version group.

II - Getting and modifying a document

Student B makes a modification to the document's latest bound configuration and saves it.

When the text is checked in, CoEd discovers which parts have been modified. For all the modified units it calls the VTML engine to have new versions created and stored.

VTML handles and stores each single change that has happened to a document between saves. This means that, after each editing session, the VTML engine must determine what has changed since the last saved version. Since there are presently no plans of integrating a VTML-aware editor into CoEd, the difference is determined by making a diff of the two versions. The output of the diff program is then converted into VTML commands, and passed back to the VTML engine. The VTML engine now can choose between using the internal format, and creating a single VTML file containing all the existing versions of the document, and using the external format, which can then be stored independently of the rest of the document, in an autonomous file. The choice is done according to reasons of efficiency and availability of the new version.

III - Comparing different versions

Student C accesses student B's bound configuration and wants to compare it with a previous bound configuration.

The CoEd interface transforms this command in a request to the VTML engine for two different versions of the document. The VTML engine verifies whether those versions of the document are stored externally. In this case internalises them and generates the compact internal representation of the selected versions of the document. Then it transforms the relevant change instructions in colour choices for the text of the document display, thereby allowing the comparison of the two versions. This is simply done by eliminating version information for those bits that belong to both version, and converting the version information into colour instructions for those bits that have been modified in either version.

This information is then visualised in a separate window by the CoEd GUI.

IV - Parallel access to a document

Students A and C want to make modifications to the same bound configuration at the same time.

Any check out of text in CoEd is done within the context of a bound configuration. It is possible to make more than one check out from the same bound configuration – either in parallel or sequentially. CoEd notices that a branch has to be created and handles it at both the structural and the textual level. The structural level is handled internally, while managing parallel variants of text is handled by the VTML engine.

Since the VTML engine easily allows branching, neither student is blocked from accessing in write mode the document. We are not planning to use VTML-aware editors or notification mechanisms, so at save time the two versions are autonomously accepted by the VTML engine and put in two parallel variants. Since VTML allows parallel variants to coexist without requiring to merge the incompatibilities, and since VTML is able to provide any selection of versions even if belonging to different version branches, there is no pressure to resolve the inconsistencies that may have been created during the parallel edits. Once the need to harmonise the differences becomes paramount, the merge operation can be activated from the CoEd GUI. A merge can either be done automatically or manually. In both cases a person or an algorithm will select, for each edit that appears in either relevant branch, whether it should belong to the final version or not. The merge version therefore is an optional operation that reconciles different version branches of the same document without loosing information on each composing branch.

5 Conclusions

The CoEd environment has proven to be robust and useful in many collaborative situations. On the other hand, the simplicity of the underlying storage engine has prevented interesting functionality to be added.

It was an important decision to maintain CoEd interface characteristics and versioning policies, and improve on the underlying storage and composition mechanisms. VTML provides the sophistication needed in the management of the versions, and thus allow to improve the feature set of CoEd. Furthermore, the significant space savings available with the VTML format may easily make CoEd usable in heavily real-life situations.

CoEd is currently a monolithic working environment. Work is in progress to move it to a client-server architecture. The WebDAV extensions to HTTP for distributed authoring ([SVWD98] and [GWF*]) would help by providing a standard way for clients and servers to interoperate. The Delta-V working group, derived from the WebDAV working group, is currently establishing the extensions to HTTP needed for versioning and configuration management. Within both groups, VTML has been proposed and extensively discussed. Unfortunately, the consensus within the working group has been that change management operations, being media-dependent, are out of scope, and will not be covered by the forthcoming standards [AC99].

Acknowledgement

This work has been supported, in part, by the Danish Research Council, grant no. 9701406.

References

[AC99]: J. Amsden, G. Clemm: Web Versioning Model, *INTERNET DRAFT, draft-ietf-webdav-versionmodel-00.html*, in the version of February 1, 1999 expiring August, 1999. http://www.ics.uci.edu/pub/ietf/deltav/model/model990209/

[BLNP97]: L. Bendix, P. Larsen, A. Nielsen, J. Petersen: CoEd - A Tool for Cooperative Development of Hierarchical Documents, Technical Report R-97-5012, Department of Computer Science, Aalborg University, Denmark, September 1997.

[BLNP98]: L. Bendix, P. Larsen, A. Nielsen, J. Petersen: CoEd - A Tool for Versioning of Hierarchical Documents, in *Proceedings of SCM-8* (Bruxelles, Belgium, July 1998), Lecture Notes of Computer Science, Springer Verlag.

[Berliner90]: B. Berliner: CVS II: Parallelizing Software Development, in Proceedings of USENIX Winter 1990 (Washington, DC, 1990).

[Durand93]: D. Durand: Cooperative Editing without Synchronization, in *Hypertext '93 Workshop on Hyperbase Systems* (Seattle, WA), Technical Report n. TAMU-HRL 93-009, Hypertext Research Lab, Texas A&M University, College Station TX

[DHHV94]: D. Durand, A. Haake, D. Hicks, F. Vitali (eds.): *Proceedings of the Workshop on Versioning in Hypertext Systems,* held in connection with The European Conference on Hypertext, ECHT94. Available as GMD Arbeitspapiere 894, GMD - IPSI, Dolivostrasse 15, 64293 Darmstadt, Germany.

[GWF*]: Y. Goland, J. Whitehead, A. Faizi, S. Carter, D. Jensen: HTTP Extensions for Distributed Authoring - WEBDav, *Internet Informational Request for Comments(IETF RFC) 2518,* ftp://www.ietf.org/rfc/rfc2518.txt

[HHDV95]: D. Hicks, A. Haake, D. Durand, F. Vitali (eds.): *Proceedings of the ECSCW'95 Workshop on the Role of Version Control in CSCW Applications,* available as http://www.cs.bu.edu/techreports/96-009-ecscw95-proceedings/Book/proceedings_txt.html, Boston University Technical Report 96-009.

[MA96]: B. Magnusson, U. Asklund: Fine Grained Version Control of Configurations in COOP/Orm, in *Proceedings of SCM-6* (Berlin, Germany, March 1996), Lecture Notes of Computer Science, Springer Verlag.

[RLJ98]: D. Ragget, A. Le Hors, I. Jacobs: *HTML 4.0 Specification,* W3C Recommendation, http://www.w3.org/TR/PR-html40/

[SVWD98]: J. Slein, F. Vitali, E. J. Whitehead, Jr., D. Durand: Requirements for a Distributed Authoring and Versioning Protocol for the World Wide Web, *Internet Informational Request for Comments(IETF RFC) 2291.* February, 1998. Also as *ACM StandardView* 1 (5), 1997, p. 17-24. ftp://www.ietf.org/rfc/rfc2291.txt

[Tichy85]: Tichy, W. F. RCS - A System for Version Control, Software - Practice and Experience, Vol. 15 (7), July 1985.

[Tichy88]: Tichy, W. F. Tools for Software Configuration Management, in *Proceedings of SCM-1* (Grassau, Germany, January 1988).

[VD95]: Vitali F., Durand D., Using versioning to support collaboration on the WWW, in *The World Wide Web Journal,* 1(1), O'Reilly, 1995.

Global Names: Support for Managing Software in a World of Virtual Organizations

Michael L. Van De Vanter[1] and Tobias Murer[2]

[1]Sun Microsystems Laboratories, 901 San Antonio Road
Palo Alto, CA 94303 USA
Michael.VanDeVanter@Eng.Sun.COM
[2]TIK (Computer Engineering and Networks Laboratory)
ETH Zürich, 8092 Zürich, Switzerland
murer@acm.org

Abstract. Emerging technologies such as the Internet, the World Wide Web, Java[TM] technology, and software components are accelerating product life cycles and encouraging collaboration across organizational boundaries. The familiar coordination problems of large scale software development reappear in a context where tools used by collaborators must be less tightly coupled to one another than before. To the traditional notion of scale, based on the size of software systems, must be added a new dimension of scale: organizational complexity. Designing configuration management systems that scale well over both dimensions requires difficult trade-offs between reliability and flexibility. At the heart of these trade-offs is the aggregate information shared by collaborators: how it is represented, maintained, and understood by the people and tools using it. While designing a prototype development environment intended to scale in both dimensions, we have revisited the role played by naming. A proposed extension to the prototype's naming system addresses issues such as which objects should be named and how the shared naming system is constructed.

1 Introduction

Software product life cycles are accelerating and increasingly take place within so-called virtual organizations that require cooperation across a variety of organizational boundaries [4]. This trend is supported and encouraged by emerging technologies: the World Wide Web, software components, and Java[TM] technology [6]. Consequently ever more software is shared across organizational boundaries and assembled in increasingly dynamic and varied ways, such as with components and plug-ins.

Highly evolved tools for configuration management, which address familiar problems of scale, have become indispensable. However, these tools, even when reworked for the Internet, often fail to address the diversity of collaborating organizations. To the traditional notion of software size, which we characterize as *compositional complexity*, must be added a new dimension of scale: *organizational complexity*. Tools must now address both dimensions.

The Forest project at Sun Microsystems Laboratories has been developing JP, a prototype environment designed for reliable development of compositionally complex systems written in the Java programming language. Complementary issues of organizational complexity and the broader software life cycle are being addressed, in collaboration with the Virtual Software House project at ETH Zürich, by the *application web*. The application web supports the software life cycle across organizational boundaries, striking a balance between autonomy and collaboration [13].

It became clear that the application web depends critically upon global naming of shared information. JP supports a simple naming system that operates both in the small (editing based on names for individual sources [15]) and in the large (configurations of arbitrary size and complexity shared across multiple JP repositories [9]). Sharing data among multiple organizations and tools, however, demands a richer naming system.

It also became clear that design decisions for such a naming system encounter trade-offs between reliability and flexibility: for example what to name at what granularity and how to support reliable bindings. These decisions require careful thought about the roles played by naming.

A design strategy was adopted in which names are only given to objects as needed, and whose bindings are as reliable as possible. The results of this strategy reflect goals for different parts of the system:

- core configuration management and build systems are designed for utmost reliability, and rely on object structures, not names;
- development tools use a simple, global naming system for JP environments, designed to make information intelligible; and
- the application web uses names to support dynamic and flexible information sharing across organizational boundaries.

The system is cast as an instance of a general framework for naming, the Java Naming and Directory Interface^{TM} (JNDI) standard [8].

This paper discusses the design issues that arose in the development of this strategy, as well as the resulting concrete proposal. Section 2 begins with background on scaling issues, in particular the different demands of compositional vs. organizational scale. Section 3 takes a closer look at specific design issues concerning names in JP and the application web. Section 4 describes the proposed extension to JP naming, followed by a discussion of related work and conclusions.

2 Technologies for Scale in Software Development

The JP programming environment and the application web are designed to solve problems of scale for tools supporting the software life cycle, but along fundamentally different dimensions.

2.1 Compositional vs. Organizational Scale

"Scale" for programs was once measured in lines of code, but the real issue here is complexity. Configuration management systems (including JP) address the *compositional complexity* of systems: the number of modules, versions, variants, platforms, and languages that it takes to construct them. *Organizational complexity*, on the other hand, arises in the presence of virtual organizations (dynamic networks of organizations that cooperate for mutual benefit [4]) and involves the whole life cycle of products. Autonomy drives organizational complexity; single software development organizations don't face the differences of culture, infrastructure, methods, tool preferences, and skills one finds at organizational boundaries in virtual organizations. The application web addresses these aspects of scale.

Tools for compositional complexity must be reliable; tools for organizational complexity must be flexible. Tools that address both aspects of scale (organizational complexity often implies compositional complexity too) face design trade-offs. For reliability, information is best managed in a tightly coupled fashion, as if in a single global data structure with complete referential integrity and type safety. Flexibility, on the other hand, requires information that is less tightly coupled and more open [13] so that information may be created and managed by autonomous organizations, selectively shared, and structured simply for intelligibility. General naming systems, for example URLs, achieve flexibility at the cost of reliability.

The challenge is to find a useful balance. JP was designed to scale with compositional complexity; the application web addresses the additional requirements of organizational complexity.

2.2 The JP Programming Environment

JP is a prototype programming environment for the collaborative, reliable development of compositionally complex systems written in the Java programming language. It is based on close coupling among federated JP repositories, and tool integration via object-oriented interfaces. Implementation simplicity and reliability derive from architectural orthogonality among core services, functional programming, and aggressive use of abstract object interfaces.

Central to the JP approach is the notion of uniquely named, reusable, independently versioned packages [9]. JP packages play many roles:

- *System Structure.* Package versions act as software modules: they contain human-created artifacts such as source code and can use specific versions of other packages by *importing* them.
- *Storage Management.* Package versions and *derived* objects built from them, as well as tools such as compilers and editors, reside in repositories of orthogonally persistent objects [1].
- *Building.* A package version is built by interpreting its *build script*: a functional program that recursively invokes the scripts of imported packages. Previously derived objects are reliably shared via function caching, a mechanism that is largely orthogonal to the type of objects and the tools that create them.
- *Versioning.* Versions of a package are managed by a simple version system that is orthogonal to version content.
- *Configuration Management.* JP configurations are implemented as packages whose role is to import particular versions of other packages, including other configurations. Each version of a configuration specifies an immutable, arbitrarily large, aggregation of packages.
- *Analysis.* Tools for analyzing and visualizing software need not be separately configured, since they have direct access to configuration contents and derived results.

2.3 The Application Web

The *application web* complements JP by addressing problems of organizational scale [13]. Organizational boundaries discourage tool-based collaboration, in the absence of which information must be copied and shared manually. The application web fills the gap between the informality of copying and the tight coupling of conventional tools.

The application web provides an infrastructure for sharing information and supporting collaboration across boundaries within virtual organizations. This brings the character of the WWW into the software life cycle, where information can be autonomously maintained at its origin, but can also be shared through simple protocols. A software application can consist of parts originating at many sites.

The application web provides rich *connectivity* that spans the life cycle of software products, beginning with construction and continuing through deployment and ongoing management. For example a deployed, possibly running, application can be queried for complete, precise, and relevant information about its configuration, available via links back to the organizations in which the parts were created.

Autonomy is just as important. Shared data models are as simple as possible, following the lead of the World Wide Web, enabling dynamic and loosely coupled collaboration.

Flexible collaboration is supported by multiple layers of access. Closely related organizations might construct software jointly, using distributed authoring tools or JP's federated build system. Loosely related organizations might have limited HTTP access to the others' repositories. In between might be application loading services, bug reporting and tracking, querying for component interoperability, and reference information in support of debugging.

3 Naming Systems: Roles and Requirements

Naming is central to the shared information upon which the application web is built. The design strategy adopted for the naming system reflects the importance of a balance between competing requirements for reliability and flexibility. This section discusses general issues, as well as choices made for different parts of the system.

3.1 Design Issues for Naming

The first question when providing name-based access to complex data is whether to do it at all.

Closely coupled tools access data via *object references*, whose referential integrity and type safety derive from modern programming languages. The persistent object system used by JP makes object references suitable for reliable, long-term data storage, but such references are not available outside system boundaries.

In contrast, a *naming system* typically offers access to data from "outside" system boundaries. Names are legible to people (names often encode contextual information and may be redundant) and portable (they can be written down and emailed), but this flexibility comes at the cost of decreased reliability when compared to object references.

At one extreme, every object might be named, mirroring an object reference structure; for example, every element in a hierarchical file system is named. Conversely, only a small number of objects might be named, as with "persistent root" objects in object-oriented databases, requiring that further access be structural. These choices depend on the information clients need and what they know about the structure of the data. Other design issues include the lifetime and mutability of name bindings as well as lookup mechanisms and accessibility guarantees.

Unfortunately developers routinely suffer *too many naming systems* that are badly suited for the task: one for the target language (e.g. class names), another for storage (location dependent file names), possibly a third for modules (often modeled weakly as directories), and others for versioning and configuration. Not only must developers understand all these naming systems, they must keep them arranged in complex relationships just to keep the tools working. The problem is made worse by *naming too many things*, for example by cluttering the name spaces for sources with derived objects.

The proposed strategy is to name as few objects as possible, depending on specific requirements. The rest of this section describes the roles played by names in different parts of the system. Whereas the JP build system uses no names at all, the JP tool interface layer uses a unified naming system that spans multiple JP repositories. The former approach permits reliable building for configurations of arbitrary complexity, and the latter provides a comprehensible user model that abstracts away inessential information. Extending JP into the application web, requires a third approach to naming, one that will serve also as a bridge to non-JP tools.

3.2 Naming in the JP Build System

At the heart of JP is a build system that provides stronger guarantees of reliable and repeatable builds than is now common. Several technologies support these guarantees, but naming is not among them.

In order to be built, a *package version* must be committed to the repository, and it must completely specify its build computation. In its build script (a functional program) source objects (those created by humans using tools such as editors) appear as literal data values of the scripting language in declarations equivalent to:

```
JavaSource myStack = <the text written by a developer>;
```

JP source objects, known as *parts*, are implemented with *functional objects*: they are immutable and can be treated as pure values whose object identity plays no role [2]. JP parts are context-free and not intrinsically named and can thus be safely shared by many contexts.

Perhaps surprisingly, it is also necessary that package versions themselves be represented as functional objects; they participate in build scripts as literal values in import declaration equivalent to:

```
import <reference to contents of an existing package ver.>;
```

To the extent that parts do have names in the build system, it is only for the internal purposes of the computation, for example as in the declaration of **myStack** in the first example. These local bindings, within the computation engendered by each JP package version, are isolated from the rest of the environment and from other versions.

Objects created during building are likewise bound for the duration of the computation. Such bindings persist only to the extent that they are captured in a returned *build result*. The result is generally not named; tools invoke the **build()** method on package versions and operate structurally on the returned value.

3.3 Local Names in the JP Environment

It is one thing to exploit the power of a purely functional build system computing over a repository of context-free objects treated as values; it is quite another to help developers create, understand, and manage such objects. People and their work are inherently contextual and must be able to understand data in their own context.

Tools in a JP repository use a simple, unified name system for versioned packages and their contents [9], as shown in Example 1 and described further in Section 4.1.

Example 1. JP Names

`com.sun.labs.forest.jp.util`	a JP package
`com.sun.labs.forest.jp.util/7`	a JP package version
`com.sun.labs.forest.jp.util/7#Stack`	a source ("compilation unit") in a JP package version

These are the only names a developer normally sees, based on the design decision that names do not need to carry any other information, and that no other objects need names.

Unlike many naming systems, these names are reliable: name bindings, once created, are eternal, immutable, and always accessible. This makes names redundant, strictly speaking, but they help make a crucial connection between abstract, buildable values and the work being done by developers. This separation between internal representation and user-visible names permits the design of each to be optimized for its own purposes. For example, the package name space is aligned with names in the Java programming language, eliminating any distinction between storage and language names. The version name space in JP supports a simple branching and numbering model, but any name space would do; version names can therefore be aligned with local software development processes, once again eliminating name distinctions.

Names are used to good advantage by JP's framework for editor coordination [15]. This framework allows JP developers to commit new package versions, which can then be built if desired. Constructing a version involves creation of new source objects, based on editing activity, as well as new folder-like containers that represent changed contents. The framework makes this process nearly transparent, even in the presence of multiple editors that are not version-aware. It also arranges that unedited parts be shared by successive versions. Although the framework operates structurally, editors appear to be operating in the JP name space. Other tools, for example for navigating, searching, and creating new objects, operate similarly.

3.4 Implementation Challenges

Supporting both structural and name-based access to information has its costs. JP exploits the implementation of parts as immutable values and permits a value to be bound to many names, for example in successive versions of a package in which the part has not been touched. Consequently, any human view of a part must supply appropriate context.

For example, from the perspective of the build system an import is bound to the *content* (value) of a package version, not a name for the content. A person examining a build script, on the other hand, expects to see the human *intention* behind the import, which is best captured by the name used when the import was created. Thus, the internal representation of a build script import must carry this extra contextual information, however inessential to the builder.

Likewise, build errors cannot be reported usefully when a compiler sees source code only as byte arrays embedded in a graph of functional objects. Each invocation of the build system must be given a way to "re-contextualize" any parts mentioned in communication with humans, for example so that programming errors can be located and corrected.

JP editors, like the builder and compilers, traffic only in object values: old values are copied into buffers, and new parts are created when needed. The editor coordination framework maintains context that explains the meaning of data in each editor buffer. The framework informs each editor of the current name for each buffer, which routinely changes as versioning progresses, even though its only purpose is to give the developer contextual information.

Bridging different areas of JP's architecture has deeper implications in the underlying implementation, since a JP repository must be able to manage parts created by different versions of editors and derive results using different versions of compilers. This requires, in effect, a separate type system for each configuration, the consequences of which are beyond the scope of this paper. These issues do not arise, of course, in systems where tools and data are not strongly typed.

3.5 Global Names in the JP Environment

In order to support development of large systems, JP must permit collaboration among developers using multiple, federated JP repositories. The challenge is to approximate as closely as possible the guarantee of reliable, repeatable builds made by JP in single repositories.

The organizational aspect of the problem requires a global naming policy. JP aligns package names with the emerging *global name space* for Java packages, which begins with reverse DNS names. This grants organizations exclusive authority to create names in owned domains, which they can subdivide as needed. JP makes the aggressive presumption that a name, once created, has constant meaning, viewed from any JP environment, anywhere in the world, for all time.

JP imports are permitted to cross repository boundaries, which presents implementation choices for the representation of a non-local import. Two solutions are being explored, functionally similar but with very different architectural implications:

- At the platform level, an experimental mechanism supports persistent remote references to persistent objects.
- At the application level, package version names can, when combined with a locator service, implement the same binding.

Although neither of these mechanisms can guarantee that remotely implemented bindings are either eternal or accessible, it is possible to check that bindings are immutable. Object *fingerprints*, upon which JP's function caching is based, can be stored with the representation of an import, making it possible to verify that the retrieved value of a remote import, if available at all, is the intended one.

3.6 Naming Requirements for the Application Web

Whereas JP embeds names in a closed world designed for reliable, federated building, the application web is designed for more flexible forms of collaboration that span organizations, phases of the life cycle, and tools [13]. The application web captures interconnected information associated with software development, and makes it available via a variety of tools throughout the software life cycle. Collaboration requires some common understanding about software systems and their structure, as reflected in a shared naming system. Such a naming system must balance requirements for expressiveness (for effectiveness), reliability (for compositional scale), and flexibility (for organizational scale). The goal of expressiveness suggests that the JP name space be extended by naming objects that otherwise would only be treated structurally. Examples include build results and the internal structure of configurations.

The World Wide Web is an example of a scalable, global name system that meets many of these requirements. However, the application web presents additional requirements such as versioning and configurations, such as those used in JP.

Equally important is the reliability of names in a well-defined life cycle, where names are guaranteed to persist and be immutably bound. Confidence that bindings will be available and will not change encourages effective and efficient communication among people and tools *by reference* to objects. It also permits reliable name-based caching. On the other hand, it must be understood that bindings can be subject to service interruptions and expirations.

Authentication, trust, and access control are also essential, but are beyond the scope of the current work.

4   The Extended JP Naming System

The extended JP naming system addresses the goals of the application web and is based on experience with a simple prototype. This required recasting the original as a composite naming system, making some syntax adjustments for scalability. It also involved extending its scope, and defining more carefully such issues as the life cycle of names.[1]

---

1. This description uses the terminology of the Java Naming and Directory Interface (JNDI) standard [8]. Name syntax is described on an EBNF notation that includes '['..']' for options and '{'..'}' for zero or arbitrary repetitions.

4.1 Package Versions and Contents

Editing, versioning, system modularity, and building all operate at the granularity of package versions.

- Every package and package version has a *canonical name* that identifies it uniquely in the global package name space.
- Every part within a package version may also have a *canonical name* that identifies it uniquely.
- This *composite naming system* includes separate naming systems for packages, package versions, and parts.

Canonical_Name = Package_Name ['/' Version_Name ['#' Part_Name]]

The Package Naming System. This naming system mirrors the increasingly accepted global name space for Java packages [6], based on reverse DNS names. The hierarchy implies no inclusion relationships, either in the Java programming language or in JP; for example **a** and **a.b** name unrelated packages.

Package_Name = Atomic_Name { '.' Atomic_Name }

Example 2. Package Naming System

COM.sun.labs.forest.jp	canonical package name

The Version Naming System. This naming system identifies each version relative to its package. JP version names are hierarchical, with alternating numbers and names, as in Example 3. However, other versioning models can be used to suit particular development processes, as mentioned in Section 3.3. This freedom permits organizations to share information based on names, even when the semantics of particular version names are not shared.

A canonical name includes at most one version name, reflecting the decision to version packages only *in toto*. Packages in which contents are to be versioned independently must be constructed as configurations of other packages.

Version_Name = Number { '.' Atomic_Name '.' Number }

Example 3. Version Naming System

1.murer.4	version name
COM.sun.labs.forest.jp/1.murer.4	canonical package version name

The Part Naming System. This naming system identifies human created source objects within the content of a version. In contrast to package names, hierarchy *does* imply inclusion. Version content is managed as a single compound document, whose root part name is null, and in which embedded parts may or may not be named.

Part_Name = Atomic_Name { '.' Atomic_Name }

Example 4. Part Naming System

`model.layout`	part name
`COM.sun.labs.forest.jp/1.murer.4#model.layout`	canonical part name

Alternatives. The above syntax is influenced by URLs. Other approaches could be used, so long as package names match the name space for Java packages, and composite names can be parsed unambiguously. An earlier JP naming system used the separator '`.`' exclusively, as in Example 5:

Example 5. Old JP Naming System

`COM.sun.labs.forest.jp.1.murer.4.model.layout`	canonical part name

The simplicity of the old approach is appealing, but it promised to become confusing with increasing richness of the naming system, since boundaries between the individual naming systems are not immediately obvious.

4.2 Configurations

An extension to the JP naming system makes more of the internal structure of configurations visible through naming.

Projections. The global package name space is immense. Developers work in subsets that include just the package versions aggregated into systems under development. These subsets are defined by configurations: package versions that recursively aggregate other package versions, as in Example 6:

Example 6. Configuration Names

`CH.ethz.ee.tik.vsh/8`	configuration version name

`import COM.sun.java.JDK/2.mac.3`
`import COM.sun.labs.forest.jp/4`
`import CH.ethz.ee.tik.vsh.services/9`
	imports of package versions in the configuration

The contents of a configuration version can be treated as a projection of the global name space in which names can be used that have meaning only relative to the particular context of the configuration, as in Example 7. In this example a part appears in a configuration version because its containing package version is explicitly imported; three different names refer to the same part:

- The canonical name, which is independent of any configuration.
- A configuration-relative name, based on an extended syntax as shown. All such names can be unambiguously translated to canonical names.

Example 7. Configuration-relative Names

`CH.ethz.ee.tik.vsh/8`	configuration name
`COM.sun.labs.forest.jp/4#Main`	canonical part name
`CH.ethz.ee.tik.vsh/8/COM.sun.labs.forest.jp#Main`	part name embedded in configuration context
`COM.sun.labs.forest.jp#Main`	part name relative to implied configuration context

- A configuration-sensitive name that only identifies the part uniquely in a context where the configuration version is implied. These shorter names are the ones JP tools might display when a developer is working in the context of an evolving configuration. In situations where even more context is implied, even shorter names might appear, for example `jp#Main`.

The particular projection used in Example 7 is only one of many that could be designed to suit various needs for visualizing and working within the context of configurations.

Complete system descriptions. Configurations capture more than sources. For example, they contain a complete prescription for building it, including the precise version of a compiler (which also comes from a JP package version), compiler options, and which version of important libraries it is compiled against. These are all examples of *meta-information* relevant to the configuration. Other kinds of parts might also be present, for example design documents and test case specifications. Some kinds of information might not be naturally represented as parts, in which case the naming system might be extended explicitly.

4.3 Derived Parts

Information created by building a configuration, although guaranteed by JP to be well-defined, is not canonically named and is understood to have no meaning outside of its originating configuration. For the purposes of the application web, any build result should contain enough information to identify its configuration, perhaps by links leading back to the repository in which it was originally created.

Access to derived information is structural within the JP environment, but access can also be provided by describing each build result as a new name space in the composite naming system, relative to its configuration version. This might name such useful information as compiled classes and Javadoc HTML files. A function applied to a given configuration builds the naming context for a *derived parts naming system*. This is another hierarchical naming system, for example:

Derived_Part_Name = Atomic_Name { '.' Atomic_Name }

In Example 8 **compile** is a distinguished name that refers to the derived name space. The names that follow can be simple, in situations where build scripts explicitly

Example 8. Derived Part Naming System

`util.Connection`	derived part name
`CH.ethz.ee.tik.vsh/8/com-` `pile#util.Connection`	derived part name in context of a configuration's build result

define such names, or they might be expressions whose evaluation would provide something approximating structural access to the information. The names are reliable in either case, a considerable advantage when caching derived information.

4.4 The Life Cycle of Names

The use of global names within the application web requires a set of rules about how names are created and managed. These rules may be summarized in terms of the *life cycle* for canonical names; projected and derived names are always well-defined in terms of canonical names, as discussed earlier.

- *Creation.* A new name is explicitly created by an autonomous organization participating in the application web. Intellectual work is recorded in JP by committing a package version to a repository, and this requires that it be named; likewise, information cannot be shared in the application web until it is named.
- *Uniqueness.* A newly created name is presumed never to have been used before. The authority to create valid names is managed at the topmost level by partitioning the global name space into DNS domains that organizations own and can subdivide as needed.
- *Persistent Binding.* A name is bound to a value when created, and this binding may never change. This permits loosely coupled organizations to communicate reliably using names, and permits reliable caching of bindings.
- *Unavailability.* No non-local lookup service can be constantly available. The bound value of a name may not be available in situations where there are system failures and there is no local cache available.
- *Eternal Names.* A name, once created, must live forever. Even if a binding expires at its source (see below) caches may live on; names must be remembered so that they will not be rebound.
- *Binding Expiration.* Although names live forever, the storage of accumulated bindings may not always be practical or desirable. Expiration dates would help organizations negotiate the lifetime of their storage services, much as other artifacts in the software business eventually expire.

The rules of the life cycle for names cannot be strictly enforced in the world for which the application web is designed. The success of names used this way must rely on the motivation of participating organizations to follow the rules for their own interest, combined with end-to-end tests to ensure that bound values never change.

5 Related Work

The Vesta project [10], from which JP's core build technology is derived, implemented functional building over a repository of immutable versioned packages. Its package name space is flat, local, and not related to language names, and there is no integrated support for integrated editing.

Distributed configuration management systems have been developed, some commercial such as ClearCase Multisite [3]. These generally presume every site is running the same tools. This restriction can be lifted by designing *middleware* to glue together different systems, for example by Kaiser and Dossick [5]. These approaches address compositional complexity, but often neglect the difficulties of organizational complexity.

Noll and Scacchi address much the same goals as ours with a shared distributed CM system that connects to each organization's tools with adapters [14]. Their design emphasizes a shared model to be understood by all organizations, whereas the application web address a much simpler, open ended model; the application web is less expressive, but may have greater potential for organizational scale. The GIPSY project addresses organizational complexity by proposing a simple, unified model that represents software product, process and organization form [12].

Collaborative authoring tools presume close organizational coupling, although WebDAV aims to bring some of this functionality to the more loosely coupled World Wide Web [16]. Although this is necessarily embedded in a less expressive name space than is needed for the application web, WebDAV could serve as an appropriate infrastructure for parts of the application web.

The application web proposes life cycle connectivity of software to its origin; this permits copying to be replaced by reliable caching. These features allow for reliable software deployment as well as other business opportunities within a Virtual Software House. Such opportunities might include consistent, up-to-date, connected software catalogues as well as component seeking and matching. The Software Dock proposes a sophisticated deployable software description format and an agent based deployment engine to support the software deployment life cycle [7]. Castanet, a product of Marimba, offers incremental software deployment services based on channels, mirroring and fingerprinting technology [11]. In contrast to more sophisticated approaches, the application web promotes the simple "web" idea of connectivity where information relevant for the whole software life cycle is directly accessed from its original source.

6 Conclusions

Reliable, scalable configuration management is essential for developing the next generation of large software systems. Traditional tools fail to help organizations cooperate in emerging models for virtual organizations. Java technology makes some of this easier, but reliable, scalable tools are still needed. Tool strategies for software require a balance between addressing compositional and organizational complexity; names play an important role in these strategies.

The application web, an extension to a reliable, scalable development environment for Java software, addresses the emerging challenge of organizational complexity. It does this in a simple, scalable, collaboration framework based on global naming that permits connecting a wide variety of services, applicable to many phases of the software life cycle. This approach presumes that reliable configuration management and repeatable building are among the core services, but it also conspires to make available a wide variety of related meta-information about software.

Early versions of the JP environment are in use, and a simple prototype of the application web, based on HTTP-coupled tools, has been developed for demonstration purposes. It supports several of the anticipated services, for example loading and running applications directly out of their originating repositories, and navigating via information present in running applications back to the sources and documents in the precise configuration in which they were built.

7 Acknowledgments

This work benefits greatly from the vision of Mick Jordan, Principal Investigator of the Forest Project at Sun Microsystems Laboratories and coauthor of JP. The VSH project is supported by Professor Albert Kündig at ETH Zürich and funded by the Swiss Priority Program of the Swiss National Science Foundation. Yuval Peduel and anonymous reviewers made helpful comments on this paper.

8 Trademarks

Sun, Sun Microsystems, Java Naming and Directory Interface, and Java are trademarks or registered trademarks of Sun Microsystems, Inc. in the United States and other countries.

References

1. Atkinson, M., Daynès, L., Jordan, M., Printezis, T., Spence, S.: An Orthogonally Persistent Java. ACM SIGMOD Record **25** (1996) 68-75

2. Baker, H.: Equal Rights for Functional Objects or, The More Things Change, The More They Are the Same. ACM OOPS Messenger **4**,4 (October 1993) 2-27

3. ClearCase MultiSite http://www.rational.com/products/cc_multisite/

4. Davidow, W., Malone, M.: The Virtual Organization: Structuring and Revitalizing the Corporation for the 21st Century. Burlingame Books (1992)

5. Kaiser, G., Dossick, S.: Workgroup Middleware for Distributed Projects. IEEE Seventh International Workshops on Enabling Technologies: Infrastructure for Collaborative Enterprises (June 1998) 63-68

6. Gosling, J., Joy, W., Steele, G.: The Java^{TM} Language Specification. Addison-Wesley (1996)

7. Hall, R., Heimbigner, D., Wolf, A.: A Cooperative Approach to Support Software Deployment Using the Software Dock. Proceedings of the International Conference on Software Engineering, Los Angeles, CA. (May 1999)

8. JAVA NAMING AND DIRECTORY INTERFACE^{TM}(JNDI), http://java.sun.com/products/jndi/, Sun Microsystems, Inc. (1999)

9. Jordan, M., Van De Vanter, M.: Modular System Building With Java Packages. In: Ebert, J., Lewerentz, C. (eds.): Proceedings 8th Conference on Software Engineering Environments. IEEE Computer Society Press, Los Alamitos, CA, USA (1997) 155-163

10. Levin, R., McJones, P.: The Vesta Approach to Configuration Management. Research Report 105. Digital Equipment Corporation Systems Research Center (1993)

11. Marimba Inc. Castanet Product Family. http://www.marimba.com/ (1998)

12. Murer, T., Scherer, D.: Structural unity of product, process and organization form in the GIPSY process support framework. In: Ebert, J., Lewerentz, C. (eds.): Proceedings 8th Conference on Software Engineering Environments. IEEE Computer Society Press, Los Alamitos, CA, USA (1997) 93-100

13. Murer, T., Van De Vanter, M.: Replacing Copies With Connections: Managing Software across the Virtual Organization. 2nd Workshop on Coordinating Distributed Software Development Projects at IEEE Eighth International Workshops on Enabling Technologies: Infrastructure for Collaborative Enterprises WETICE-8, Stanford University (June 1999)

14. Noll, J., Scacchi, W.: Supporting Distributed Configuration Management in Virtual Enterprises. Proceedings 7th International Workshop Software Configuration Management (ICSE 97 SCM-7), Lecture Notes in Computer Science, Vol. 1235. Springer-Verlag, Berlin Heidelberg New York (1997) 142-160

15. Van De Vanter, M.: Coordinated editing of versioned packages in the JP programming environment. Proceedings System Configuration Management, ECOOP '98 SCM-8 Symposium. Lecture Notes in Computer Science, Vol. 1439. Springer-Verlag, Berlin Heidelberg New York (1998) 158-173

16. IETF WebDAV Working Group, World Wide Web Distributed Authoring and Versioning, http://www.webdav.org/

Distributed Objects
for Concurrent Engineering

Jacky Estublier
Laboratoire Dassault Systèmes / LSR.
Actimart, Bat 8, Av de Vignate
38610 Gieres France
Jacky@imag.fr

Abstract. The growing size of Software Engineering teams (up to a thousand people), combined with shrinking software life cycle duration (a few months) have created considerable pressure to increase concurrency. Concurrent work in Software Engineering. leads to find the same "object" simultaneously in multiple copies, locations and formats. Concurrent engineering support means the definition, control and automation of all these copies and how cooperative work policies are defined and managed.

We believe the paper contributes in two ways, first in showing that the SCM community has to break with some traditional approaches, if scalability and efficiency issues really are of concern; secondly that the approach we propose is a step toward making a new service available on top of conventional middleware (CORBA like), which could constitute a new and wide commercial field for SCM vendors.

1 Introduction

The growing size of Software Engineering teams (up to a thousand people), combined with shrinking software life cycles (a few months) have created considerable pressure for more concurrent work in Software Engineering. We have addressed this issue from a configuration management perspective, but the experience shows that the problem spans in almost all areas of computer supported concurrent activity.

In SCM, each engineer needs a large number of files (for exemple for compiling), and changes only a tiny sub-set of these files. Apparently unchanged files can be shared; but experience shows this is not realistic for three reasons:

- Efficiency. With many files and high performance demand (compilation), only local copies of all files can provide enough efficiency.
- Name and directory. The same file can be located under different names and directories depending on the platform (NT or Unix) or on the product version (restructuring).
- Internal format. Some file need to be translated from a format to another depending on the tool and activity which use it.

These reasons make that each file, even when not changed, has to be physically copied on the machine and workspace where it is used.

Objects of concern are distributed over the network (because the Software Engineers who manipulate them are spread over the network), in multiple copies (because of the concurrent work), and stored in different repositories (because many tools own or require specific storage).

2 Object management in concurrent engineering

One of the major difficulties in Software Engineering is to define each representation, the evolution rules governing the whole environment, and to enforce these definitions.

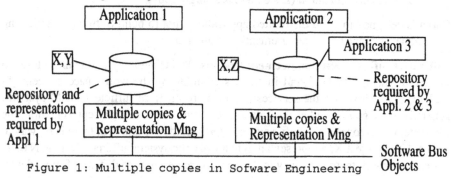

Figure 1: Multiple copies in Sofware Engineering

The requirement is to have, for a given object:

    1 Multiple locations (the users and tools locations)
    2 Multiple representations (needed by tools and environments)
    3 Multiple copies (one for each involved user)
    4 Evolution control (for disciplined concurrent work)
    5 Synchronization control (for synchronizing concurrent work).

Unfortunately, the current technologies do not provide the expected services.

2.1 Current technologies for distributed objects

Techniques like NFS (in a LAN) allow an object (in fact a file) to be shared between different machines and different platform, but this applies only for file system representations and for sharing policies. It only solves point 1.

In a Corba like approach, objects have a single definition (its IDL definition) and a single location at any point in time. An object does not move; Corba allows distributed access to a single copy of an object. Object changes are performed by applications which know only the IDL format. Each application may transform the object from IDL to its local format if required. Corba, to some extent, provides the opposite of our requirements. Each object has:

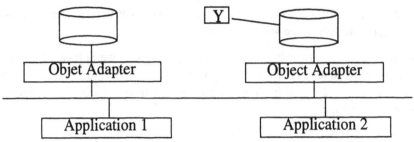

Figure 2: Corba Approach

1   A single location.
2   A single representation (the IDL)
3   A single copy.
4   No evolution control (applications are free to make the object evolve)
5   No synchronization (since there is a single copy).

Corba is designed to build distributed applications, not to build Software engineering environments. None of our requirements are satisfied.

Software configuration management systems. The technology that comes closer to our requirements can be found in SCM systems using the work space concept [5] [12][13] [17]. However, the services provided are far from sufficient. SCM systems, generally, manage *files* rather than objects, and thus know a single representation: the file system. Moreover a single file system representation is allowed: there is no way to define, for an object X, a representation in a Unix file system different from an NT file system; a fortiori, there is no way to define a test representation different from a development one, or a process representation in another DB repository. Finally, evolution constraints are missing or un clearly stated[6].

Requirements 1 and 3 are satisfied, partially 5.

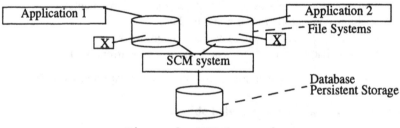

Figure 3: SCM Approach

Databases. The view technology, developed in Databases share some aspects of the problem: an object may be seen simultaneously through different definitions. Unfortunately it is still the same object. Some work has defined sub-databases, which looks similar to SCM work spaces, [2][3], which allows different copies to evolve differently, but still with a predefined format and location. There is a single evolution strategy: the transaction!.

Current databases satisfy only requirement 4 limited to a single strategy: serialization.

2.2 Proposed architecture

The architecture we propose consists in four layers (Figure 4). The first one deals with the problem of presenting to each user (and his/her tools) at current location, the needed objects in the right format; it is the basic Work Space manager. The second layer provides basic functions for transferring / synchronizing objects between any two work-space. The third layer provides concepts for concurrent activities consistency, for structuring the workspaces, and for defining and enforcing cooperative work policies which satisfy some consistency requirements. The fourth layer deals with general process support, and will not be developed here; see [1][4][7] [14][15].

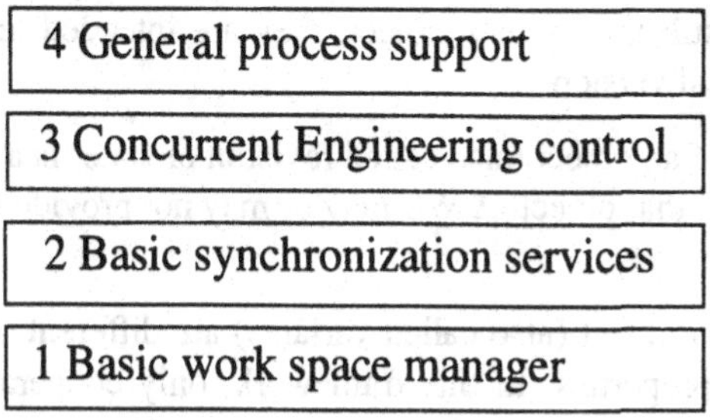

| 4 General process support |
| 3 Concurrent Engineering control |
| 2 Basic synchronization services |
| 1 Basic work space manager |

Figure 4: Layered architecture

2.3 Concepts and definitions

An *object* is an instance of a class in which is defined the content and the behavior of each instance. An object instance contains attributes. Attributes domains can be literals (i.e. strings, integers, file), or another object type; in the later case we say the attribute is a composition attribute, and the object a complex or composed object.

We adhere to this definition, and have added a few features like explicit relationships and versioning (revisions only), as exemplified bellow (Java extension).

```
class SoftComponent extends Component ;
  relation SourceFile sourceCode inverse inObject;
  relation File set Binary ;
  Common Stringowner ;
  Common Date creationdate ;
  relation SoftComponent set components {boolean shared} inverse partOf ;
  ....
```

That language is not the point of this paper and will not be described, it extends java and borrows some aspects from ODMG [16], but relationships have attributes in our case. Unless preceded by key word *Common*, attributes pertains to revisions. Navigation on relations in both directions is allowed.

However, even with the above extensions, this definition is too imprecise in our context, because an object type may have a different definition in each different WS type and an object instance may simultaneously have different values and definitions (its cooperative versions).

A *Workspace* (WS) is a sub-set of a public repository[1] in which (part of) the objects to be controlled are stored.

We call *repository* any system which can store persistent information. It can be a file system or any kind of DB.

An *object representation* is an object instance found in a WS. A single object instance may have simultaneously different representations; one in each WS which contains it.

An *abstract object*, or simply an object, is the whole of all its current representations.

Three levels of versioning apply to each abstract object [8]:

Each object representation is a *cooperative version* of that object. By definition, cooperative versions are still the «same» object; they are intended to converge toward a single persistent logical version.

A *historical version* of an object (also called revision or state) is a stored snapshot of a cooperative version of that object. A WS may or may not provide historical versioning capabilities.

Logical versions of an object (also called variants) are different objects sharing some logical or historical properties. In this framework, only cooperative versions are of concern.

3 Basic WS manager

In our architecture, no repository is the main one, no one owns objects. An object has a (potentially different) definition in each WS (attributes may be missing, others may be specific to that WS); and a WS manages a single object representation.

The fundamental goal of the basic WS manager is to provide the objects in the representation required by the tools working in this WS, irrespective of the other possible representations, and let applications change the object in that specific format, (apparently) irrespective of the changes performed by other applications on the same object in other WSs.

A WS manages two areas. The first one is a part of a public repository i.e. directly accessible by users and tools, in which *some* of the objects attributes are mapped; the other area contains the objects stored in an internal format only accessible through specific

---

1. Access to the objects in the public repository is performed by tools and users using the native repository functions **without any need to be wrapped**. It does not prohibit the representation for controlling these accesses, nor prevent undesired access, as long as this is done in a transparent way.

functions provided by the WS. The former is called the *projection*, the later the *local store*.

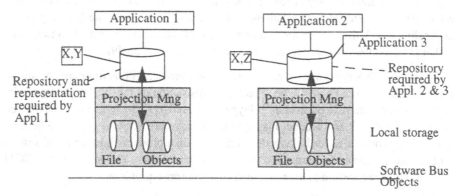

Figure 5: Basic WorkSpace manager

A *WS type* is defined by:

- **Object types definitions**, for objects allowed to be contained in this WS.
- **Repository type** (Unix FS, NTFS, Oracle,...).
- **Projection functions**. Manages the relationships between the object part and the projection part.

For each type of object, the following projection functions must be provided:

- **Projection**: A function translating an instance of that type from its object definition into the local repository and may apply filters to change the content format. In general it is a partial function; some attributes may not be mapped, others can be added.
  Example: attribute *content* of object *foo* of type *c*, is mapped to file *foo.c*; attribute *owner* is not mapped, attribute *protection* is added.
- **Reverse projection**: A function translating entities of the local repository into objects and attributes in the object format. If the repository data model is weaker than the object one, this function will require conventions or additional information.
  Example: File *foo.c* is attribute *content* of object *foo*, which is a component of X through relationship *partOf* (*partOf* and *X* may not be projected).
- **Change mapper**: A function translating a change performed on the entities of the local repository to changes on the corresponding object(s). If the repository data model is weaker than the object one, this function is in theory non deterministic. This function usually requires conventions and heuristics or changes to be performed through a specific interface.
  Example: If file *foo.c* is renamed or is moved into another directory, what does that mean for object *foo*?

Existing SCM systems support a single WS type where these functions are predefined and trivial. Either there is no object model at all, thus the local model is the repository model, or conventions are simple enough to compute the functions trivially. For example name identity (object *foo* of type *c* maps to file *foo.c*); a single composition relationship mapped into the relationship between directory and file (e.g. if *foo.c* is under directory *X* then object *foo* is a component of object *X*). The direct consequence is that (1) the object models are poor, and (2) WS type is unique[9].

In our system, WS types are formally defined, and projection functions are part of the type definition of each object type. There is no restriction on the WS types that can be defined in our system. In particular, WS types proposed by SCM vendors can be defined easily which allows any product managed under any current SCM system to be integrated. It provides also for linking the work done on a product under an SCM system with the work done on the same product, under another representation, by another SCM system. This way we aim to address the virtual enterprise problem.

This approach is in complete opposition with current work in SCM (as well as our own previous work [9]) on at least the following:

- There is no longer any *central* repository. Experience have shown that no centralized approach can scale to very large projects (like the Dassault Systèmes one).
- There is *no generic* WS manager, because there is no generic projection function, and because efficiency requires WS manager to be tailored to take benefit from current company conventions.
- Basic WS managers are indeed SCM systems providing simple functionality at almost no cost. They can be compatible with current habits and revision control tool like RCS or CVS.

Basic WS managers can be simple, but unlike RCS or CVS, our solution is scalable toward high functionality levels, huge software products and very large and distributed teams. This is the topic of the next chapters.

4 Basic synchronization services

There is a need to define the way different WSs communicate. In our approach, all communications between WSs, whatever their type, relies on a normalized definition of the objects described in our Interface Definition Language (IDL). Each basic WS manager must be capable of translating an object from its IDL definition to its local definition (often much simpler).

The fact we enforce a definition to be "universal" may be seen as a scalability limiting factor. We believe this is not true for at least two reasons. First, we do not expect an object definition to be shared by the whole world (we are "only" addressing SCM for a world wide company). Second, remember that each WS manager only has the knowledge of a sub-set of the objects it manages.

In our prototype, the IDL is simply a Java interface defining an SCM meta model. It slightly extends Java with file attributes, historical object (a sequence of object states), relationships (to/from objects or object states) and complex object (with multiple composition relationships) concepts. A product model is an interface making use of the SCM meta model. We provide a Java pre-processor which generates standard Java from these few new keywords.

Note that not only the approach applies to any meta model (other than SCM), but it also includes Java itself. The prototype can be used, as is, as a general upper layer to Corba and Java for multiple copy / multiple representation management.

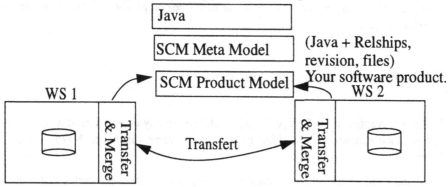

Figure 7: Basic coordination

When WS1 asks WS2 for object X, it sends the relevant definition of X to WS2 i.e. which attributes and components of X it needs. WS2 only sends these attributes back to WS1. For example, a test WS manager may want only the binary attribute of X and X test-suite components; a development WS may require instead the source attributes and all its components. This facility is required for any large development and/or distributed development.

Concurrent changes imply there is a way to reconcile different values of an attribute. We call that function the *merge* function. If we note $A_1,... A_i$ the different value of attribute A, and $A_i = Ci(A_0)$ the value of A after change Ci is performed on A_0, then a merge function M is such that $M(A1, A2) = C1(C2(A_0)) = C2(C1(A_0))$.

This means the result of the merge is the same as if changes C1 and C2 has been performed in sequence, on A_0, irrespective of the order. If an exact merge function exists for each attribute, concurrent engineering always leads to consistent results!. Unfortunately, for a given attribute, such a merge function either (1) exists, (2) is an approximation, or (3) does not exist at all. In our example, *partOf* attribute has an exact merge, file merge is an approximate function, *owner* has no merge.

Merge, in our work, is understood at the IDL *object* level. We provide the functions to merge complex object (composition relationship merge) as a standard feature, as well as the usual file merge. This contrasts with SCM traditional approaches where only *file* merge is available.

This approach contrasts with current work in SCM, on at least the following aspects.

(1) The meta model is high level, but since it relies on a standard language, we have compilers, interpreters, and object transfer (Java IDL) "for free". A WS manager is simple to implement.

(2) Each WS manager ignore the formats and models used by the other WS managers; SCM system heterogeneity is possible.

(3) Transfers are partial. Only the relevant information is transferred, which is critical in distributed work.

(4) We provide *object* merge instead of *file* merge. Our customers are unanimous in saying that object merge is a major enhancement (the composition relationship merge is an exact merge).

5 Concurrent engineering control

Nothing prevents each WS to perform any change on any object, thus at a given point in time, each attribute of each object may have a different value in each WS in which it is present.

Concurrent engineering control means ensuring that collectively performed work is consistent. Unfortunately, for concurrent access to information, there is a single real consistency criteria: serialization i.e. ACID transactions as found in databases i.e. conrurrent changes are prohibited.

These values apply only to *files* while, in this work, we deal with *objects* (files are atomic attributes in our object model). Our experience shows that concurrent changes to the same attribute (like file or composition) as well as different attributes of the same object (like responsible, state, name, namefile, protection etc) are very common. Merging must address the two levels of granularity : the same attribute and the different attributes of an object. For example, restructuring, renaming and changing files are common and independent activities. Raising the granularity from file to object makes appear new kinds of concurrent changes, which may produces new kinds of merges. It is our claim that object concurrent change control subsumes traditional file control and provides homogeneous and elegant solutions to many difficulties which currently hamper concurrent software engineering.

5.1 The group approach

We call a *group*, a set of Work Spaces (WS) the goal of which is to make an object evolve in a "consistent" way. Each group contains a WS playing the role of reference repository for the group called the *integration* WS.

For consistency to be enforced in a group, it must behave in a way similar to an ACID transaction applied to the *integration* WS, each WS playing the role of local transaction caches.

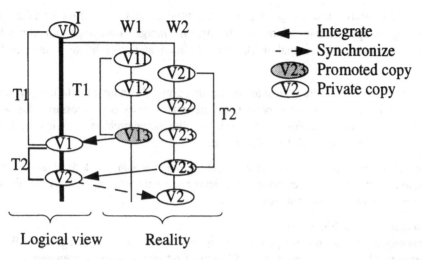

Figure 8: Consistent Concurrent

In Figure 8, Transaction T1, executed on V0 (in W1) provides value V13, while transaction T2 provides value V23 (in W2). Concurrent changes by T1 and T2 are consistent only if it is possible to compute the value V2, the result of applying T2 to V1 instead of V0. If this is possible, the group G = (I, W1, W2) behaves as a single WS, (I) to which all the transactions really performed concurrently on the different WSs of that group are applied in sequence.

Let us call O/Wi and $O.A/Wi$ the current values of object O and attribute A of O as found in WS Wi. We have defined the following atomic functions:

$P(O/Wi)$, for propose O, informs that the current value for O in Wi is available to become the current value of the group.

$I(O/Wi)$, for integrate O, merges $O/Integration$ with O/Wi, providing a new value for O in the *Integration* WS.

$S(O)$, for synchronize O, when performed by Wi merges in Wi O/Wi with $O/Integration$.

$R(O.A/Wi)$ and $F(O/Wi)$, for Reserve and Free A, together define a critical section for attribute O.A. At any point in time, a single WS can be in the critical section for a given attribute.

For the sake of simplicity let us denote C(A) any change performed on attribute A, and «,» any other action (involving or not O).

5.2 Basic policies in a group

A basic concurrent engineering policy means defining and enforcing

- who has right to perform a change on what (not anyone on anything at any time),
- what is to be merged and when,
- who has to merge.

Experience shows that merge control is a central point when the merge function is missing or approximate. More specifically, file merge is an approximation which requires, potentially, manual work (for conflicts) and to validate if the result is consistent.

This becomes even more critical as soon as in a group the integration task is performed by a dedicated person. That person, the integrator, does not necessarily know the changes performed and would not be able to solve merge problems, nor is it its duty to fix the bugs that can result from the merge.

We claim that basic concurrent engineering policies can be defined as the valid sequences of operations performed on objects and attributes in a group. A definition of a few of the most useful policies follows:

Exclusion. O.A: (SR),C,PIF.
This sequence states that the policy to be applied to attribute O.A in a group of WSs. It means that before changing A (C), a WS must first synchronize (S) then reserve (R) A. If reserve fails, the couple SR must be repeated at a later time. After the change, the WS promotes (P), integrates (I) and frees (F) the object. This policy implements an ACID transaction; *Integrate* and *Synchronize* simply replace the old value by the new one (no merge). In practice any attribute for which no merge function exists should be managed in this way.

Delayed reserve: O.A: C,R,C,S,C,PIF.
This sequence states that changes on attribute A can be done before to reserve it. As a consequence the synchronize operation (S) may require a merge (because meanwhile, a change on A may have been integrated). But since S is performed in the critical section (i.e. between R and F), operation I (integrate) will never require a merge (because since the reserve only that WS can integrate a change on A). That policy has the property to never produce any merge in the *integration* WS for attribute A. This is a consequence of any sequence in which S is before P and in a critical section.

Delayed reserve and integration. O.A: C,RSP,I,F.
This sequence expresses that attribute A can be changed concurrently, but it must be *reserved* immediately before being *proposed*. As soon as all *reservations* for O are obtained, the object is *resynchronized* (i.e. updated) and immediately *proposed. Integration* however is deferred; which means the integrator is free to select which proposed change to integrate, when and in which order. Since the *free* operation can also be delayed, it means the integrator has the opportunity, for example, to run the test suite before validating the changes (F). With respect to the previous policy, flexibility is provided to integrators, not to developers.

Note that no merges are ever needed in the Integration WS. In other words, multiple concurrent changes are allowed but their integration is sequentialized and merges are performed in the WS which performed the changes, never in the integration WS.

Remember that a policy is defined on an attribute basis. For example, the management of source code objects in development groups can use **exclusion** for the *filename* attribute, **Delayed reservation and integration** for *sourceCode* attribute and default (no control) for the *components* attribute.

This approach contrasts with all other SCM cooperation strategies in the following ways:

- A policy can be defined independently for each attribute (default means no control). For instance, in a development group, it is possible, for the same object, to have three WS changing the file (*sourceCode*) another one changing that file name (*fileName*) and a third one changing which complex object it pertains to (*components*). Subsequent synchronization will consistently merge all these changes.
- A policy is declared on a group type basis i.e. all WSs in a group share the same policies; but each group can have different policies over the same objects. Typically, the *development* groups have more relaxed policies than the *release* group.
- A policy is formally defined (as the valid sequence of commands), and some "classic" policies have been studied so that their properties have been proved and used to optimize the implementation. In the above policy examples, each command involves only 2 WSs, not all the group WSs, which is critical in distributed development.

The integration WS plays the role of the coordinator for the whole group, it knows the policies and thus enforces and optimizes the controls, based on the properties of each policy.

5.3 Company concurrent work policies

The *integration* WS behaves as the representative of the whole group, and can thus be a component of another higher level group (potentially of another type). In this way, the whole company can be organized in a hierarchy of WSs.

It can be proven that the properties identified inside a single group hold for any sub-hierarchy with the single condition that reserving an attribute in a WS is considered as reserving that attribute in the *integration* WS of that group. It makes the *reserve* command transitive between groups which include the *reserve* command for that attribute in their policy.

The strict application of the previous strategy leads to a tree of groups, with data flow following the edges. Experience have shown this strategy is too limited. Data flow between siblings is common and needed, as well as data flow between almost any arbitrary groups (as long as it is accepted by the process in place).

We have shown that synchronization between siblings in a group is possible, while still satisfying the coordination properties, provided some constraints, but at the cost of more inefficient algorithms (many optimizations are no longer valid); demonstration is out of the scope of this paper.

The system keeps track of "abnormal" object synchronization (any synchronization that does not follows the tree). This is needed since it invalidates the assumptions used for optimization, and is required for performing subsequent merges (relationship merges require to store information). This "simple" enhancement, as well as the facility allowing to "undo" complex operations like *synchronize* or *integrate* are responsible for significantly increase the complexity of the whole system (remember that these commands can involve very complex object, often the whole WS, which amounts to hundred of thousands files).

6 Conclusion

A major issue faced by SE is that time to market pressure, combined with the increasing size of software teams make concurrent engineering critical. To face that issue, copies of the same object are created and given to SE engineers, with modification rights for everyone.

In many fields like databases, operating systems or networks, creating and managing object copies is usual, but in a transparent way (in caches) in order to provide the user the illusion that a single object copy exists. In SE the issue is different, users **want** to be able to ask for a private copy, to say for how long, to decide when changes performed by others are to be integrated, and when their changes are ready to be used by others. Copy management must be explicit and part of the working paradigm. Further, each copy of an object may have a different structure, content and format depending on the tools, operating system, or platform on which it will be used.

It is shown that a copy facility, to be realy usable, must provide the services we have identified in the three layers of Figure 4: basic work space manager, resynchronization and concurrent engineering control. We believe this kind of copy facility is needed each time concurrent object management is required, which covers a very wide range of applications. We also think that this papers have shown that such a facility is far from trivial to design and implement, at least if generality and efficiency are of concern. It is a waste of energy to redo that work in each application domain and even in each vendor tool.

The large community around CORBA is designing a number of general purpose services and facilities, but none adressing our issues. We claim that a copy management facility, similar to what is presented in this paper, should become a Corba/OMG facilities. Currently no work we know goes in that direction.

We illustrate the approach in a specific area: Software Configuration Management. But this paper claims that a new generation of SCM systems, breaking with most traditional approaches, can provide general and efficient concurrent engineering facilities as a "natural" extension of current middleware.

The paper has shown the approach, architecture and concepts that have been put in place and investigated. We think that our experience shows at least two things: (1) SCM systems have to be redesigned if scalability, efficiency and generality issues faced in that field are to be solved, (2) Instead of focussing on a specific area, anew generation of system should target a much wider commercial segment: middleware supporting concurrent object modification.

References

[1]   *"ClearGuide: Product Overview"*. Technical report, Atria Software, Inc.

[2]   A. Bjornersledl and C. Hullen. *Version control in an Object-Oriented Architecture*. In Won Kim and Frederick H. Lochowsky. editors. Objects-Oriented concepts, databases and application. Chapter 18, pages 451-485, Adisson-Wesley. 1990.

[3]   E. Bratsberg. *Unified Class Evolution by Object Oriented views*. Proc of the 11th Conf on the relationship approach. LNCS N0645, Spronger Verlag, Oct 1992.

[4]   S. Dami, J. Estublier and M. Amiour. *"APEL: a Graphical Yet Executable Formalism for Process Modeling"*. Automated Software Engineering journal, January 1998.

[5]   S. Dart. *"Concepts in Configuration Management Systems"*. *Proc. of the 3rd. Intl. Workshop on Software Configuration Management*. Trondheim, Norway, june, 1991.

[6]   J. Estublier. *"Workspace Management in Software Engineering Environments"*. in SCM-6 Workshop. Springer LNCS 1167. Berlin, Germany, March 1996.

[7]   J. Estublier and S. Dami and M. Amiour. *High Level Process Modeling for SCM Systems*. SCM 7, LNCS 1235. pages 81--98, May, Boston, USA, 1997

[8]   J. Estublier and R. Casallas. *"Three Dimensional Versioning"*. In SCM-4 and SCM-5 Workshops. J. Estublier editor, September, 1995. Springer LNCS 1005.

[9]   J. Estublier and R. Casallas. *"The Adele Software Configuration Manager"*. Configuration Management, Edited by W. Tichy; J. Wiley and Sons. 1994. Trends in software.

[10]   B. Gulla, E.A. Carlson, D. Yeh. *Change-Oriented version description in EPOS*. Software Engineering Journal, 6(6):378-386, Nov 1991.

[11]   M. Hardwick, B.R. Dowine, M. Kutcher, D.L. Spooner, *"Concurrent Engineering with Delta Files'*, IEEE Computer Graphics and Applications, January 1995, pp. 62-68.

[12]   D. B. Leblang. and G.D. McLean. *Configuration Management for large-scale software development efforts*. In Proceedings of the workshop on Software Environments for Programming-in-the-Large. Pages 122-127. Harwichport, Massachussets, Jume 1985.

[13]   D. B. Leblang. *"The CM Challenge: Configuration Management that Works"*. Configuration Management, Edited by W. Tichy; J. Wiley and Sons. 1994. Trends in software.

[14]   D.B. Leblang. *Managing the Software Development Process with ClearGuide*. SCM 7, LNCS 1235. pages=66, 80, May, Boston, USA, 1997

[15]   J. Micallef and G. M. Clemm. *"The Asgard System: Activity-Based Configuration Management"*. In SCM-6 Workshop, Berlin, Germany, March, 1996.

[16]   R.G.G Catell & All. *The Object Database Standard: ODMG 2.0*. Morgan Kaufmann Publisher. ISBN 1-55860-463-4, 1997.

[17]   Walter F. Tichy. *Tools for software configuration management*. In *Proc. of the Int. Workshop on Software Version and Configuration Control*, pp. 1–20, Grassau, January 1988

Goals for a Configuration Management Network Protocol

E. James Whitehead, Jr.

Dept. of Information and Computer Science
University of California, Irvine
Irvine, CA 92697-3425 USA
Tel: +1 949 824 4121
E-mail: ejw@ics.uci.edu

Abstract. Experience from research on integrating versioning and configuration management support to the Web has shown that building such support on the basic Web infrastructure leads to undesirable architectural choices. This paper presents goals for a standardization effort called Delta-V which is extending the Web infrastructure, specifically the core network protocols HTTP and WebDAV, with capabilities for remote versioning and configuration management. Important goals include providing equal support for all content types, allowing versioning unaware applications to participate, supporting both mutable and immutable revisions, ensuring that human-readable strings are internationalizable, and provision of strong authentication and transport security. These goals are currently being used to develop the Delta-V protocol within the Internet Engineering Task Force.

1   Introduction

What if you were an employee of a small design firm called DesignHaus, working on a Web site update for a client whose pages are *very* time sensitive. To benefit from a broad pool of design talent, DesignHaus draws its designers from around the world, and you're working in a team active 24 hours a day — Kenji supplies graphics and icons from Tokyo, Denise provides page layout in Paris, while simultaneously Peter writes custom JavaScript in New York. You're in Los Angeles, in charge of content, working closely with the client to fine tune the Web site's message.

Though unaware of this fact, you are using a network protocol called Delta-V, a series of extensions to the Web's core protocol, the Hypertext Transfer Protocol (HTTP) [9] and the WebDAV protocol [13] (itself an extension of HTTP) which open the Web for collaborative authoring and versioning. From your perspective, you are simply collaborating over the Internet using your favorite tools. After finishing a phone call with the client, you start your Web page editor, and start editing a product information page by typing its URL into the "File... Open" dialog box. Behind the scenes, the tool makes a network protocol request to check out the Web page from the group's work area located in the URL space of a Web server at the DesignHaus corporate headquarters in New York. The editor learns this check out will result in parallel development, so it pops up a dialog box indicating that Denise is also working on this Web page at the same time. Not a problem — you decide to work in parallel with Denise. In the background, the editor sends a network request to download the Web page, and you see the Web page quickly appear on screen, ready for changes.

Once you've finished altering the content based on the client's feedback, you save it using the "File... Commit" dialog in the editor. The editor saves the final version by writing over the network directly to the URL, and then sends a network request to perform a check in. The check-in succeeds, and the editor discovers that Denise has also committed her latest changes. It pops-up a dialog box asking you if you want to merge your changes with Denise's. You select yes, and the tool brings up a merge utility. The editor already has a copy of your latest changes, but it has to perform a network request to retrieve Denise's latest revision, and then check-out the Web page to make the merged revision. Since Denise was altering layout while you were altering content, there are few conflicts which are easily resolved. When done, you select "File... Commit", and the editor makes two network requests to write back the Web page to its URL, and check in the new merged revision.

Since you've been editing directly in-place on the Web, you're now ready to call back your client, tell them the URL, and get their feedback on the new revision.

Developing the network protocol which makes this scenario possible is the goal of the Delta-V working group of the Internet Engineering Task Force (IETF). While work on the Delta-V protocol is still underway, and the final design is still in flux, there are many interesting preliminary results. This paper reports on the initial experience of the Delta-V working group in developing a network protocol for remote versioning and configuration management of Web sites, software projects, and other complex information artifacts.

Adding versioning support to WebDAV will support the following capabilities:

- Development teams can collaboratively develop complex information artifacts in-place on the Web, using locking to prevent overwrite conflicts, and versioning to support parallel development. Due to the distributed nature of the Web, these workgroups can have members from within the same organization, or across organizational boundaries.
- All the types of artifacts in a typical software development lifecycle or encountered in a typical Web site can be remotely versioned, including requirements, design documents, test cases, code, GIF and JPEG images, CGI scripts, Java code, and much, much more. The protocol will support versioning of HTML and XML just as easily as it supports versioning of existing word processing, spreadsheet, text, graphics, and all other formats.
- The protocol will provide a common interface to a wide range of repositories, such as configuration management systems, file system based versioning systems (e.g. RCS [26]), databases, document management systems, etc. In essence, WebDAV makes the Web look like a versioned, large-grain network-accessible file system. But, unlike a conventional file system, a WebDAV-enabled repository provides Internet access, and allows all "files" to be viewed using a standard Web browser.

The paper is organized as follows. It begins with highlights of the Web's client-server architecture, including a description of the existing capabilities of HTTP and WebDAV. Next is a presentation of key high-level goals that have been identified by the Delta-V group, interspersed with some discussion of significant technical challenges and initial design choices. The paper ends with discussion of related work.

2 Delta-V, a Client-Server Architecture

The Delta-V protocol is a series of extensions to the WebDAV protocol, which itself extends HTTP, a client-server protocol. Figure 1 shows three different Delta-V clients interacting via the HTTP/DAV/Delta-V protocol with a hypothetical Web server that provides interfaces to several different storage repositories. The advantage of this client-server architecture is *distribution*. In the case of WebDAV and Delta-V, by allowing the client/server information flow to take place over the Internet, clients, which author and version Web resources, and servers, which provides persistent storage for these resources, can be physically separated by thousands of miles. Furthermore, the network protocol in a client/server system acts as a bridge across organizational and system boundaries, allowing remote cooperative authoring by collaborators located in different organizations (or different divisions of the same organization), using different hardware platforms.

To perform an action in HTTP, a client opens a network connection to a server, then creates a request message, which is divided into three parts, the request-line, a series of headers, and a request body. The client issues a command, called a *method*, by encoding the command in the request line. Parameters for the method are passed in two forms, as attribute-value pairs, called *headers*, and as Extensible Markup Language (XML) [7] in the message request body. Once the request is complete, it is sent to the server, which unpackages the request and executes the command. After processing the request, the server creates a response message, which contains a status line, a series of headers, and a response body. Success or failure is indicated by a status code, a three digit number located in the status line.

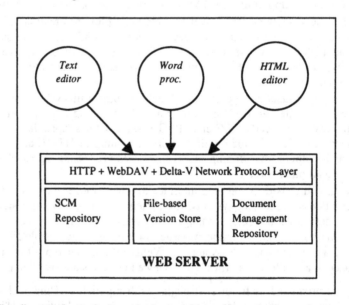

Fig. 1. This diagram shows three versioning capable remote authoring tools communicating via the HTTP protocol using WebDAV and Delta-V extensions to a Delta-V capable server. The server shows three different persistent storage interfaces, highlighting the ability to map Delta-V operations across a wide variety of repositories. Typically no one server will implement so many storage interfaces simultaneously.

The basic object within HTTP/WebDAV/Delta-V is the *resource*, which represents a network accessible data item which provides a set of operations, its methods. A resource contains two kinds of state, state associated with the *body*, and *property* state. The body is the content retrieved by a read request on a resource, and is a *representation* of the body of the resource, not necessarily the exact contents of the body state. This extra abstraction permits dynamic behavior of resources, allowing a read request response to be the output of a computational process, like a CGI script or an active server page (ASP). A resource also contains properties, name/value pairs, where the value of a property is a sequence of well-formed XML.

Table 1. Methods supported by HTTP and WebDAV

HTTP METHODS	
GET	Retrieve a resource and simple metadata, such as its length, MIME type, and cache tag.
HEAD	Retrieve just the simple metadata, but not the contents of a resource.
POST	Submit form data. Often used for tunneling other RPC schemes.
PUT	Write a resource.
DELETE	Remove a resource.
OPTIONS	Discover which methods are supported by a resource.
TRACE	Debug method.
WEBDAV METHODS	
PROPFIND	Retrieve properties (complex metadata) from a resource, or a tree of resources.
PROPPATCH	Set and remove properties on a resource.
MOVE	Move a resource, or a tree of resources.
COPY	Copy a resource, or a tree of resources.
MKCOL	Create a new collection.
LOCK	Lock a resource, or a tree of resources, preventing overwrite conflicts.
UNLOCK	Remove a lock.

As Table 1 highlights, HTTP provides operations for retrieving Web resources, the most frequently used HTTP operations. HTTP also provides basic authoring capabilities with the PUT and DELETE methods, which are only now starting to enjoy widespread client support as WebDAV is adopted. WebDAV extends base

HTTP with capabilities for overwrite prevention, properties, and namespace management, which are described briefly below, with details available in [28].

Overwrite prevention. Keeping more than one person from working on a document at the same time. This prevents the "lost update problem" in which modifications are lost as first one developer, then another writes changes without merging the other developer's work.

WebDAV provides overwrite prevention via its shared and exclusive lock capability. This dual lock support provides sufficiently flexible locks to accommodate a wide range of collaborations, with shared locks best supporting collaborators who have a lot of awareness of each other's activities, and exclusive locks providing a more stringent guarantee of conflict avoidance for less aware collaborators, or during periods of high contention for a resource. Locks may have a scope of a single resource or a hierarchy of resources, such as a source code tree. A lock discovery mechanism (a WebDAV property) allows authors to find out if any locks exist on a resource. Since the Web is designed so that no lock is required to read a Web page, there is no concept of a read lock.

Properties. Creation, removal, and querying of information about resources, such as its author, last modified date, etc. Also included is the ability to make hypertext links between resources of any content type.

WebDAV properties are name, value pairs where the name is a URI, and the value is a sequence of well-formed Extensible Markup Language (XML) elements. Using URIs as property names provides a globally unique property namespace. Since property names can be URLs, which have a domain name as a component of the URL, property names can be given uniqueness without central registration by using URL property names chosen from within a domain whose name is controlled by the party defining the property. So, for example, a company which controls a given domain name, like "widgets.com" can chose a property name from within this domain, like "widgets.com/properties/color".

Name space management. Creation, removal, and automatic consistency maintenance of the membership of collections containing sets of Web resources. Also, the ability to copy and move Web-accessible artifacts, and to receive a listing of resources in a collection (similar to a directory listing in a file system).

Functional goals for the capabilities which will be provided by the Delta-V protocol are described in the next section.

3   Functional Goals for a Web Versioning and Configuration Management Protocol

This section describes the primary functional goals for the Delta-V protocol. Due to space limitations, it is not possible to list all goals. A complete listing is given in the Delta-V working group's consensus goals document [24]. Where appropriate, text in this section is quoted from the working group's goals document.

Throughout this paper, the terms *revision* and *versioned resource* will be used. Informally, a versioned resource is an abstraction representing all of the revisions of a particular resource over time, such as all of the revisions of the HTML page "index.html" over its lifetime. A revision is a persistently stored specific instance of a resource, for example, the contents of "index.html" as checked-in at a specific moment in time. Formally, a versioned resource is an abstraction for a resource which is subject to version control, a resource having a set of revisions, relationships between those revisions, revision identifiers and labels, and named branches that track the evolution of the resource. A revision is a particular version of a versioned resource

3.1 Equal support for all content types

The Web is composed of documents, images, and objects of many content, or Internet media types [11]. The Web is composed of more than just text. *It must be possible to version resources of any media or content type, that is, a Web versioning and CM protocol must treat all content types equally.*

A protocol which only provides operations for resources of one preferred content type, such as HTML, would have limited applicability due to its lack of support for the wide variety of other content types. Furthermore, since many common content types are in constant evolution, in order to ensure stability of the protocol a strict separation between the protocol, and the format of the objects operated upon by the protocol, must be maintained. For example, during the development of the WebDAV protocol itself, new standards for HTML 3.2, 4.0, and XML were issued, highlighting how quickly these document formats can develop and evolve. Tailoring an authoring protocol too closely to any one content type would rapidly make the protocol obsolete.

3.2 Versioning aware and non-versioning aware clients must be able to interoperate

Many WebDAV authoring clients are expected to be in use by the time the Delta-V protocol is supported in shipping products. There are also some authoring tools which just use HTTP, and are not even WebDAV aware. To aid adoption of the Delta-V protocol, it is important to provide a minimal level of versioning support to these clients, so they can interact with a versioning server without having any knowledge of the versioning protocol. This allows people to gain versioning capability without having to change their tools, and provides a ready-made base of clients when versioning servers first become available. It does, however, raise the design challenge of ensuring that versioning-aware and versioning-unaware clients can smoothly interoperate, preventing unforeseen negative interactions.

Non-versioning aware clients should be able to request the contents of a versioned resource without specifying a revision and receive a well-defined default revision. A non-versioning aware client should be able to write to a versioned resource and have a new revision automatically be created. It is expected that a write operation will perform an implicit check-out, write, and check-in to maintain versioning semantics and avoid lost updates. A subsequent read on the same versioned resource by this client will return the new revision. However, the versioning operations available to non-versioning clients will be very limited. For example, such clients will not be capable of submitting comments or properties on check-in or check-out, and will be limited to either linear versioning, or working on only a single branch.

3.3 Configuration management capability is an optional extension to versioning capability

Two kinds of clients are expected to support the Delta-V protocol. The first is an authoring client, such as a text editor or a word processor, which will only provide versioning capabilities, allowing a check-out, edit, check-in style of interaction. The second type of client is a configuration management "control panel" application, which understands all of the configuration management capabilities of Delta-V. For Delta-V, a *configuration* is a versioned resource that contains a set of specific revisions of versioned resources, thus making a each versioned resource a configuration item. One example of a configuration is a snapshot of a Web site, where the configuration records the revision of every Web page and graphic image in the site. A Delta-V configuration management control panel application can perform actions like creating configurations, check-out and check-in of configurations, and reverting to a previous configuration. Though these control panel operations are not expected to appear in authoring tools, it should be noted there is nothing to prevent an authoring tool from supporting these configuration management capabilities.

The major benefit of this two-tier approach is that it provides a simple initial set of functionality which, if supported, provides useful versioning features. By limiting the scope of functionality initially required to be Delta-V compliant, it is much easier to convince tool makers to add Delta-V support, thus boosting adoption of the protocol. The same logic works on the server side too. Since some use situations do not require configuration management support, such as a small set of artifacts being developed by a small, closely knit team, a versioning-only server might provide all the support they need. Existing versioning systems can provide Delta-V support without having to add configuration management capabilities to their system, thus creating a versioning-only server which can be used by these smaller projects.

However, as sometimes happens when projects grow, if a versioning-only team discovers they need configuration management capabilities, using their versioning-only authoring tools, they can trade up to a server which supports configuration management capabilities in addition to versioning operations. The only additional tool required is a configuration management control panel. Thus, supporting this requirement creates two stable plateaus of functionality, a versioning level, and a configuration management level, which give tool and server makers an easy, full-featured entry level for small to medium scale projects, and a clear upgrade path to configuration management capability for large-scale projects.

3.4 Revisions may be mutable or immutable

Versioning support for software development has traditionally emphasized the creation of revisions which, once checked-in to the control of the versioning system, can never be modified again, making them immutable. This makes sense for software development due to the machine-readable nature of program code, where every change needs to be tracked. However, versioning support for documents within document management systems is often more relaxed about tracking every possible change. In these systems, it is more important to maintain the logical name of a revision (e.g., "June Sales Brochure") than to track every small change that has been made. As a result, these systems do allow changes to a revision, *even after it has been checked-in*. Users of these systems appreciate the ability to make minor changes to these mutable revisions, like fixing a spelling error, without having to create an entire new revision. For these use cases, the immutable style of versioning is just not appropriate.

A common, but misguided, approach to mutable revisions is to simulate mutable revisions using immutable revisions. One technique is to provide a mechanism that performs a check-out, modification, and check-in in one convenient operation, thus preserving the immutability of revisions, while still allowing easy changes. However, the ease of making changes isn't the main point. The intent of mutable revisions is to avoid creating a new revision for a small change, and to have each revision maintain a stable logical value. For example, with mutable revisions, a version history for a monthly sales brochure need only have 12 revisions, one for each month. In many use environments where there are minimal archival storage requirements, there is little need for storing intermediate revisions as the next month's brochure is developed. Similarly, if minor spelling or grammatical errors are fixed in a brochure before a second printing is made, storing the original, error-containing document has little value.

Since configuration management systems have a fundamental constraint that revisions must be immutable, it is expected that a mutable revision will not be a permissible member of a configuration. In fact, it is likely that servers which support mutable revisions will only support versioning, and will not provide any configuration management support. This is due to the semantics of configurations that require the ability to revert to a previous revision of the configuration and get exactly the previous contents. For many use environments, especially software and system configuration control, the ability to revert and get exactly the previous contents is critical for providing control over large systems. However, there are many use environments where such stringent control is not needed, and is in fact burdensome. Since the Delta-V protocol is intended to be used in environments that vary in their configuration control requirements, both immutable and mutable styles of versioning should be supported.

3.5   Revision history support

Storing previous revisions of resources, along with descriptive comments for each revision, is a major benefit for versioning Web resources. Therefore, retrieving a revision history which lists all of the revisions of a versioned resource, details predecessor relationships among the revisions, lists comments submitted on each revision, and gives the URL for each revision, is an important feature. This information can be used by versioning-aware clients to display a graphical representation of the version history, and allow direct navigation to an individual member of the revision history.

A significant design choice in Delta-V is to make the Web server the control point for consistency maintenance of the predecessor and successor relationships in the revision history of a versioned resource. Some systems, such as NUCM [14] and the NTT web versioning system [19] place the client in control of creating and updating these relationships, providing the significant benefit of allowing version histories to span multiple servers. However, an implicit design goal of Delta-V is to provide a

Web gateway to existing configuration management and document management systems, where the expected use environment will have some people using these systems via the Delta-V protocol interface while others simultaneously use the system via its local access interface. Since these existing systems maintain the consistency of predecessor and successor relationships that are stored within their repository, they were unwilling to cede this consistency control to clients. Furthermore, if consistency control were the purview of clients only, the possibility exists that a single poorly implemented, or poorly behaving client could disrupt version histories created by other, well-behaved clients. This was considered unacceptable.

One implication of having the versioning relationships controlled by the server is the difficulty of providing version histories which span servers. Indeed, in the server-controlled scheme, server-spanning version histories require a server-to-server protocol for transmitting messages to coordinate these histories. Since no such protocol exists or is planned, server-spanning version histories are a feature awaiting future work. However, it is a goal to ensure that nothing in the current design of Delta-V makes it impossible to add cross-repository version histories in the future, primarily requiring Delta-V to ensure identifiers used in version histories are unique across all servers, not just a single server.

3.6 A revision is a resource, with its own URL

The HTTP protocol operates on resources, hence this goal has the result of making each revision an object which can be operated on by the HTTP/WebDAV/Delta-V protocol. This provides two important benefits. The biggest benefit is that a revision can be the target of an HTML link, allowing hypertext browsing of previous revisions of a resource. Close behind is the ability to perform other protocol operations on revisions, such as retrieving properties.

3.7 A mechanism must exist for giving a human readable name to a single revision

Version control systems often reserve the right to give individual revisions an identifier (e.g., "1.5"), and this identifier may not be intelligible to a human user. As a result, it is useful to be able to associate a human-readable *label* to a revision. This label is unique within a revision history, and can be used to identify a specific revision.

The introduction of labels may seem confusing at first, since, due to the previous requirement, a revision must have its own URL, and one of the design requirements for a URL is human readability. Hence it might seem that the per-revision URL meets this requirement. However, labels and URLs differ in their uniqueness requirements. The URL for a revision must be globally unique, since it identifies just a single resource. In contrast, a label need only be unique within a versioned resource, identifying a single revision among the set of revisions in a versioned resource. The same label is expected to be used across multiple versioned resources on the same server, and can be used in revision selection rules by workspaces and configurations to select, for example, all the revisions that make up a particular release. Furthermore,

while revision URLs are expected to refer to the same revision over time, a label may
be moved across revisions of a versioned resource.

3.8 Versioning should not disrupt relative URLs

Documents on the Web in HTML format often employ hypertext links or image tags
whose target location is expressed relative to the URL of the current resource. One
typical use of this feature is to create a directory of images and icons containing a
common appearance for a site. A link to one such image might look like
"../images/logo.gif". To ensure that versioning support will not break links in HTML
documents containing relative URLs, versioning support should not disrupt relative
URLs. A corollary of this requirement is, if a set of resources is arranged in a URL
hierarchy before they are placed under version control, then this hierarchy should be
the same after the resources are version controlled.

The primary effect of this requirement is to constrain the types of changes that can
be made to the URL namespace to support versioning. URLs do not have any support
for adding revision identifier information, and several schemes have been proposed to
address this deficiency. One commonly suggested scheme is to place all the revisions
of a versioned resource in a collection that has the original name of the resource. In
this scheme the URL for revision 1.1 of "index.html" would be "index.html/1.1".
However, such a scheme would disrupt relative URLs, since it introduces an extra
hierarchy layer. This particular scheme also has the drawback of not handling
versioned collections well.

In the design of the protocol, there is a tension between giving every revision its
own URL, and not disrupting relative URLs. Since URLs do not have provisions for
expressing revision identifier information, once each revision is given its own URL,
every resource which used to have a single URL before it was versioned now has
multiple URLs, one for each revision. These URLs need to go someplace in the URL
namespace, and it is likely they will not end up at the original URL of the resource.
Current designs address this tension by creating separate spaces for the revision URLs
and the "edit" URL, the location where the resource is actually edited. At the edit
URL location, the behavior of relative URLs in links will be preserved, while relative
URL links may not work at the revision URL location.

Providing configuration management support for Web sites containing relative
URL links has the implication that these links depend on a specific hierarchical
structure of the site. Since the site hierarchy is expected to change over time, it does
raise the possibility that a configuration of web pages could be created where the
relative URL links are broken. This could occur in a snapshot of a Web site that is in
the middle of modifications during a site redesign. As a result, the requirement that
versioning should not disrupt relative URLs is interpreted as meaning if the relative
URLs worked when the resources were not versioned, then once the same set of
resources is placed under version control, relative URLs in the same configuration
should still work. Or, put another way, if the relative URL links do not work, this
should be the result of an operator action, and not the result of URL namespace
restrictions imposed by the Web versioning system.

Once a separation is made between the edit URL space, and the revision URL
space, the edit URL becomes a window, or a view, onto a versioned resource,

associated with one of the revisions in a versioned resource. This leads to the following requirements on the capabilities supported by the edit URLs.

3.9 Read requests on a URL to a versioned resource should return a default revision

If a non-versioning aware client, such as a current generation Web browser, makes a read request at the URL for a versioned resource (a.k.a., an edit URL), it is desirable for the server to reply with some default revision. Likewise, it is desirable to be able to set this default revision. This goal is a subset of the following, more general requirement.

3.10 A mechanism must exist for associating a particular revision to a URL for a versioned resource

When a request is made against a URL for a versioned resource (a.k.a., an edit URL), which specific revision is returned? The answer to this question depends on the current work being performed. When making a change, the answer will be the latest stable configuration, except for the changes just made.

To address this goal, the Delta-V design employs the notion of a *workspace*, which acts as a mediator between the edit URL space and the revision URL space by using a set of revision selection rules to choose a specific revision for each edit URL. The expectation is that each user will have their own workspace, and as a result, workspaces support parallel development since each user can have the semblance of their own private working space. The server performs the action of evaluating the revision selection rules of the workspace, associating a revision URL with each edit URL. To perform an action inside a workspace, a client passes both an identifier for the workspace (as the value of an HTTP header) and a specific edit URL to the server. The server evaluates the revision selection rule, and applies the operation to the selected revision.

3.11 Some properties on revisions may be changed without creating a new revision

This goal is motivated by the recognition that there are two types of properties. The first type contains metadata about the resource, and this metadata is directly dependent on the content of the resource. The second type of property is used for protocol operations, typically to expose some system-maintained information about the resource. Access control permissions are a commonly discussed example of this kind of property, motivated by the desire to modify the access permissions of a revision even after it has been checked-in.

3.12 A mechanism must exist for logically grouping sets of changes to one or more versioned resources

Frequently a single logical change, such as updating a link whose destination has changed, requires modifications to multiple resources. A mechanism for mapping a logical change to actual changes provides several benefits. It allows these mappings to be preserved; without it, this information would need to be stored in comments, and would be difficult to reconstruct. This mechanism can also be used to merge together parallel work.

The Delta-V design makes use of the *activity* concept to support this goal. An activity contains a set of versioned resources, and for each of these, one or more revisions. An activity is not versioned. The Delta-V protocol allows an activity to be merged into a workspace, supporting parallel work. If the act of merging an activity into a workspace causes change conflicts, a *conflict report* is generated. A client is expected to resolve these conflicts.

3.13 A mechanism must exist for creating versioned sets of specific revisions of versioned resources

A primary feature of configuration management system is the ability to freeze important configurations of the system for later retrieval and manipulation. While similar to activities, configurations do have some differences. A configuration is versioned, an activity is not. A configuration is used to create and store persistent views of the state of an entire system, while an activity is used to represent a single logical change to a part of the system.

3.14 Revision Operations

Goals for operations that should be supported by revisions are:

- Create a versioned resource from an unversioned resource and set its initial revision to the contents of the unversioned resource.
- Check-out a revision in an activity
- Check-in a resource and either create a new revision (immutable revisions) or update the existing revision in place (mutable revisions)
- Cancel a check-out
- Describe a revision with human-readable comments

These goals provide the operations needed to place an unversioned resource under version control. A Delta-V enabled Web server will typically have part of its URL namespace that is not versioned, part that is versioned, and part that is a mix of versioned and unversioned resources.

Delta-V will use the library model for versioning, using a check-out operation to make a versioned resource suitable for editing, and check-in operation to create a new revision. It will be possible to cancel a check-out, if the entire edit operation needs to be cancelled. Since it is a typical versioning operation to associate human-readable comments with a particular revision, Delta-V will also provide this capability.

3.15 Label Operations

Goals for operations that should be supported by labels are:

- Apply a label to a particular revision
- Change the revision to which a label refers
- Retrieve all labels on a particular revision

An important use of labels is to provide a consistent, human-readable name that can be used to decorate specific revisions in multiple versioned resources. These labels can then be used within a revision selection rule by a workspace to create a consistent set of resources that can be edited.

3.16 Activity Operations

Goals for operations that should be supported by activities are:

- Create and name an activity
- Check-out a revision in an activity
- Merge an activity into a workspace, possibly creating a conflict report
- Get a list of the resources modified in an activity
- Apply a label operation to all resources in an activity

Within Delta-V, activities are created by authors to organize related changes to resources, and to provide a basis for parallel development and merging concurrent changes to the same resource. An activity can contain revisions of multiple versioned resources, and/or multiple revisions of the same versioned resource along a single line-of-descent. The activity operations listed above give the critical functions a protocol must support to provide activity functionality.

3.17 Configuration Operations

Goals for operations that should supported by configurations are:

- Create/delete a configuration
- Add/remove revisions from a configuration
- Use a configuration in a workspace's revision selection rule to choose revisions in that configuration.
- Determine the differences between two configurations by listing the activities in one and not the other.

These operations provide the base set of capabilities needed to support configurations. They allow a configuration to be created and populated with revisions. Once created, a configuration can be used by a workspace's revision selection rule so to only select revisions within the configuration, thus providing the ability to revert to a previous configuration.

3.18 Internationalization

Since the Internet is in use around the world, it would be arrogant and inappropriate to hard-code dependencies on any human language into the protocol. For the Delta-V protocol, internationalization support means that any string used within the protocol that would typically be displayed to a human operator must store sufficient information such that it can display that string in most known human character sets. Recent protocol specifications have met this requirement by supporting one of the encodings of the ISO 10646 [16] standard, which encodes most known human character sets. The contents of the string also needs to be augmented with the human language of the string, so that it can be properly displayed, an issue with ideographic languages where the display of the same character may vary across languages.

One aspect of the protocol affected by this requirement is revision labels, which are definitely exposed to a human operator. Instead of using just an ASCII string, internationalization requirements require a label to be a tuple of string, encoding, and language. Storing multiple variants of each string (e.g., a Japanese and an English representation of the same label) is not a requirement.

3.19 Security

Typically, configuration management systems operate within a single organization where most users are known, and have often met other users in person. There is inherently more trust in this situation than will exist on the Internet, where collaboration may be taking place across organizations, or within a virtual organization comprised of people from diverse geographic locations. These collaborators may never have met each other in person. As a result, *a protocol for versioning and configuration management over the Internet needs to support strong authentication* so users can correctly be identified. This needs to be backed-up by operational procedures that ensure authentication credentials are given to appropriate people.

Furthermore, on the Internet the possibility exists that the traffic across a connection may be spied upon. Since source code is often proprietary, and may contain trade secrets, it is important that source code contents not be exposed during transmission across the Internet.

The Delta-V protocol intends to leverage existing HTTP technologies to address the dual problems of authentication and transport security. Digest authentication [10], developed as an alternative to HTTP Basic authentication and mandated by WebDAV, allows a client to send a multiply one-way hashed username/password pair to the server to authenticate the client to the server. Since Delta-V uses HTTP, the Transport Layer Security (TLS, more widely known as SSL) [8] standard can be used to encrypt a connection between client and server to prevent eavesdropping.

4 Related Systems and Protocols

Systems which are similar to those which would employ the Delta-V protocol can roughly be categorized as either Web-based or distributed versioning and configuration management systems. Though the Web-based systems can rightly be viewed as a subset of the class of distributed systems, they are examined here separately due to the focus on Web support in this paper. Selected systems from each category are described below to highlight their differences and similarities to the Delta-V work.

4.1 Web-based Systems

There has been interest in providing versioning support for the Web from its very inception. Tim Berners-Lee, in his original design notes on the Web describes as important the issue, "keeping track of previous versions of nodes and their relationships." [6].

Initial work on Web versioning concentrated on browsing the contents of version repositories. An early paper describing this capability is [20], where the authors highlight the need for version support in digital libraries, and provide this support via a CGI script which interprets ",{version identifier}" at the end of a URL as a request to retrieve that revision from an RCS repository. This idea has recurred in the literature, most recently in [25], which presents a module for the popular Apache Web server [2] that interprets URLs appended with a ":{version identifier}" or a ":{date}" as a request to retrieve either the specific revision, or the revision that was current as of the date. This approach suffers from two drawbacks which preclude their use in a versioning protocol standard. First, URLs are intended to be opaque, with no meaning encoded into their syntax. Since there are relatively few reserved characters in URLs, if meaning is encoded into URLs, this extra meaning will likely use these reserved characters, and over time lead to semantic collisions between extensions. While an individual server may choose to constrain its URL namespace and use one of these extensions, it is improper for a standard to constrain *all* server namespaces in this way. The second drawback is that the interior path elements of a URL cannot be easily extended, and hence the technique falls short when identifying a specific revision of a versioned collection.

Another common architecture for adding versioning services to the Web is the "form fill-in" style. Examples of this type of system are BSCW [4] and WWRC [23]. These systems share the approach of using HTML pages to create the user interface to a revision control system. Commands are either appended to URLs, or sent to the system using the HTTP POST method, which has a sufficiently broad definition that different remote procedure call mechanisms can tunnel through it. Internet content types attuned to helper applications on the client side help the transfer of information from server to client for editing.

A more sophisticated architecture for adding versioning to the Web is the "Java helper app." approach. In this technique, a Java application is downloaded into the browser, and acts as an intermediary between a version control repository and the user's local environment. This technique is employed in the WWCM [15] and MKS WebIntegrity [18] systems. Similar to these is the WebRC system [12], which uses the CORBA RMI protocol instead of HTTP. WWCM will be discussed as an exemplar of this approach. In WWCM, a Java application running in the browser initiates most versioning and CM operations, but due to the security model of Java which prevents a browser-based application from writing to the local filesystem, it also requires the use of a second helper application which is free from this restriction.

Since direct communication between the browser application and the helper application is not permitted, WWCM must employ a circuitous sequence of three to four network round trips to perform check-out and check-in operations. While WWCM is an exemplar of the kind of CM functionality which can be integrated with the Web using only existing standards, the awkwardness of the two applications and the multiple network round trips highlights the need for developing extensions to the core standards to better support this capability.

Web-based versioning and CM systems assume that the Web server is responsible for maintaining the predecessor and successor relationships between revisions. However, one proposal [19], based on research at NTT Labs., suggested using the (now deprecated) LINK method in HTTP to have client-maintained relationships between resources in a version history. Though not adopted by the Delta-V effort, the idea has the advantage that version graphs can span multiple servers without requiring cooperation between these servers. However, it has the drawback of making operations that span the version history expensive. For example, in such a system it would be difficult to use labels, since ensuring the uniqueness of a label requires a traversal of the version history, an action which may span many servers, some of which may be unavailable due to network outages at any given moment. It also has the drawback that clients must be well-behaved — a single misbehaving client could corrupt a revision history.

A different take on client-side versioning is VTML [27], which augments HTML to store all modifications to an HTML file internal to the HTML file, essentially making each HTML file its own version store. Clients which support authoring of VTML documents are responsible for maintaining the internal revision structure. One major benefit of this approach is that it easily supports simultaneous collaborative authoring of the same HTML file. Since VTML stores all changes to a file, no locking is necessary as the overwrite problem cannot occur because no data is ever overwritten.

4.2 Distributed Configuration Management

A common problem faced by Delta-V, ClearCase [22], and by n-DFS [3], is the desire to improve a pre-existing system by adding CM support. Both ClearCase and n-DFS add this support to the filesystem, and hence the low-level interface to data stored in the system is via operating system library calls. In contrast, since Delta-V is building upon the Web, access to data is via HTTP, not operating system calls, and this introduces new design flexibility — for example, the semantics of namespace bindings (akin to Unix hard links) can be tailored to the needs of versioning. However, unlike ClearCase multisite [1], and n-DFS, Delta-V is not initially planning on providing facilities for repository to repository replication, although one design goal for Delta-V is to ensure adding such services in the future is not prohibitively difficult.

NUCM [14] is a client-server CM system in which a NUCM client interacts with a remote NUCM repository server using primitive operations, upon which are implemented higher-level CM styles. In this respect, NUCM is similar to the NTT Labs. work [19] in that the client is responsible for maintaining the consistency of relationships in the remote repository.

Remote CVS [5] is a client-server CM tool in wide use on the Internet today, with a proven track record of supporting open source development projects. It uses its own human-readable non-HTTP protocol [17], which consists of a stateful connection where the client issues one-line commands that may elicit a reply, depending on the command. The cvsweb [29] utility provides a Web forms-based interface to a CVS repository. Another recent non-HTTP protocol for remote CM is [21] which presents a client-server protocol which uses ASN.1 as its marshalling syntax.

Acknowledgements

The discussion of goals in this document was based on the consensus goals document developed by the Delta-V design team, Jim Amsden, Alan Babich, Geoff Clemm, Bruce Cragun, Chris Kaler, Jeff McAffer, Bradley Sergeant, John Stracke, and the author. The author has contributed to, but is not solely responsible for the content of this consensus goals document. The current goals document is itself based on an earlier goals document by Judith Slein, Fabio Vitali, and David Durand. Discussions on versioning with the WebDAV design team, Yaron Goland, Asad Faizi, Steve Carter, and Del Jensen also helped crystallize my understanding of these issues.

References

1. L. Allen, G. Fernandex, K. Kane, D. Leblang, D. Minard, J. Posner, "ClearCase MultiSite: Supporting Geographically-Distributed Software Development." In J. Estublier (ed.) *Proc. SCM-4 and SCM-5, Software Configuration Management: Selected Papers*, LNCS 1005, Springer-Verlag, SCM-4 and SCM-5, 1995, pages 194-214.
2. Apache Server Project, "Apache Project" Web site. http://www.apache.org/, April, 1999.
3. D. Belanger, D. Korn, H. Rao, "Infrastructure for Wide-Area Software Development" In I. Sommerville (ed.), *Proc. SCM-6, Software Configuration Management: Selected Papers*, LNCS 1167, Springer-Verlag, ICSE'96, SCM-6, Berlin, Germany, March 25-26, 1996, pages 154-165.
4. R. Bentley, T. Horstmann, J. Trevor, "The World Wide Web as enabling technology for CSCW: The case of BSCW" In *Computer Supported Cooperative Work: The Journal of Collaborative Computing*, vol. 6, nos. 2-3, 1997, pp. 111-134.
5. B. Berliner, "CVS II: Parallelizing software development" In *Proc. Winter 1990 USENIX Conference*, January 22-26, 1990, Washington, DC, pages 341-352.
6. T. Berners-Lee, "Versioning", A Web page that is part of the original design notes for WWW. http://web1.w3.org/DesignIssues/Versioning.html
7. T. Bray, J. Paoli, C. M. Sperberg-McQueen, "Extensible Markup Language (XML) 1.0" World Wide Web Consortium Recommendation REC-xml, February, 1998.
8. T. Dierks, C. Allen, "The TLS Protocol Version 1.0" Certicom. Internet Proposed Standard Request for Comments (RFC) 2246, January, 1999.
9. R. Fielding, J. Gettys, J.C. Mogul, H. Frystyk, T. Berners-Lee, "Hypertext Transfer Protocol -- HTTP/1.1" U.C. Irvine, DEC, MIT/LCS. Internet Request for Comments (RFC) 2068, January 1997.
10. J. Franks, P. Hallam-Baker, J. Hostetler, P. Leach, A. Luotonen, E. Sink, L. Stewart, "An Extension to HTTP: Digest Access Authentication" Northwestern University, CERN, Spyglass, Microsoft, Netscape, Spyglass, Open Market. Internet Request for Comments (RFC) 2069, January, 1997.

11. N. Freed, N. Borenstein, "Multipurpose Internet Mail Extensions (MIME) Part One: Format of Internet Message Bodies" Innosoft, First Virtual. Internet Request for Comments (RFC) 2045, November, 1996.

12. P. Fröhlich, W. Nejdl, "WebRC: Configuration Management for a Cooperation Tool" In R. Conradi (ed.), *Proc. SCM-7, Software Configuration Management*, LNCS 1235, ICSE'97, SCM-7, Boston, MA, May 18-19, 1997, pages 175-185.

13. Y. Goland, E. Whitehead, A. Faizi, S. Carter, D. Jensen, "HTTP Extensions for Distributed Authoring -- WEBDAV" Microsoft, U.C. Irvine, Netscape, Novell. Internet Proposed Standard Request for Comments (RFC) 2518, February, 1999.

14. A. van der Hoek, "A Generic Peer-to-Peer Repository for Distributed Configuration Management" In *Proc. 18th International Conference on Software Engineering (ICSE 18)*, Berlin, Germany, March, 1996, pages 308-317.

15. J. J. Hunt, F. Lamers, J. Reuter, W. F. Tichy, "Distributed Configuration Management via Java and the World Wide Web" In R. Conradi (ed.), *Proc. SCM-7, Software Configuration Management*, LNCS 1235, ICSE'97, SCM-7, Boston, MA, May 18-19, 1997, pages 161-174.

16. ISO/IEC, "Information Technology — Universal Multiple-Octet Coded Character Set (UCS) — Part 1: Architecture and Basic Multilingual Plane", May, 1993, with amendments.

17. J. Kingdon (and others at Cygnus Support), "CVS Client/Server", a description of the CVS client/server protocol distributed in the CVS source distribution in file "cvsclient.ps", initially written 1994, with ongoing revision.

18. Mortice Kern Systems, "Web Integrity" Web site. http://www.mks.com/solution/wi/, April, 1999.

19. K. Ota, K. Takahashi, K. Sekiya, "Version management with meta-level links via HTTP/1.1" Internet-Draft (expired), draft-ota-http-version-00, November, 1996. http://www.ics.uci.edu/pub/ietf/webdav/draft-ota-http-version-00.txt

20. R. Pettengill, G. Arango, "Four lessons learned from managing World Wide Web digital libraries" In *Proc. of the Second Annual Conference on the Theory and Practice of Digital Libraries*, Austin, TX, June 11-13, 1995.

21. S. Ramaswamy, "Version Control Protocol" Internet-Draft, work-in-progress, draft-ramaswamy-version-control-00, February, 1999. http://www.ics.uci.edu/pub/ietf/webdav/versioning/draft-ramaswamy-version-control-00.txt

22. Rational Software, "ClearCase: Configuration Management, Software Development Teams" Web page. http://www.rational.com/products/clearcase/, April, 1999.

23. J. Reuter, S. Hänßgen, J. J. Hunt, W. F. Tichy, "Distributed Revision Control Via the World Wide Web" In I. Sommerville (ed.), *Proc. SCM-6, Software Configuration Management: Selected Papers*, LNCS 1167, Springer-Verlag, ICSE'96, SCM-6, Berlin, Germany, March 25-26, 1996, pages 166-174.

24. J. Stracke, J. Amsden, "Goals for Web Versioning" Internet-Draft, work-in-progress, draft-ietf-webdav-version-goals-00, February, 1999. http://www.ics.uci.edu/pub/ietf/webdav/versioning/draft-ietf-webdav-version-goals-00

25. J. Simonson, D. Berleant, X. Zhang, M. Xie, and H. Vo, "Version augmented URIs for reference permanence via an Apache module design" In *Proc. WWW7, Computer Networks and ISDN Systems*, vol. 30, nos. 1-7, Brisbane, Australia, April 14-18, 1998, pages 337-345.

26. W. Tichy, "RCS - A System for Version Control" *Software - Practice and Experience*, vol. 15, no. 7, July 1985, pages 637-654.

27. F. Vitali, D. Durand, "Using Versioning to Provide Collaboration on the WWW" In *Proc. WWW4, Fourth Int'l World Wide Web Conference Proceedings*, World Wide Web Journal, Vol. 1, No. 1, Boston, MA, USA, 1995, pages 37-50.

28. E. J. Whitehead, Jr., Y. Y. Goland, "WebDAV: A network protocol for remote collaborative authoring on the Web" In *Proc. of the Sixth European Conf. on Computer Supported Cooperative Work (ECSCW'99)*, Copenhagen, Denmark, September 12-16, 1999.

29. H. Zeller, B. Fenner, and H. Nordström, "Hen's cvsweb CVS Repository" Web page, http://linux.fh-heilbronn.de/~zeller/cgi/cvsweb.cgi/, April, 1999.

CM Strategies for RAD

Version 1.0

Darcy Wiborg Weber
darcy@continuus.com

Continuus Software Corporation
108 Pacifica, 2nd Floor
Irvine, CA 92618

Abstract. SCM provides many well-known benefits for traditional software development. It enables software teams to develop quality software in a timely and predictable manner. However, some teams who are doing Rapid Application Development, also known as RAD, sometimes feel that standard SCM processes have too much overhead for their quickly moving team members. In fact, some teams choose to forego SCM altogether when in rapid development mode, because they think it slows them down. Is RAD really incompatible with SCM? This paper explores the relationship between SCM and RAD, provides some strategies to keep SCM from hindering RAD, and describes some ways in which SCM can help teams develop applications more rapidly.

1 Introduction

Software is being developed more quickly than ever before. Environments such as Visual Studio provide fully integrated development tools and packaged controls that enable rapid prototyping of complex applications. Tools such as Rational Rose can generate application code based on system models. GUI builders abound, both for traditional software development and web development. Software that once took months or years to develop can be put together in just weeks or even days. Companies publish changes to their web sites daily, sometimes hourly.

These rapid methods of software development are known as Rapid Application Development, or RAD. RAD teams may have many of the following characteristics:

- They are working on a new product that has not yet been shipped.

- Developers often must work closely together on new features.

- Team members are adding new files on a regular basis.

- They have a general sense of the tasks that need to be done, but often discover additional tasks as the features they implement become better defined. The project plan may not be as detailed or well-defined as for traditional software projects.

- Developers may be using tools to quickly prototype or generate their software, such Microsoft's Visual Studio or FrontPage, or Rational Rose.

- The team is not doing exhaustive product testing, and may not even have a regular build cycle yet.

The benefits of SCM are well known. However, some RAD teams feel that standard SCM processes have too much overhead for their quickly moving team members. Typical SCM capabilities such as tracking each change individually, insulating developers from each others' untested changes, and managing build areas may be more than a RAD team needs at a given point in time, especially when developing a new application. RAD teams need to be able to relax tight SCM restrictions when it makes sense; likewise, it is important for them to understand the tradeoffs of doing so, so they can make informed decisions about the risks involved. In addition, some processes that look like overhead can actually help you develop more rapidly.

This paper describes some SCM process alternatives for RAD teams and discusses the tradeoffs of using those strategies. Ultimately, the paper offers some ways that SCM tools can help teams meet their rapid application development goals.

2   SCM Process Alternatives for RAD

One option for RAD teams is no SCM at all. Although most of us would never even consider this an option, many RAD teams do, because they feel that SCM practices slow them down. Of course, the drawbacks of this decision are numerous: the team has no insurance against lost work, bugs may reappear in later versions of the software after they were fixed, developers may overwrite each others' changes, the product quality may suffer, and the team may not be able to reproduce and maintain the software after it is released. To be successful, it is essential for a RAD team to follow some SCM practices even if they do not use an SCM tool.

At Continuus, we've noticed that RAD is becoming much more common at our typical customer site, and we've spent some time working with those teams to find ways they can be successful while using SCM. Although we cannot recommend these alternatives as best practices for SCM, they are practices that enable RAD teams to accomplish their goals and yet incorporate some important benefits of SCM. These practices are not specific to any particular SCM tool, although some of them assume the SCM tool or environment has certain features.

The process alternatives for RAD teams discussed here fall into the following categories:

- Alternative build and test cycles
- Less formal change management
- Closer sharing between developers
- Ways to manage rapid configuration changes

Each of these topics is discussed in detail on the following pages.

2.1   Alternative Build and Test Cycles

Mature traditional software development teams often have a process that incorporates two or more stages of testing. The first stage might be categorized as integration testing, where changes from different developers are gathered and tested together.

Later stages might involve regression testing, system testing, performance testing, and so on. [Con98a] SCM enables you to configure the software that will be tested in each of these phases and implement the build-and-test process. All these test stages are probably overkill for some RAD teams, especially those working on prototypes or brand new systems.

- **Add Test Stages as Needed.** Although most teams will need a full test process before the software is eventually released, you will probably want to start out small and grow the build-and-test process as you need it. You can start out with only unit testing by the developers. Later, as developers start to spend a fair amount of time solving integration problems when they get each others' changes, or when it becomes difficult for each developer to build the system for unit testing, it is probably time to add an integration testing stage to the process. Later, as your team needs to prepare for a release, you can add more testing stages as needed, in order to insulate a particular configuration of the system and add only the changes that are approved for the release.

  For each testing stage, all the standard SCM principles apply: the integration build process should be automated and repeatable, it should use a clean environment, it should analyze dependencies and rebuild everything that has changed, and so on. [Con98a] Many commercial SCM tools can help you implement the build-and-test process, whether you have one test stage or ten.

- **Have a Way to Roll Back.** If your team doesn't have time for in-depth testing before releasing changes, it is critical to have a way to roll back to the last good configuration. This is typical for teams who develop and maintain web sites; they may publish updates to the live site multiple times per day, sometimes without even trying the change in the context of the entire site. In case of a critical error, a saved copy of the last good configuration can save the day.

2.2 Less Formal Change Management

Here the term change management means the overall process of managing changes to software [Con98b]. This includes a combination of change tracking (tracking software defect reports and enhancement requests) and change packages (the actual code changes, grouped into packages that represent logical changes) [Ovum96].

- **Use Relaxed Change Tracking.** Most RAD teams don't need a complex lifecycle for tracking changes or a formal change review process; rather, they want the developers to be able to fix problems immediately upon finding them and prototype enhancements as they get new ideas. They need a simple, lightweight representation for logical changes: not much more than a short description of the change and a reference to the files that have changed. (We will call this a task.) For RAD, the task lifecycle could be very simple: its only states might be assigned and completed. Developers must be able to create and assign their own tasks, preferably in one step.

  The drawback here is that there is not much control over what changes go in - but that's exactly the point! The change management policies can change when there is a need for tighter control.

- **Use Less Granular Change Packages.** Some developers in RAD mode will find using one task for every individual software change too much overhead. Developers may be working quickly, working out details of designs that were not broken down into specific tasks, making unanticipated changes, or switching between many different changes in progress. While there are many benefits to tracking every change by task, it is extra work for developers to remember to create new tasks when needed, and to remember to use the appropriate task every time they switch to working on a different change. In this case, a developer may choose to use one task for multiple changes, for example, one task for a group of loosely related changes that take a day or two to implement. He would create a task when he starts the set of changes, and then complete the task (thus checking in its related code changes) when he reaches a logical breaking point. This way he doesn't need to do so much "accounting," but his changes are kept together and are made available to other users on a regular basis.

  Developers should be sure to check in sets of changes that are complete and will build, so as not to break other developers' work areas. They should also complete their tasks frequently, every day or two if possible, to prevent divergence from and ensure ongoing integration with other developers' changes. [Ber96] (These issues are not so important if developers are working on modular sections of the application and don't need each others' code in order to build, or if they are working on an application such as a web site where their changes don't deeply affect the quality of other users' work.)

  The main drawback is that you won't see the complete benefits of change packages, since the units of work represented by these tasks are not as meaningful as they would normally be. For example, you cannot pull out or propagate an individual change that is bundled in with others; a developer must do it by hand. Likewise, the system cannot report on exactly which changes are included in a configuration, and will not be able to detect configuration conflicts on a detailed level. In addition, you won't be as successful at tracking the progress of tasks against your project plans and schedules. These drawbacks may be insignificant during the early development stage of your project, and you can use more meaningful tasks later in your project.

- **Work Offline and Reconcile Changes.** Some developers may find working directly in an SCM environment to be too much overhead, especially if they are in a prototyping phase where it is common to throw away changes and start over frequently, or if they use a tool that generates unpredictable numbers of files, files with unpredictable names, or both. They don't want to track every change or check in every new file until they reach a point where they are ready to save what they have developed. In this case, they may choose to work offline from the SCM system, perhaps in a work area that was prepared by their SCM system, and then reconcile the differences between the work area and the SCM repository when they reach a point where they want to save those changes. [Con98c] This is a variation of the last option (use less granular change packages) because the task represents the set of changes made between reconciliations.

This methodology includes the drawbacks described earlier for less granular change packages, plus a more serious one: users may lose valuable changes and cannot fall back to intermediate versions. However, this may be an acceptable risk for the sake of less overhead. Teams who use this methodology should ensure that their work areas are backed up on a regular basis.

- **Don't Use Change Packages.** Some teams may choose to forego using change packages altogether, and simply check in individual objects. In doing so, they give up a myriad of benefits: the relationships between the objects that changed and which depend on each other, the ability to easily share a specific change with another developer or build a configuration containing a particular set of changes, progress tracking, reporting, automated conflict detection, and the conveniences provided by tasks, such as the ability to check in a set of changes in one step. [Web97]

2.3   Closer Sharing between Developers

Typical SCM methodologies insulate developers from each others' changes until the changes have passed testing, or at least until the changes are complete. (It is very difficult to test your own changes when your work area is changing without your knowledge. [Con98b, Per98]) However, in RAD, it is common for developers to work closely on features, and to want to share changes with one another before those features have passed testing or even before they are complete. Also, some RAD projects, such as web development, do not share the same need for insulation as traditional software development. [Con98c]

You will probably want developers to share changes using one of the following alternatives:

- **Share Completed Changes.** When you update your personal work area, include all tasks that have been checked in by other users, regardless of whether they have been tested. Often, RAD projects have no formal integration testing process, so this is necessary. The drawback is that a developer's productivity can be affected by quality problems in other users' work, and he may end up spending significant time integrating incompatible changes that aren't even his.

- **Share Partial Changes.** When you update your personal work area, pick up all individual objects that have been checked in up to the moment. Note the difference between this alternative and the previous one: with this alternative, developers will pick up each others' changes even for tasks that are still assigned, as long as the individual object associated with the task has been checked in. They will not see each others' checked-out objects (those objects that are still changing) in either case.

  The drawback is that it is even more likely for developers to break each others' work areas, because they will be seeing partial changes. However, they can coordinate with each other by checking in only those changes that others need to see, and keeping the rest checked out until the change is complete and will build correctly.

- **Share Changes in Progress.** Note in the previous scenario that developers saw each others' changes only after the changes were checked in. If your team needs to work together even more closely, you may choose to share code even while others are still modifying it.

Of course, including objects in your work area that other developers are still modifying is likely to break your builds on a regular basis. Only developers who truly need to work this closely should use this methodology. (This alternative is safer for certain types of projects, such as web content development, where there is no build process and incompatibilities do not typically have a catastrophic effect on team members.)

- **Share Work Areas.** It is possible for two or more developers to share a single work area for their work. In this case, they see all of each others' changes immediately. This works well only for projects in which developers do not need to build (for example, a web site), or projects that are modularized such that each developer works in his own area and the areas do not overlap. It is important to select an "owner" for each shared work area who is responsible for administration activities such as updating the work area. He can coordinate with the other team members so that these activities do not interfere with their work. At Continuus we've found that shared work areas work well for web content developers, but not very well for more traditional software development. It is important to understand the issues and consider carefully before trying this alternative. [Con98c]

2.4 Ways to Manage Rapid Configuration Changes

When a team is working on a new software application, developers often create new files frequently, perhaps many per day. Developers may be generating new files or creating them manually.

Some advanced SCM systems manage your directories as well as your files. They can keep track of which files are contained in each directory. Whenever a file is added to a directory, the directory will be checked out, since it is being modified. [Con98b] (Some SCM systems let you use other types of groupings in addition to directories, but the issues - and recommended solutions - are the same.)

Therefore, if your site allows parallel check out, it is possible for several developers to check out parallel versions of a given directory if they need to add files to that directory at about the same time. For example, if Chris adds the file colors.h to the incl directory, and before he has checked in his change, Gennie adds the file defaults.h to the same directory, each will have a checked out version of the directory, and the versions will be parallel. Alternatively, if your site does not allow parallel check out, Gennie would need to wait until Chris has checked in his change before she could add her new file.

Managing directories in this way enables the SCM system to save earlier versions of your configuration, and to detect missing files that should be in a directory. [Web98] However, you can imagine that the notion of having parallel versions of a directory and of merging two directories is pretty foreign to most developers. Likewise, waiting until someone else checks in his change before you can make yours does not make for rapid development. Because of this, you should consider one of the following strategies to help your team either avoid creating parallel directories or ensure that they get merged.

- **Create Files Up Front.** Think about your project structure ahead of time and create all the files up front. Create them empty, and developers can check out from them to add the contents later. This is the best strategy for handling this situation; however, it is not always possible to anticipate every file you will need, or to know the names of the files if you are using a tool to generate the files. Even if you are able to create many of the files up front, consider one of the strategies below for handling parallel versions of directories if they should occur.

- **Add the New File First, then Update It.** Whenever a developer adds a new file, have him add the new file first, then check in the task (and associated empty file and updated directory) immediately. After that, he can check out from the empty file to make his changes. This way the directory is checked in and available to other developers immediately, so they are less likely to create parallel versions and will not need to wait to make their changes.

- **Work Offline and Reconcile Changes.** This methodology was described on page 4. It is worth mentioning again here because it enables the developer to make a change and unit test it without checking out any directories. The directories get checked out when the developer is finished and reconciles the work area with the repository. This works well in Java development environments where the number and names of the files that will be produced by the compiler are unpredictable. [Gei98]

- **Appoint a Directory Merge Guru.** Appoint one team member (possibly the team lead) to keep an eye on directories and merge any parallel versions he finds. This user needs to understand why parallel directories can occur and how to merge them. He should check for parallel checked-in directory versions at least once per day and merge them at that time, so that other developers will get all the latest changes when they update their work areas.

- **Use Open Directories.** It may be possible in your SCM system to set up directories so that all developers can modify them. This prevents parallel directories from occurring. However, before choosing this strategy, you should be aware that it has some serious drawbacks: it may be possible for developers to overwrite each others' changes if they modify the directory at exactly the same time. It is also possible that developers will break each others' builds, since they will get changes to these directories immediately as they occur, before the other developer's change is complete or tested.

3   How SCM Can Help

The previous section described some ways to keep SCM from hindering your team on a RAD project. At this point, SCM may seem like the antithesis of RAD! Luckily, it's not. We've found that there are many ways SCM can make application development more rapid.

There are a number of well-known best practices for developing high-quality software as quickly as possible. They may not necessarily speed the individual developer's personal tasks, but they do cut overall development time and improve productivity for the team. They cross a wide variety of activities, from software development to planning to scheduling to tools. These practices can enable you to deliver software faster, reduce schedule risks and overruns, and make progress visible, dispelling the appearance of slow development. [McC96a]

This section describes a number of practices that you can implement with SCM. You will see immediate results from some of the practices, while others have a learning curve or require some investment in infrastructure before you begin to see the benefits. If your team is already using an SCM tool or process, you have already made an investment in infrastructure that can be leveraged to help you develop software faster and more efficiently. If your team is not using SCM, this section highlights the benefits it can help you achieve. The practices described here include:

- Choose a software lifecycle.
- Don't make developers stop working while the software is tested.
- Build and test the software daily.
- Set small milestones.
- Use a stretch list.
- Measure your progress.
- Inspect your software.
- Reuse components.

Each of these practices is discussed in detail below.

3.1 Choose a Software Lifecycle

A software lifecycle describes the process you go through to plan, develop, test and release your software. The benefit of a software lifecycle is that it provides a roadmap for all team members, so that everyone knows how they fit into the big picture and what happens next. [McC96a]

This practice decreases schedule risk by helping to define the steps in the schedule and ensure that none are overlooked, and by avoiding confusion about what activities should be happening at different phases of the project.

SCM directly supports the development, testing, and release portion of the lifecycle. It can also help you integrate the planning phase with development, since tasks on your schedule map to tasks that will become software changes. You can also use SCM to version your requirements and functional specification documents, and then relate those documents to the corresponding code for traceability. Some SCM tools provide out-of-the-box development methodologies that support a variety of lifecycle models; some also are integrated with scheduling or planning tools.

3.2 Don't Make Developers Stop Working While the Software is Tested

When preparing software for a release or delivery, your goal is to achieve a particular quality standard. To do so, you must restrict ongoing changes to the software while it is being tested; the only changes that should be added are those that are approved for that release. Unless you lock down the changes, your team may very well continue introducing and fixing defects long past your scheduled release date. [Con98a]

On some teams, when it's time to lock down the code for testing, the developers must stop checking in their changes; developers may do nothing in this phase but wait to be assigned bug fixes that are approved for the release. The whole team comes almost to a standstill while the release wraps up.

SCM can provide insulated areas for building and testing configurations, so that developers can continue developing and checking in changes without affecting the software to be released. It enables teams to work on parallel code streams in order to develop two or more releases at the same time. Essentially, it enables your team to multi-task.

3.3 Build and Test the Software Daily

\This involves building your entire software product on a daily basis and running a series of tests (sometimes called "smoke tests" [McC96b]) to verify its basic operations. If defects are found, developers fix them immediately.

This process has several significant benefits. The first is that your team finds basic defects immediately after they are introduced. It is much easier to isolate the cause of defects, and developers can fix the defects while the code changes are still fresh in their minds. Another benefit is that your team integrates their changes on a daily basis, rather than putting off integrations until late in the cycle. Integrating on a daily basis is much less time-consuming than waiting, and minimizes schedule risks. One more benefit is that your team can use the result of the build as a public test area, and see the state of the software at that point in time. [McC95] This provides progress monitoring, since everyone can immediately see how close the software is to completion. Overall, this practice improves product quality and reduces the risk of schedule overruns due to unexpected integration or quality issues.

Setting up insulated build/test areas and automating the daily build and test cycle is an integral part of SCM.

3.4 Set Small Milestones

Small milestones are fine-grained targets on a schedule. Rather than tracking the schedule by milestones that are weeks or months apart, you can set small milestones by breaking every project into one- or two-day tasks.

In order to break down a project into one- or two-day tasks, you must analyze the project well enough to understand each task and how long it will take. This lowers your risk of having an inaccurate schedule. Another benefit is that you can see slips in your schedule as they occur, and immediately take steps to correct the situation. You can identify unrealistic estimates or bottlenecks early in your project, and recalibrate your schedule or adjust resources accordingly. A third benefit is that the visibility of the milestones will help to motivate developers to meet their targets. Not only will it be obvious when a developer misses his targets; it will also be visible when he meets them.

Each small milestone can be treated as a task (a logical change) within SCM. If you can store additional properties on a task, you can mark tasks with information such as the priority and the estimated and actual time to complete each task. You can report on the time estimates for all tasks assigned to a particular release or developer. You can use the assigned tasks and their time estimates to measure progress against your schedule, and possibly even to sync up your schedule with the current state of the project.

3.5 Use a Stretch List

A stretch list is a list of enhancements that you'd like to include in a release but that are not strictly required. These enhancements are typically scheduled near the end of the development phase, so that they can be safely dropped off the schedule if the team runs out of time.

A stretch list creates a safety buffer for your team in case of schedule slips or changing requirements. More important, it makes hard decisions at the end of the development cycle easier, because the team has agreed up front which items can be cut.

If you treat each scheduled change as a task within SCM (as described earlier), you can set a lower priority on stretch list tasks. Developers can use the priority to decide which tasks to work on first.

3.6 Measure Your Progress

Software products and projects can be measured in a number of different ways. Such measurements are often referred to as metrics. Examples of some useful metrics follow:

- Milestone progress
- Accuracy of time estimates for development tasks
- Areas of code that have many defects or change frequently
- The rate of defects being found in the software both before and after release
- How quickly defects are addressed

Metrics give you information that helps you improve your software and process. This benefit may not be fully realized right away, but it will pay off in the long run. It helps you analyze which practices work well and which don't, and where you should devote more resources to get certain types of gains. For example, software teams who are working on a product release typically track the rate of defects detected in the software over the final QA cycle. Although many teams don't even realize it, they are using metrics to predict how many defects are still in the product to determine when the software is stable enough to ship to customers.

When you begin using SCM, you begin accumulating raw data that can be used to measure the team's results. For example, you might track estimated and actual time to complete each task. This information enables you to note how accurately your team is estimating its work and use it to adjust your estimates. If you find that the whole team is falling behind schedule, you should review the estimation process used to create the schedule. You can use this experience to improve your team's estimating skills and correct schedule errors early in the project.

Your SCM system also provides valuable data on potential improvements to areas of the code:

- Review areas of code that have many defects or change frequently for excessive complexity or design flaws.
- Review areas with many enhancement requests or rejected problems (defects closed as "working as designed") to identify potential usability problems.
- Determine which areas have many open problems but few closed ones, signifying possible neglect.

You will probably want to inspect the code to look for potential improvements or consider whether it needs a rewrite.

3.7   Inspect Your Software

An inspection is a formalized review of software or related artifacts. Prior to the meeting, participants inspect the review materials using checklists of common errors. During the meeting, they discuss the errors and point out potential problems. The responsible developer uses this information to fix any defects that were found and investigate potential issues.

Data shows that inspections are more effective at finding defects than execution testing. Well-run inspections typically find between 50% and 70% of the defects in a program. In addition, it takes less time to fix a defect found in a code review than one found in execution testing, because execution testing finds only the symptom; the developer must still locate the source of the error. And possibly the most compelling reason for inspections is that the average cost of finding and fixing a defect increases about 10 times with every step of the development process. [Hum97] Ultimately, inspections will help you produce a higher quality product and minimize schedule risks due to quality problems. In addition, inspections help to cross-train your team and encourage code sharing and reuse.

SCM can make inspections a part of your process. It can trigger inspections by informing users when a task is completed (and the corresponding objects are checked in). You can also measure the effectiveness of your inspections by tracking the defects in a change tracking system, marked as having been discovered during inspections.

3.8   Reuse Components

This involves building a repository of useful components and using them in different software products. This practice enables you to quickly assemble new programs from existing components.

Reuse takes initial investment and planning. Before you can employ this practice, you must develop (or purchase) a reuse library. The components must be developed in a generic and standard manner. But in time, planned reuse can produce significant schedule and effort savings. [McC96a]

By storing software and artifacts in a repository, SCM systems typically enable you to reuse or share objects that were created by someone else. SCM systems also enable you to store and track vendor code, helping you to customize it and merge your changes into later releases.

4 Conclusion

This paper has suggested some ways RAD teams can use SCM without hindering their rapid development. It also discussed some ways that SCM helps teams develop applications more rapidly.

The moral of this story for SCM tool vendors is that SCM tools must be flexible enough to let users employ a variety of processes, from simple to advanced. This flexibility enables a team to start out with a simple process that requires only minimum overhead, and grow into a more mature process later when they need it, perhaps as their software nears release and maintenance.

The moral for RAD teams is not to give up on SCM, but instead consider alternative methodologies. However, while doing so, it is important to consider the tradeoffs of these alternative processes in order to recognize the risks and make an educated decision about what is best for your team. And finally, SCM processes that, at first glance, look like almost pure overhead can help you ship quality code faster.

Above all, remember that a process is not permanent. If an approach doesn't work well for your team, you can reconsider and try a different approach. Pick an SCM tool that is flexible enough to handle different alternatives and support ongoing process improvement.

References

[Ber96] Steve Berczuk. *Configuration Management Patterns*. Proceedings of the 1996 Pattern Languages of Programs Conference. Washington University Technical Report# WUCS-97-07. Available online at http:// world.std.com/~berczuk/pubs/PLoP96/plop96.html.

[Con98a] Continuus Software Corporation. 1998. *Build Manager's Guide*.

[Con98b] Continuus Software Corporation. 1998. *Change Management for Software Development*. Available online at http://www.continuus.com/ developers/developersACED.html.

[Con98c] Continuus Software Corporation. 1998. *Shared Projects*.

[Dart96] Susan Dart. *Not All Tools Are Created Equal*. Available online at http:// www.adtmag.com/pub/oct96/fe1002.htm.

[Gei98]   Barry Geipel. 1998. *Java in the Enterprise: Managing Java Development with Continuus/CM.*

[Hum97]   Watts Humphrey. 1997. *Introduction to the Personal Software Process.* Addison Wesley Longman Inc. Reading, MA.

[McC96a]   Steve McConnell. 1996. *Rapid Development: Taming Wild Software Schedules.* Microsoft Press. Redmond, WA.

[McC96b]   Steve McConnell. 1996. *Best Practices: Daily Build and Smoke Test.* IEEE Software, Vol. 13, No. 4. Available online at `http://www.construx.com/stevemcc/bp04.htm`.

[McC95]   Jim McCarthy. 1995. *Dynamics of Software Development.* Microsoft Press. Redmond, WA.

[Ovum96]   Clive Burrows, George George, and Susan Dart. 1996. *Ovum Evaluates Configuration Management.* Ovum Limited. London.

[Per98]   Laura Wingerd and Chris Seiwald. 1998. *High-Level Best Practices in Software Configuration Management.* Available online at `http://www.perforce.com/perforce/bestpractices.html`.

[Web97]   Darcy Wiborg Weber. 1997. *Change Sets Versus Change Packages.* Software Configuration Management ICSE '97 SCM-7 Workshop Proceedings. Available online at `http://www.continuus.com/developers/developersACEG.html`.

[Web98]   Darcy Wiborg Weber, 1998. *Techniques for Detecting and Resolving Conflicts in Software Configurations.*

Software Configuration Management: State of the Art, State of the Practice

Karol Frühauf[1] and Andreas Zeller[2]

[1] *INFOGEM AG*
Informatiker Gemeinschaft für Unternehmensberatung
Rütistrasse 9, CH-5401 Baden, Switzerland
Karol_Fruehauf@compuserve.com
[2] Universität Passau
Lehrstuhl für Softwaresysteme
Innstraße 33, D-94032 Passau, Germany
zeller@acm.org

Abstract. Which are the open problems in Software Configuration Management (SCM)? The purpose of this paper is to ignite a discussion on current and future SCM directions. Based on the findings of a Dagstuhl Seminar on the current state of Software Engineering, we *assess the state of SCM* with the goal to identify effective SCM tasks and solutions, to establish a core body of SCM knowledge, and to denote remaining real-world SCM problems.

1 Introduction: An Assessment of SCM

Which are the open problems in SCM? Software Configuration Management (SCM) is one of the few success stories in Software Engineering. All software organizations admit the importance of SCM as a prerequisite for a coordinated software development. Consequently, SCM is widely used—and with success. Already, the SCM tools market is expected to be worth over a billion dollars [4].

The 1999 Dagstuhl Seminar on "Software Engineering Research and Education: Seeking a new Agenda" [7] has joined experts in several Software Engineering fields to take stock of the current state of Software Engineering research and education. Within this Seminar, we have addressed this task for the SCM area—*assessing the state of Software Configuration Management*. In particular, we have attempted to cover the questions:

What do we know? Which are the *SCM tasks and solutions* that every practicing software engineer should be able to perform?
What should we teach? Which is the *core body of SCM knowledge* that has been validated as useful in practice?
What should we know? What are the most important *open SCM problems?*

In contrast to earlier approaches, we have not searched for novel ideas "that should keep researchers busy for the next several years" [31] or examined possible similarities between some area X and SCM [10, 34], but attempted to identify remaining *real-world SCM problems*—problems faced by today's practitioners, yet not sufficiently addressed by SCM research. This paper summarizes our results; its purpose is to ignite a discussion on current and future SCM directions.

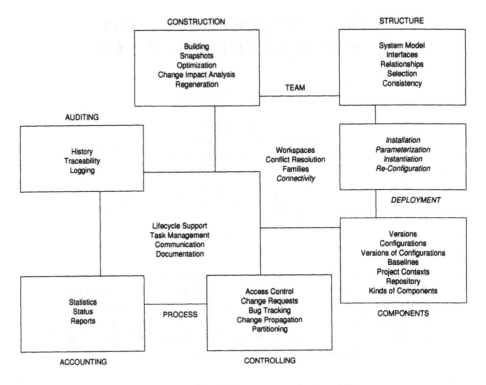

Fig. 1. SCM Functionality Areas (after Dart [6])

2 Assessing SCM Solutions

In this paper, we have focused on those SCM solutions that are provided or supported by some automated SCM tool or system, be it a research prototype or a full-fledged commercial system. (This is just a matter of economy; if some solution has only been proposed, but never realized, we will not regard it here.) Note that we do not consider SCM organisational matters. The reason is not their irrelevance; in fact we are convinced that SCM work procedures need to be defined in an organisation before any SCM tool can be selected (which will of course backfire on the work procedures). The difficulty is that as every organisation has its own flavour of work procedures, there is no such thing as a solution.

Relying on Dart's survey [6], the functionality of SCM systems can be grouped into two major *functionality areas,* as shown in Figure 1.[1] The *team-centered* functionality areas deal with the *technical aspects* of SCM:

Components. Identify, classify, store and access the components that form the product.
Structure. Represent the architecture of the product.
Construction. Support the construction of the product and its artifacts.
Team. Enable a project team to develop and maintain a family of products.

---

[1] Areas in *italic* are areas not covered in [6] that are now considered part of SCM.

Deployment. Support the remote installation and maintenance of the product.

In contrast to the team-centered areas, the *process-centered* functionality areas cover management issues:

Auditing. Keep an audit trail of the product and its process.
Accounting. Gather statistics about the product and its process.
Controlling. Control how and when changes are made.
Process. Support the management of how the product evolves.

For each of these areas, we shall discuss the state of the art, assessing available and proposed SCM *solutions*—means that solve specific SCM tasks. Following the *assessment categories* as elaborated at the Dagstuhl seminar [7], each SCM solution is ranked according to five categories:

Effectiveness. How well does the solution work? This considers factors such as how much of the task it covers and how good a solution it is to the problem posed by accomplishing the task. Ratings are
- *high* (the solution is very effective),
- *medium* (the solution is somewhat effective), and
- *low* (the solution is hardly effective at all).

Affordability. The extent to which a typical software development organization can afford to perform the solution. (Note that it may be that a solution is high cost, but that an organization cannot afford not to use it.) Ratings are
- *high* (the solution is very affordable),
- *medium* (the solution is somewhat affordable), and
- *low* (the solution requires relatively high investment).

Teachability. The extent to which the solution can be taught in a university, including the body of knowledge that must be conveyed to students and how well we understand how to convey that body of knowledge. Ratings are
- *high* (we know how to teach the solution very well),
- *medium* (we know how to teach the solution to some extent), and
- *low* (we do not really know how to teach the solution).

Use in Practice. The class of users who have adopted the solution:
- *laboratory users* (LU) – researchers developing prototypes and models,
- *innovators* (IN) – willing to use early prototypes of the solution,
- *early adopters* (EA) – willing to use advanced prototypes
- *early majority* (EM) – willing to be the first users of industrial-quality versions of the solution
- *late majority* (LM) – not willing to use the solution until there is considerable industrial experience with it.

Research Potential. The extent to which further research is supposed to increase effectiveness, affordability, teachability, or use in practice. Ratings are
- *high* (major breakthroughs can be expected),
- *medium* (substantial improvements are likely), and
- *low* (details may be improved).

3 SCM Team Tasks and Solutions

We begin with a discussion of the solutions available in the team functionality area; Table 1 on the next page summarizes our findings.

3.1 Team

The notion of a *workspace* that isolates a developer from other's work is crucial to SCM. Generally, workspaces should provide their own structure, states for the configuration items and configurations, and access rights for the different functions in the project [14]. The extent to which these requirements are met by SCM systems varies from file-based checkin/checkout mechanisms as in RCS [28] over virtual file systems as in CLEARCASE [18] or in n-DFS [13] to database-supported workspaces in ADELE [9].

However, since every SCM system provides means to generate, propagate, and apply changes, every SCM system allows to *simulate* workspaces—even if the "workspace" is but a developer's private directory or a branch in the version graph. This problem is thus considered solved.

With an uncontrolled propagation of changes, the chances for two or more people's changes interfering with each other are high; this leads to *conflicts* that must be resolved. This *merging* of changes is still manual work. Textual merging is considered too unsafe for many environments; the effectiveness of syntactic merging [33, 3] and semantic merging [16, 2] has not yet been validated. Any solutions that ease the pain of manual conflict resolution are likely to save valuable developer time; here is still work to do.

A group working together needs *connectivity* to propagate changes. Given a small group with good interconnection, a central repository suffices for all project sizes. Things get more difficult for multi-site, multi-organization software developments (so-called *virtual software corporations*). Here, local copies of shared resources must be replicated and cached; remote access must be designed such that cooperation is possible while avoiding total project disclosure. Although several commercial SCM tools such as CLEARCASE [18] offer support for wide-area connectivity, the area remains subject to further research.

3.2 Components

Managing the history of individual components is a well-understood SCM task. Tools like SCCS [25] and RCS [28] are being used for more than two decades now. Efficient means to store and retrieve huge amounts of versions in a *repository* are available and have been thoroughly validated [17]. *Identifying* and reconstructing a configuration by means of its components or changes applied to a baseline is a task easily solved with all available SCM tools. SCM at the component level may well be the SCM area that is best understood of all.

3.3 Structure

Versioning of structures, i.e. systems of related components, is still not completely solved. Let us start with the inventory of components—the *system model*. Most SCM

SCM Tasks	Ranking of SCM Solutions				
	Effectiveness	Affordability	Teachability	Practical Usage	Research Potential
Team					
— *Workspaces* (individuals, groups)	high	high	high	LM	low
— *Conflict resolution* (parallel work as the rule, automated merging)	low	low	med?	IN	high
— *Local area connectivity*	high	med	high	LM	low
— *Wide area connectivity* (remote access, replication, caching)	med	med	med	EA	med
Components					
— *Version management for components* (revisions, branches, checkout/checkin, identification)	high	high	high	LM	low
— *Repository* (storage issues, deltas)	high	high	high	LM	low
— *Configurations* (baselines, parts lists, identification)	high	high	high	LM	low
Structure					
— *System model* (interfaces, relationships)	med?	low	low	LU	med
— *Version management for structures* (renaming, reorganization, retiring of subsystems with whole history)	med	high	high	EA	med
— *Selection* (baselines plus change sets, generic configurations)	high	high	high	EM	low
— *Consistency* (compatible versions)	med?	low	low	LU	med
Construction					
— *Building* (snapshots, optimization, dependencies)	high	high	high	LM	low
— *Regeneration* (integrated with SCM)	high	med	med	IN	med
Deployment					
— *Replication* (on a medium)	high	high	high	LM	low
— *Installation* (in a consistent manner)	med	med	low	EM	high
— *Parameterization* (customizing)	med	med	low	IN	med
— *Instantiation* (running)	med	med	low	IN	med
— *Reconfiguration* (dynamically)	low	low	low	IN	high

Table 1. SCM Team Tasks

systems do not go beyond simple part lists; relationships and interfaces are barely supported, let alone versioned. (Exception to this rule are *build dependencies,* as discussed in Section 3.4.) The extent to which system modeling is part of SCM is still being discussed [32].

Although several commercial SCM systems and even free tools like CVS [1] allow decent versioning of file hierarchies, issues like renaming or reorganizing structures are still not handled in a fully satisfying manner.

All SCM systems offer methods to *select* specific configurations; the range goes from tags as in RCS or CVS to elaborated rules as in CLEARCASE [18] or ADELE [9]. The organization of versions (or changes) within an SCM system, the *version model,* has considerable impact on the way users interact with an SCM system [5]. Although it has been shown that all existing versioning models can be unified to applying constrained changes [37], the quest for user-friendly and intuitive SCM interaction continues.

A still open problem is how to identify and denote consistent configurations in presence of multiple variants. So far, systems like ICE [36] or CMA [24] are confined to lab use only. On the other hand, one must ask whether variability at construction time—that is, permanent variants—is still an SCM issue. In general, product variability is best handled *by the product and within the product.* The more we design for change, the more we abstract from system issues, the less variability we have at construction time, and the more variability we have at run time. Although consistency issues may rise again within the scope of *dynamic reconfiguration* (see Section 3.5), efforts spent in variability may thus better be directed towards software design.

3.4 Construction

The SCM task of building products can be summarized as "MAKE rules". Virtually every software product is built using MAKE [12] or one of its numerous descendants. Significant improvements on the original MAKE include smart recompilation [29], parallel and distributed building [27], automatic dependency tracking [18], or caching of derived versions [18]. All of these are widely used today, and it is difficult to see room for further improvements.

A more important problem is the traditional distinction between construction tools (i.e. MAKE) and SCM tools (i.e. RCS), as this separation hampers the *regeneration* of derived files. A notable exception and an example of good integration is the build facility integrated in CLEARCASE [18].

3.5 Deployment

Deployment is a new field of SCM, traditionally subsumed under "maintenance". According to Heimbigner and Wolf [15], deployment encompasses *installation, parameterization, instantiation,* and *reconfiguration;* ISO 9000-3 also lists *replication.*

Replication means to make sure that the intended configuration is correctly and completely copied on the medium chosen for delivery. Copying from master to an EPROM, preparing a package with CD and paper documents, and putting the files to an area from where they are electronically transferred to the customer site are all techniques for replication. This is evidently a topic for process engineering in an organization. The main challenge is to define (and apply) it as a process with self-check so that the mistakes can be detected before delivery. We cannot see research opportunities in this area.

Installation is the task of transferring the product to the user. Basic installation is easy—a set of files is copied to places reachable by users. But this task becomes the more difficult the more the product depends on other products, maybe in specific versions. Managing these dependencies and denoting consistency is only partially solved today; the more applications depend on each other, the more the need for installation support will increase.

Parameterization is the task of adapting the product to the user's context—a task either done on site (by the user) or in the factory (especially when hardware is part of the delivery). Parameterization is traditionally carried out by customization files and environment variables; more recently. tools like GNU AUTOCONF [19] are used to determine system properties automatically. In future, such checks will be increasingly carried out at run time and will thus need system support; the Windows registry is a yet rudimentary form of such capabilities.

Instantiation is the task of starting the product into execution. This is trivial (and solved) for simple, monolithic applications, but becomes a challenge as soon as multiple components interact with each other; trading services like the ones specified for CORBA [22] can serve as base for determining a consistent configuration.

Reconfiguration means adapting the product to new requirements while it is executing. This includes all decisions made during installation, parameterization, and instantiation, and may also mean that the product entirely re-creates and replaces itself. This problem is well-understood when speaking of isolated applications: uploading software releases dynamically to space probes or telecommunication switches is common usage. However, dynamic reconfiguration will gain even more importance as more and more software products interact with each other for an undetermined time. The challenge for SCM is to see how far classical SCM concepts can be applied dynamically.

Our observation is that the aspects of deployment are considered late in the life cycle of a software product, usually after the software is finished and somebody discovers that it has to be shipped to the customer site. Very few requirements specifications contain paragraphs for requirements on deployment issues. Most software producers can improve in this area; complex software systems offer new research issues.

4   SCM Process Tasks and Solutions

Let us now turn to the process functionality area. Our findings are summarized in Table 2 on the following page.

4.1   Process

How far should the SCM system support the user's lifecycle model and their organization's policies? Although every SCM system comes with a built-in process in the small

SCM Tasks	Effectiveness	Affordability	Teachability	Practical Usage	Research Potential
	Ranking of SCM Solutions				
Process					
– *Lifecycle Support* (process enforcement)	low?	low	med	LU	med
– *Task management* (identify current and pending activities)	med	high	high	EM	low
– *Communication* (relevant events)	high	high	high	IN	low
Auditing (history, traceability, logging)					
– *of individual items*	high	high	high	LM	low
– *of structures* (related documents)	high?	med?	low	LU	med?
Accounting (status, statistics, reports)	high	high	high	LM	low
Controlling					
– *Access control* (no unwarranted changes)	high	high	high	EM	low
– *Change requests* (automatically)	med	high	high	EM	low
– *Bug tracking* (automatically)	high	high	med	IN	med

Table 2. SCM Process Tasks

(i.e. checkin/checkout-cycle, long transactions, etc.), the degree to which large-scale processes are supported varies.

Our experience tells us that the big leap forward is the clear *definition* of software processes. Use of tools is beneficial only if they are really supportive; often they take the role of bureaucrats increasing the number of required interactions for the developers. Consequently, SCM systems that are too rigid in enforcing a process will be cursed by developers and reduce effectiveness. The distinction between support and discipline and thus the effectiveness of lifecycle support remains to be validated.

Rather than *enforcing* activities, more advanced SCM systems offer means to *track* current and pending activities. *Task management* is an area overlapping with (project) management. If tools are used it must be carefully decided which type of information is kept in the SCM tool and which in a project management tool. The interface is thin if the SCM system handles the states of the configuration items (and configurations) and this information is used by the (project) management for the progress control. Tight coupling of work activities with the state control of the work results leads to sluggish SCM systems.

Ultimate process support is achieved with automated *work flow systems*. These are not widely used (yet); their validation is a pending research topic. In practice, work flow is typically organized by informal communication. Most SCM systems support *triggers* that are associated with specific events—such as automatic notification by e-mail whenever a change occurred. These *communication* features are well-understood, cheap and effective means for a simple work flow support [9].

4.2 Auditing

Every SCM system provides features to inquire the change history of specific config-uration items; these features are mature and widely used. A yet unsolved problem is the traceability of *related documents:* How does one trace a change in implementation back to the design and back to the requirements? How is a change in the implementa-tion related to a change in the documentation? Although *change-based versioning* or *activity-based SCM* [21] allows these changes to be associated with each other, there is still room for improvement here.

4.3 Accounting

Accounting facilities let users (and managers) inquire about the status of a product. SCM systems at least allow classifying components and versions according to specific properties (i.e. experimental, proposed, or stable); it may well be this simple tagging method is already sufficient. Again, we know of no research that has addressed pending problems in this area.

4.4 Controlling

Access control is one of the fundamental principles of automated SCM. Every SCM system features some kind of access control, typically via *locks* (only one user at a time can edit a file). Several SCM systems also support *access control lists* (only specific users are allowed to do changes); others rely on the security features of the underlying repository. Access control is widely used; it has never been a SCM research topic.

Tracking of change requests and defect reports is at the heart of the maintenance process, starting as soon as independent testing begins. The process of handling these, especially responsibility for decisions and definition of records to be kept, determines the responsiveness of an organization on user needs. In small organizations, a simple Excel sheet will provide enough support; bigger organizations require an elaborated data base with dedicated queries.

Advanced SCM systems like LIFESPAN [35] offer an elaborated management of *change requests;* in fact, the whole development process is organized along the pro-cessing of change requests. Although the effectiveness of the process remains to be validated, improvements are more likely to come from SCM vendors than from SCM researchers.

An important SCM topic is the tracking of *product defects,* as it provides immediate insight on the current product quality. Bug-tracking tools frequently come as stand-alone tools, from the freely available GNATS [23] to elaborated commercial systems. However, the integration with SCM repositories as well as automated testing facilities still leaves to be desired—a challenge for SCM vendors and researchers.

5 Conclusion

SCM is a mature discipline. It is mature in practice, as it is successfully used. And it is mature in research, since there is much to be taught—and not so much left to be researched. The only two research areas that are considered to have high potential are automated change integration and deployment issues; major improvements are also feasible in wide area connectivity, version management of structures, system modeling, consistency issues, lifecycle support, and integration issues.

Although several well-understood solutions are available, no single SCM system provides a solution to all problems. Integration and flexibility are thus still issues for SCM users and SCM vendors—maybe also for SCM researchers, provided they find a way to validate the practical benefits of new SCM models.

Validation is also an issue for this paper, and the state of SCM in general. Upon compiling the tables, it was amazing to see how few hard facts were available to back specific judgements. The most important result of our assessment is that many more SCM experience reports and experiments are needed—*we need to know what we know before we can move on*. We thus encourage the SCM community to prove us right or wrong and look forward to fruitful discussions.

Acknowledgments. We thank the participants and organizers of the Dagstuhl Workshop on Software Engineering Research and Education [7] for their suggestions and contributions. Gregor Snelting provided useful comments on an earlier revision of this paper. Walter F. Tichy initiated the discussion on the state of SCM and helped a lot in ranking the individual SCM solutions.

References

1. BERLINER, B. CVS II: Parallelizing software development. In *Proc. of the 1990 Winter USENIX Conference* (Washington, D.C., 1990).
2. BINKLEY, D., HORWITZ, S., AND REPS, T. Program integration for languages with procedure calls. *ACM Transactions on Software Engineering and Methodology 4*, 1 (Jan. 1995), 3–35.
3. BUFFENBARGER, J. Syntactic software merging. In Estublier [8], pp. 153–172.
4. BURROWS, C., AND WESLEY, I. *Ovum Evaluates: Configuration Management*. Ovum, Inc., Burlington, MA, 1999.
5. CONRADI, R., AND WESTFECHTEL, B. Version models for software configuration management. *ACM Computing Surveys 30*, 2 (June 1998), 232–282.
6. DART, S. Concepts in configuration management. In Feiler [11], pp. 1–18.
7. DENERT, E., HOFFMAN, D. M., LUDEWIG, J., AND PARNAS, D. L. Software engineering research and education: Seeking a new agenda. Workshop Report 230, Dagstuhl, Feb. 1999.
8. ESTUBLIER, J., Ed. *Software Configuration Management: selected papers / ICSE SCM-4 and SCM-5 workshops* (Seattle, Washington, Oct. 1995), vol. 1005 of *Lecture Notes in Computer Science*, Springer-Verlag.
9. ESTUBLIER, J., AND CASALLAS, R. The Adele configuration manager. In Tichy [30], ch. 4, pp. 99–133.
10. ESTUBLIER, J., FAVRE, J.-M., AND MORAT, P. Towards scm/pdm integration? In Magnusson [20], pp. 95–106.
11. FEILER, P. H., Ed. *Proc. 3rd International Workshop on Software Configuration Management* (Trondheim, Norway, June 1991), ACM Press.
12. FELDMAN, S. I. Make—A program for maintaining computer programs. *Software—Practice and Experience 9* (Apr. 1979), 255–265.
13. FOWLER, G., KORN, D., AND RAO, H. *n*-DFS: The multiple dimensional file system. In Tichy [30], ch. 5, pp. 135–154.

14. FRÜHAUF, K. Hygiene in software works—Software configuration management. In *Proceedings of the Second European Conference on Software Quality* (Oslo, 1990), pp. 1–17.

15. HEIMBIGNER, D., AND WOLF, A. Post-deployment configuration management. In Sommerville [26], pp. 272–276.

16. HORWITZ, S., PRINS, J., AND REPS, T. Integrating noninterfering versions of programs. *ACM Transactions on Programming Languages and Systems 11*, 3 (July 1989), 345–387.

17. HUNT, J. J., VO, K.-P., AND TICHY, W. F. Delta algorithms: An empirical analysis. *ACM Transactions on Software Engineering and Methodology 7*, 2 (Apr. 1998), 192–214.

18. LEBLANG, D. B. The CM challenge: Configuration management that works. In Tichy [30], ch. 1, pp. 1–37.

19. MACKENZIE, D., AND ELLISTON, B. *Autoconf—Creating Automatic Configuration Scripts*. Free Software Foundation, Inc., Dec. 1998. Distributed with GNU autoconf.

20. MAGNUSSON, B., Ed. *Proc. 8th Symposium on System Configuration Management* (Brussels, Belgium, July 1998), vol. 1349 of *Lecture Notes in Computer Science*, Springer-Verlag.

21. MICALLEF, J., AND CLEMM, G. M. The Asgard system: Activity-based configuration management. In Sommerville [26], pp. 175–186.

22. OBJECT MANAGEMENT GROUP. *The Common Object Request Broker: Architecture and Specification*, Aug. 1991.

23. OSIER, J. M., AND KEHOE, B. *Keeping Track: Managing Messages With GNATS*. Cygnus Support, 1996.

24. PLOEDEREDER, E., AND FERGANY, A. The data model of the configuration management assistant. In *Proc. 2nd International Workshop on Software Configuration Management* (Princeton, New Jersey, Oct. 1989), W. F. Tichy, Ed., ACM Press, pp. 5–13.

25. ROCHKIND, M. J. The source code control system. *IEEE Transactions on Software Engineering SE-1*, 4 (Dec. 1975), 364–370.

26. SOMMERVILLE, I., Ed. *Proc. 6th International Workshop on Software Configuration Management* (Berlin, Germany, Mar. 1996), vol. 1167 of *Lecture Notes in Computer Science*, Springer-Verlag.

27. STALLMAN, R., AND MCGRATH, R. *GNU Make—A Program for Directing Recompilation*, 0.48 ed. Free Software Foundation, Inc., 1995. Distributed with GNU Make.

28. TICHY, W. F. RCS—A system for version control. *Software—Practice and Experience 15*, 7 (July 1985), 637–654.

29. TICHY, W. F. Smart recompilation. *ACM Transactions on Software Engineering and Methodology 8*, 3 (July 1986), 273–291.

30. TICHY, W. F., Ed. *Configuration Management*, vol. 2 of *Trends in Software*. John Wiley & Sons, Chichester, UK, 1994.

31. VAN DER HOEK, A., HEIMBIGNER, D., AND WOLF, A. L. Does configuration management research have a future? In Estublier [8], pp. 305–310.

32. VAN DER HOEK, A., HEIMBIGNER, D., AND WOLF, A. L. System modeling resurrected. In Magnusson [20], pp. 140–145.

33. WESTFECHTEL, B. Structure-oriented merging of revisions of software documents. In Feiler [11], pp. 86–79.

34. WESTFECHTEL, B., AND CONRADI, R. Software configuration management and engineering data management: Differences and similarities. In Magnusson [20], pp. 95–106.

35. WHITGIFT, D. *Methods and Tools for Software Configuration Management*. John Wiley & Sons, Chichester, UK, 1991.

36. ZELLER, A. Smooth operations with square operators—The version set model in ICE. In Sommerville [26], pp. 8–30.

37. ZELLER, A., AND SNELTING, G. Unified versioning through feature logic. *ACM Transactions on Software Engineering and Methodology 6*, 4 (Oct. 1997), 398–441.

SCM: Status and Future Challenges

Reidar Conradi[1] and Bernhard Westfechtel[2]

[1] Norwegian University of Science and Technology (NTNU),
N-7034 Trondheim, Norway.
conradi@idi.ntnu.no
[2] Computer Science III, Aachen University of Technology,
Ahornstrasse 55, D-52074 Aachen, Germany.
bernhard@i3.informatik.rwth-aachen.de

This paper summarizes the state-of-the-art in software configuration management (SCM). Ten SCM themes are discussed and relevant research questions are proposed for each theme. The full version of this paper may be retrieved under http://www-i3.informatik.rwth-aachen.de/private/bernhard/westfechtel.html.

1. The version and product model: one or separate? These two models control the version space and product space, respectively. There are several research questions to clarify:

- *Q1.1: What product model to apply?* Most SCM tools are still based on files. It is highly desirable to support more sophisticated data models for representing typed objects, relationships, and attributes.
- *Q1.2: What version model to apply?* E.g. choose state-based versioning (variants and revisions) or change-based versioning (conditional compilation with more liberal delta combinations)? The two authors have proposed a unifying version model [CW97], capable of supporting both state- and change-based versioning – but limited experience exists.
- *Q1.3: Should the version model and product/object model be orthogonal to each other?* In many proposals, version model and product/object model are intermingled. Separating product/object model and version model appears attractive because the same version model can be combined with different product/object models. However, the implications on database design have still to be explored more thoroughly.

2. How to manage and evolve the meta-information, such as version rules? A software product may evolve into many revisions and variants, and many changes may be applied during its lifetime. Rule-based version construction supports the construction of consistent configurations from an intentional, high-level description. The result of version construction heavily depends on the quality of the version rules and the underlying deductive version engine. Not only does the product evolve; the version rules evolve likewise.

Research questions: Q2.1: To better understand the problem space (understanding the requirements, collecting empirical data on the structure of and evolution of version rules). Q2.2: To better understand the solution space (improving the deductive capabilities of rule-based version engines and assisting the user in managing the version rules). Q2.3: Give effective user assistance in managing the combinatorial space of configurations and the interplay between product and version structure. Q2.4: In all this, collect empirical data on the structure and evolution of such rules, both for the version and the product space.

3. New media and delta techniques

Traditionally, SCM has been applied to sequential texts only, i.e. "source programs" or other lifecycle documents. Efficient delta techniques exist for such texts, reducing the storage demand to 2-3% of the original one [HVT98]. Efficient diff/merge tools are also available. Later on, delta algorithms have been generalized to binary files.

Focusing on text and binary files is no longer sufficient. Multi-media data such as sound, pictures, and video also have to be stored efficiently. So far, this is addressed by compression techniques decoupled from versioning. In addition, we should also consider high-level deltas exploiting structural knowledge about software objects (e.g., deltas for HTML documents [WW98]).

Research questions: Q3.1: To develop new delta techniques for multi-media data. Q3.2: To explore the potential of more high-level structure-oriented deltas.

4. Workspace management and transaction control

Central issues here are *high-level (intentional) configuration descriptions* that are expanded into *low-level (extensional) part-lists* to control check-out and check-in of workspaces, either shared ones for groups or private ones for individuals.

Recently some pragmatic tools have emerged for dynamic (re)configuration of files on distributed computers (e.g., file docking, incremental downloading of executables (web-applets), e-mail attachments). In all this, there is weak control in defining and maintaining local configurations.

Research questions: Q4.1: To develop flexible workspace architectures. Q4.2: To develop efficient and pragmatical configuration descriptions to control the above.

5. Distributed and cooperative work and relation to groupware

SCM tools provide workspaces for organizing distributed and cooperative work. For example, ClearCase can support distributed workspaces with controlled check-out/in and mutual notifications. In addition, we may need temporary workspaces (bulletin boards) for short-term and dedicated communication and negotiation. Finally, SCM tools may provide cooperative transactions that allow for information interchange *before* check-in.

SCM tools tend to provide product-centered support for distributed and cooperative work. Conversely, groupware tools usually do not consider product structures, when organizing actors, groups, processes, and cooperation patterns. Thus, we have to investigate how to combine groupware and SCM support.

Research questions: Q5.1: To experiment with and assess the support from groupware tools on typical, cooperative SCM-scenarios. Q5.2: To configure and

evolve groupware support based on SCM-maintained information. Q5.3: To de-
velop and validate flexible models for cooperating database transactions.

6. Process support issues Most SCM processes are well established and
repetitive, thus ripe for computerized support. Indeed, the more advanced SCM
tools offer facilities for process support, e.g. Adele, Continuus and ClearCase.

At least five process areas must be supported: (1) change control and status reporting, which is already supported in many SCM tools; (2) management
(project planning, cost estimation, etc.), which is covered by project management tools; (3) QA and auditing, which is supported by many methods and
tools with weak coupling to SCM; (4) regeneration, which is well supported by
Make and related tools; (5) cooperation/negotiation support, which is provided
by groupware tools and some advanced SCM tools. All in all: some of the total
process support is supported by the SCM tools, some by a spectrum of other
tools.

Research questions: Q6.1: Can required process support for SCM be made in-
dependent of basic product/versioning management? Q6.2: What are the mutual
dependencies and interfaces of SCM and process tools?

7. SCM tool architecture Software architectures have attracted much attention recently. Since current SCM tools tend to grow larger and larger, developers
of such tools would clearly benefit from a well-defined architecture. However, virtually no such proposal exists, although we have outlined a layered architecture
with coarse-grained components, such as: a versioned database (the "facts"), a
rule base, a version engine for defining and evaluating rules, a workspace manager, a transaction manager, etc. in an earlier paper [CW97]. The layering is still
subject to debate — as well the scope of SCM (e.g., to what extent is process
support included?).

Research questions: Q7.1: What are kernel SCM functionalities? Q7.2: How
should the layering and interfaces be?

8. Industrial Experiences SCM is an established and recognized area of
software engineering, with a spectrum of methods, techniques and tools available.
We should then expect that there is a huge body of empirical data to demonstrate
its effectiveness – but not so.

Much data has been collected to assert the effectiveness of delta storage on
the low end. At the high end, it is much more difficult to obtain measures of
productivity improvement resulting from the introduction of SCM tools. Some
work has been done e.g. in the European ESSI program, where several process
improvement experiments were concerned with the introduction of SCM tools.
One of these reported a 36 % reduction in external reports of major errors after
ClearCase had been installed, although no strict causality can be assumed.

Research questions: Q8.1: Design a common and moderate metrics to assess
the impact of SCM tools, both on the product and process side. Q8.2: Perform
empirical studies from industry, using such metrics.

9. SCM Maturity Models Both ISO-9001 and CMM (level 2) require product management, i.e. SCM. However, there are many aspects to consider when introducing a SCM tool into an organization. Thus, it makes sense to distinguish between levels of SCM maturity, e.g.:

1. No SCM procedures – chaos.
2. Get the overall process in shape. Organize old/new versions in different catalogs.
3. Introduce simple SCM tools, such as RCS / SCCS and Make. Improve the process.
4. Upgrade to a medium-level SCM tool, like CVS, with explicit product definitions. Consolidate the process.
5. Finally introduce a more complete SCM tool, like ClearCase. Also allow a distributed process.
6. Total SCM, with complete support processes across projects and products.

Research questions: Q9.1: How to design such an maturity scale? Q9.2: How to use and validate such an maturity scale?

10. SCM technologies also for CAD/CAM, VLSI and office automation Managing consistent configurations of versioned documents is a problem that occurs not only in software engineering, but also in electrical, mechanical or chemical engineering, in office automation, etc. Although many similarities do exist, disciplines such as SCM and EDM/PDM (engineering/product data management) and corresponding tools have evolved fairly independently.

Research questions: Q10.1: To investigate whether common version- and configuration management are applicable on hybrid hw/sw products. This may assume a common base model, and how to separate domain-independent from domain-specific aspects.

Acknowledgements Thanks go to our nearest colleagues and to many discussions in the SCM workshop series.

References

[CW97] Reidar Conradi and Bernhard Westfechtel. Towards a Uniform Version Model for Software Configuration Management. In *Reidar Conradi (Ed.): "Proc. Sixth International Workshop on Software Configuration Management (SCM'7)"*, pages 1–17, Boston, USA, 18–19 May 1997. Springer Verlag LNCS 1235.

[HVT98] James Hunt, Kiem-Phong Vo, and Walter Tichy. Delta algorithms: An empirical evaluation. *ACM Transactions on Software Engineering and Methodology*, 7(2):192–214, April 1998.

[WW98] E. James Whitehead and Meredith Wiggins. WEBDAV: IETF Standard for Collaborative Authoring on the Web. *IEEE Internet Computing*, pages 34–40, Sep/Oct 1998.

New Challenges for Configuration Management

Magnus Larsson[1], Ivica Crnkovic[2]

[1] ABB Industrial Products AB, LAB,
S-721 67 Västerås, Sweden
Magnus.Larsson@mdh.se
[2] Mälardalen University, Department of Computer Engineering,
S-721 23 Västerås, Sweden
Ivica.Crnkovic@mdh.se

Abstract. More and more systems are developed using components. There is a move from monolithic to open and flexible systems. In such systems, components are upgraded and introduced at run-time, which affects the configuration of the complete system. Keeping up-to-date information about which components are installed is a problem. Updating a component also affects the compatibility of the system. It is therefore important to keep track of changes introduced in the system. In the product life cycle, CM is traditionally focused on the development phase, in particular on managing source code. Now when changes are introduced in systems at run-time and systems are component-based, a new discipline, *component configuration management* is required. This paper analyses component management and highlights the problems related to component configuration. Requirements on component configuration management are outlined, and some directions to possible solutions of the problems are given.

1   Introduction

In recent years we have recognized a new paradigm in the development process: From a complete in-house development, to a development process which has focused on the use of standard and de-facto standard components[1], outsourcing, COTS (commercials off the shelf). The final products are not closed, monolithic systems, but are instead component-based products which can be integrated with other products available on the market [3]. Developers are not only designers and programmers, they have become integrators and marketing investigators. The new paradigm increases the efficiency of development and the flexibility of delivered products, but at the same time increases the risk of losing product configuration consistency. The higher risk reduces the product reliability, which is a critical factor for certain types of systems, such as real-time and safety-critical systems. Configuration Management (CM) is a discipline, which controls the consistency between the parts of the entire system, and can increase the reliability of component-based products.

---

[1] Definitions of components are presented in chapter 3.

Software systems based on standard components are the results of a combination of pure development and integration of components. The requirements for conventional use of CM remains, but new requirements related to component management appear in all phases: in the design, integration and run-time. We can expect that the source code management will become less critical, because there is less internal development and because of the fact that source code management in CM is very well established in both theory and implementation. The integration part, i.e. configuration, and version management of the components becomes more important. New aspects of CM arise in the run-time phase, as components are usually loosely coupled, and their update is allowed in the run-time environment.

The importance of CM, and challenges in research and implementation of CM support, are emphasized in the 1998 CBSE (Component-based Software Engineering) workshop [1], as quoted: "In particular, high composeability in a product line setting amounts to mass customization and this introduces tremendous configuration management challenges and support challenges."

Although CM provides good support in the development phase, especially in the coding phase, there is a lack of CM disciplines managing components already developed. This paper points to certain new aspects of CM in managing components. Chapter 2 shows different phases in component development processes and run-time environments and their relations to CM activities. The different compatibility levels of the components are discussed in chapter 3. Chapter 4 gives an overview of the component characteristics related to CM issues. The problems, which appear due to the lack of proper CM support, are presented. Chapter 5 outlines certain models for improving the support and improving the reliability of products.

2 Using CM in Component-Based Product Life Cycles

Configuration management is applied in different phases of a component-based product life cycle. Fig. 1 shows an example of a development and run-time process. In the development phase we build libraries from the source code. A component is built by assembling libraries and collecting other types of items such as documentation and executable files. Finally, a typical component-based product consists of a set of components.

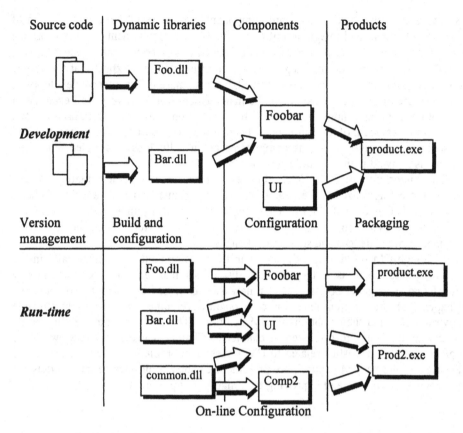

Fig. 1.   CM activities in different phases of a component-based product life cycle

In the first development phase, source code management is used to track the introduction of different versions of source code, to enable parallel development, etc. Many CM tools supporting this are available today. The building phase is also supported by CM tools such as different variants of make and configuration tools, the results of the building procedures being connected to the source code. One step closer to CM for components is to use description logic, to describe configurations, in combination with make to build a product[10]. However, this does not solve the run-time issues.

Having control over the source code and producing the system entirely from the source code makes it possible to control the target system configuration. When using imported components, we lose this control, because we only partially know their behavior. It is possible however to manage versions and configurations if we place the components under version control and deliver them as a part of the product.

When delivering components or products, which are part of a target system, we face two problems:

- We cannot predict the behavior of the entire environment of the target system. The system may contain another product, which uses the same component as our product. The relations between components, and the changes we may obtain by introducing a new version of a component, are uncertain.

- A more serious problem is the dynamic behavior of the system configuration in the run-time environment. If we permit component-updating during the run-time, by updating dynamic libraries, we could be facing a situation in which a new component version works for one product, but not for another. There are also different aspects of updating, such as moving or copying an application from one computer to another, or automatically generation of code.

CM can provide solutions to these problems, and those are new challenges for CM. To cope with the problem, the research and practical implementations must focus on the component management. The following chapters describe the mechanisms of component management and point at the problems related to their identification. Finally an outline of possible solutions for improvement of the component version and configuration management are presented.

3   Component Compatibility

There are different definitions of software components [1]: A component is a non-trivial, nearly independent, and replaceable part of a system which fulfills a clear function. A component conforms to and provides the physical realization of a set of interfaces. A run-time software component is a dynamically bindable package of one or more programs managed as a unit and accessed through documented interfaces which can be discovered at run-time. A component can be deployed independently and is subject to composition by third party.

The importance of components becomes significant where technologies for their development and integration are being standardized. The most prominent component technologies today are Java Beans, COM/DCOM and ActiveX, and CORBA. In this paper, we illustrate component-management problems using COM/DCOM technology, but the same principles are valid with other technologies.

A new component version might be added to introduce new functions in a system, or only to change its behavior, (better performance, better stability), without changing the interface. When replacing a component or a component version we must consider which type of change is permitted, and which type of compatibility is required. We define three levels of compatibility:

- *Input and Output compatibility.* A component requires input in a specific format and produces results in a defined format. The internal characteristics of the component are of no interest. An example of this type of compatibility is provided by different word-processors producing the same document format. This type of compatibility does not ensure that the interfaces or the behavior are preserved.

- *Interface compatibility* (at development time and at run time). The interface remains the same, but the implementation can be different. A typical example is given by different implementations of ActiveX objects, with the same interface.

Interface compatibility is more demanding than input and output compatibility, but it does not need to have the same behavior.

- *Behavior compatibility.* Internal characteristics of the components, such as performance, resource requirements, etc., must be preserved. Such requirements can be appropriate for real-time systems. This is the strongest compatibility requirement and it includes the previous ones.

The compatibility criteria can be used in deciding if a component can be replaced or not. This decision can be especially important in case of a replacement "on the fly" in a run-time environment. It is important to maintain the required level of compatibility to avoid the risk of interrupting the whole system.

4 Managing Components

Components typically consist of shared libraries, where the component functions are implemented. The programs using components do not refer to the libraries directly but to the component interfaces. The libraries are implementations of the interfaces. We need to keep track of changes on both logical and physical levels as well as their relations. Both libraries and interfaces must be identified. Component Configuration Management must work on both levels. Versioning of interfaces is a more difficult task, because the interface is an abstraction without information about the physical representation. For this reason, we separate the problem of managing components onto two levels: Managing libraries and managing interfaces.

4.1 Libraries

Historically there were less problems in this area as all libraries were statically linked into the executables. This prevented the executable from being updated when a new version of the library was released. An advantage of this approach is that the executables are protected from uncontrolled use by the new version of the library. A disadvantage is the necessity to re-link the executable only to incorporate a new version of the library, which is unnecessary work when the library is interface-compatible. Another disadvantage is that all executables which shared the same library must be linked with their own copies of the library. The concept of shared libraries was introduced to avoid this. This was a significant improvement since we could now share libraries and make updates without re-linking the executables while functions were interface-compatible. In Microsoft platforms, shared libraries are designated dynamic link libraries or dlls, which can be loaded and unloaded whenever needed. On other platforms, such as different Unix platforms, shared libraries are loaded together with the main executable.

Unfortunately, the concept of shared libraries introduces new problems related to the consistency of the system, as illustrated by Fig. 2.

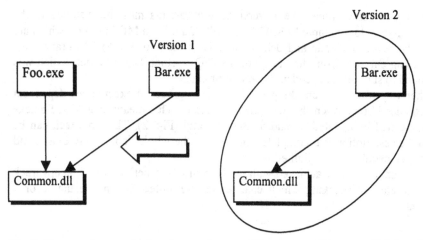

Fig. 2. Foo.exe stops work when the new incompatible version of Common.dll is introduced.

The figure shows how a new version might damage the system. Common.dll version 1 will be overwritten with version 2 when the new version of bar.exe is introduced. The replacement could be successful if version 2 of Common.dll is interface-compatible with version 1, but definitely not if the compatibility level is less. There is a risk that Foo.exe will stop working after the new version of Common.dll is introduced.

The new interface-compatible version of Common.dll may contain undetected errors as it was tested with Bar.exe only and not with Foo.exe. Foo.exe may then access some erroneous code and crash even if the library was interface-compatible.

One way to handle multiple versions of libraries is to insert version information into the actual library name as Microsoft does in MFC [9]. For example, names such as MFC40.dll and MFC42.dll can be used for version 4.0 and 4.2. This prevents name collisions problems such as developed in Fig. 2. With different names for different version, the situation may be as in Fig. 3.

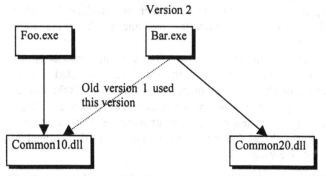

Fig. 3. Common10.dll can now coexist with Common20.dll

This solution is to some extent similar to the static linking of executables, because an executable always uses the same version of the shared library. The solution however becomes cumbersome when several versions and variants must be installed in the system. There are, for example MFC42d.dll, MFC42u.dll and MFC42ud.dll which are respectively debug, Unicode and debug/Unicode versions of the MFC library. This tight coupling emerges from the design of the C/C++ compilation model, which was not intended to support independent binary components.

Another way to circumvent the problems is to upgrade all executables dependent on a particular library when the new release is ready. This means that both Foo.exe and Bar.exe will be updated instead of Bar.exe only (Fig. 2). This approach can be taken on the assumption that complete control over the whole deployment exists, and from that perspective is very limited.

Suitable support can be achieved with the help of CM functions which keeps track of changes, and by checking which changes are permitted for an executable or a component.

4.2 Interfaces

An interface is a connection between a component and its user. If an interface is changed, the user needs to know that it has been changed and how to use the new version.

Functions exposed to the user are usually designated Application Programmable Interfaces (API). If a change is made in the API, the user must recompile his code. This is the case for compiled languages such as C/C++ but not for interpretative languages such as Smalltalk or Java.

In an object-oriented world, an interface is a set of the public methods defined for an object. Usually the object can be manipulated only through its interface. In C++ the user need only recompile the code when an interface, referred to from the code, is changed.

A disadvantage is that the user of the object must use the same programming language throughout the whole development.

Separation of the interface from the implementation is a means of avoiding this tight coupling. This kind of separation is performed with binary interfaces as in CORBA [3] and COM [6]. Binary interfaces are defined in an interface definition language (IDL) and an IDL compiler, which generates stubs and proxies to make the applications location transparent.

COM solves the interface versioning problem by defining interfaces as unchangeable units. Each time a new version of the interface is created a new interface will be added instead of changing the older version. A basic COM rule is that an interface cannot be changed when it has been released. This makes couplings between COM components very loose and it is easy to upgrade parts of the system indifferent from each other. Fig. 4 shows that it is possible to run new clients together with old server components or vice versa.

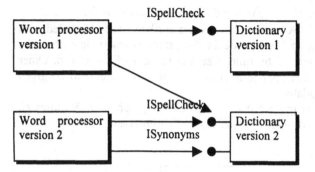

Fig. 4.   Possible combinations between old and new clients and their server component.

Even if an interface has not been changed, its implementation can be changed. This increases the flexibility of possible updates, but also introduces the possibility of resultant uncontrolled effects. For this reason, it is of interest to know if the implementation has been changed.

Today there is no support for the handling of components in the configuration management perspective. CM functions should provide information about the changes on the interface level.

5   Proposed CM for Libraries and Components

No or insufficient information is available when a system is assembled from components. There is no standard way to track the dependencies between components. When a system is upgraded with a new program, the programs running already might be affected without notice because the new program may introduce new versions of existing components in the system (see Fig. 2). It is necessary to determine which interfaces (i.e. components) are used by a program or a component.

As a component is placed in a set of shared libraries some control may be obtained by keeping the libraries under control. We propose a component configuration management on two levels, the library level and the component level.

5.1   CM for libraries

Which shared libraries are linked to another library or program can be seen. This can be used to list the dependencies between different programs and libraries. When installing a new program containing libraries the following steps shall be taken:

1. Take a snapshot of the current system configuration.

2. Install the new modules.

3. Take a snapshot of the new system configuration.

The contents of a snapshot are all programs and libraries installed in the system and are treated as nodes in a graph. A number of different attributes are associated with each library. The information for each node in the graph uniquely identifies the module. We propose that at least date, time, size and name shall be stored. Other attributes are which compatibility change is allowed or if a warning is to be given when a particular module is updated.

A snapshot of the system is presented as a dependency graph. Fig. 5 shows an example of how one of the COM libraries depends on other libraries.

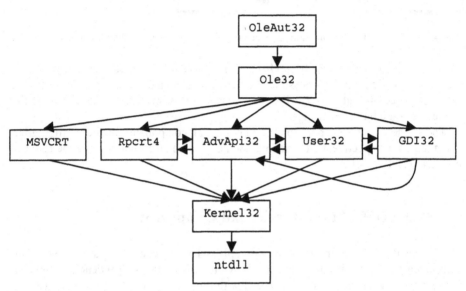

Fig. 5.   A dependency graph for OleAut32.dll.

Different versions of snapshots are placed under version control and treated as configuration items. A tool which could browse this information would present the differences graphically to the end user. The user would now gain an understanding of the effects of the introduction of new and updated libraries in the system. An alarm would be activated if a library which should not have been affected is changed. The configuration tool could browse different configurations and could label components as changeable or not changable.

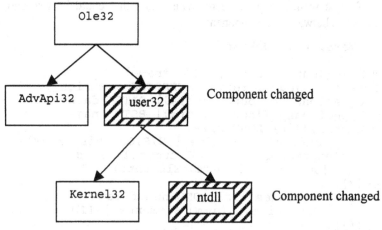

Fig. 6.   A dependency graph that shows all changed versions.

This kind of knowledge is useful if the cause of malfunction in the system is to be traced. An incorrect version of a library may have been installed by mistake. This kind of identification gives no direct information about which components are changed and which can be affected by the change, but indirect information is available since the physical representation of components are libraries.

5.2   CM for components

In this chapter, we discuss COM as an example. COM treats interfaces in a manner unlike other object models such as CORBA.

COM components expose themselves and communicate through COM interfaces only. Moreover, COM is designed to work with loose references between components. There is no requirement that the clients shall know the class declaration since every class declaration contains implementation details. Components should be able to add or remove interfaces without affecting existing clients.

As components are loosely coupled there is no information connecting different versions of components with each other. A COM component finds its fellow components through the Windows registry in which all installed components store their activation data, such as Interface id, class id, library locations and where to find their stubs and proxies. Connections between components are set up first at run-time. A client uses a unique key to find the server component in the registry and then the COM run-time will load the corresponding component or stub into the client memory.

Unfortunately, there is no capability in the target system for finding which interfaces are used by a component. This prevents us from getting proper information about all dependencies in the system.

If we do not know which components a program uses in run-time, we must request that knowledge. This can be obtained if the provider of the components implements a specific interface for version management, which we designate IVersion (Fig. 7). The IVersion interface can return facts about version, name, creation date, compatibility change, interfaces provided and components used. If the components had such an interface, it would be possible to write a tool that could browse and record the dependencies between the components.

```
interface IVersion : IUnkown
{
  HRESULT Name([out , retval] BSTR *name);
  HRESULT Version([out , retval] VERSION *version);
  HRESULT CreationDate([out , retval] DATE *date);
  HRESULT TypeOfChange([out , retval] BSTR *name);
  HRESULT History([in] LONG size,
              [out, size_is(size)] HISTORY history[*]);
  HRESULT HasInterfaces([in] LONG numOfElements,
              [out, size_is(numOfElements)] IID
interfaces[*]);
  HRESULT UsesInterfaces([in] LONG numOfElements,
              [out, size_is(numOfElements)] IID
interfaces[*]);
}
```

Fig. 7.   IDL specification of IVersion.

- `Name`, `Version` and `CreationDate` identifies the component.

- `TypeOfChange` indicates the compatibility level affected by the change.

- `History` informs about previous versions of the component and which type of change applied between them.

- `HasInterfaces` shows all interfaces provided by the component.

- `UsesInterfaces` lists all interfaces used. This list makes possible the building of the dependency tree of the components.

In the absence of a standard version interface, another method is to parse in some way the dependency data from source code files to provide a list of dependencies with the release of a new product. This has some major disadvantages. Firstly, it cannot be applied to third party components. Secondly, it might work for the first level of dependencies where there is source code, but if other third party components are included, no information can be obtained because of the lack of source code.

A possible partial solution to the problem finding dependencies between components is to track the interfaces from the registry repository. All interfaces are registered in the Windows registry with information about where to find the dynamic link library which implements the stubs and proxies for that particular interface. This mechanism provides us with the information we need to see if an interface has been changed during an update. The snapshot browsing tool has a list of all interfaces apart from the libraries and programs installed. The tool can now warn if the implementation of an interface has been changed. It is possible, using this method, to determine if new interfaces have been registered or if old interfaces have changed implementation.

6 Conclusion

We consider that there is a need for component configuration management, especially during the run-time when components can be changed on the fly. In this paper we have highlighted the different phases in component management in which CM is needed. Support from CM related to component management is rudimentary today and we propose beginning work in a new area, Component Configuration Management.

For want of standardized techniques in component management, we have proposed certain relatively simple methods to identify components and possible changes they can cause in the system. Further work will include a deeper investigation of how to snapshot a system for an insight into the interrelationships between different components. A tool capable of browsing and analyzing an existing system for this should be developed.

7 References

[1] Don Box, Essential COM, Addison-Wesley, ISBN 0-201-63446-5
[2] Alan W. Brown, Kurt C. Wallnau: An Examination of the Current State of CBSE: A Report on the ICSE Workshop on Component-Based Software Engineering, 1998 International Workshop on CBSE, http://www.sei.cmu.edu/cbs/icse98/summary.html
[3] Continuus Software Corporation, http://www.continuus.com/homepage.html, 1999
[4] CORBA, http://www.corba.org
[5] Ivica Crnkovic, Magnus Larsson, Managing Standard Components in Large Software Systems, Position paper on Second International Workshop on Component-Based Software Engineering, Los Angeles, May 1999
[6] Microsoft corporation, http://www.microsoft.com/com
[7] Microsoft Source Safe, http://msdn.microsoft.com/ssafe
[8] Rational http://www.rational.com/products/clearcase/index.jtmpl, 1999
[9] Dale Rogerson, Inside COM, Microsoft Press, ISBN 1-57231-349-8
[10] Andreas Zeller, Versioning System Models Through Description Logic, Proceedings ECOOP'98 SCM-8 Symposium, vol 1439 of Lecture Notes in Computer Science, Springer-Verlag.

The 3 Software Configuration Management Implementation Levels

Mario E. Moreira

Fidelity Investments, Boston, MA, USA
mario_e_moreira@yahoo.com

Abstract. In order to deploy effect Software Configuration Management (SCM) technology and practices, it is important to follow a roadmap of SCM tasks and to align the SCM tasks with the appropriate target level within an organization. The three primary target levels include implementing SCM tasks at the organization; the application; and the project level. By aligning SCM tasks to the appropriate level, the chances for a more effective SCM implementation may increase. It is also important to implement SCM in a practical sequence of events so that past SCM tasks can lead to more effective completion of future SCM tasks. This paper will; 1) provide a brief analysis of success & failure criteria; 2) identify SCM tasks to the appropriate target level; and 3) provide a practical sequence of SCM tasks (along with templates, procedures, policy, guidelines, etc.) to help SCM personnel improve their chances of implementing SCM successfully.

1.0 Introduction

This paper is based on the experience of performing 10+ years of over 50 SCM implementation efforts covering the commercial, DoD, and financial industries. After performing these implementations, an analysis[1] of the success criteria and of the tasks used to implement these efforts occurred. The common success criteria for an SCM implementation effort include:

- Sponsorship - management commitment to the effort
- Funding - money to purchase appropriate SCM tools and infrastructure (e.g., servers, etc.)
- Skilled SCM personnel - persons trained and experienced in the areas of SCM tools and process
- SCM Implementation Plan - a plan detailing the tasks that lead to the implementation of SCM practices (tools & process) and effective tracking and management of the plan

---

[1] The author does not claim to have performed full and in depth study of every aspect of the 50 SCM implementation efforts he has experience with.

Also, it then became clear that after an analysis of the tasks and task structures, there were 3 primary levels in which SCM can be focused to ensure an increased possibility of success. The 3 levels include:
- Organization level - initial tasks targeted toward upper management to attain commitment and raise awareness of SCM
- Application level - tasks targeted toward the application owner, SCM, and infrastructure personnel to build the appropriate SCM infrastructure for the application
- Project level - tasks targeted toward project & SCM personnel to continue usage of SCM tools and process

2.0 Approach

For the past 2 years, I have focused on SCM implementation efforts that had a reasonable level of sponsorship, funding, and skilled SCM personnel. This allowed me to focus on the SCM Implementation Plan and accompanying management/tracking aspects. I constructed an SCM planning approach that structured the organization and application level SCM tasks into a standard SCM Implementation Plan and the project level SCM tasks intoan SCM Task List (to be incorporated in a project's project plan). While the SCM Implementation Plan provides guidance for a successful implementation of SCM tools and process, the SCM task list ensured a continuation of usage of the SCM tools and process.

During the past 2 years, this approach has been used to successfully implement SCM in 8 of 12 efforts. Success criteria constitutes the adoption of SCM tools and process for 1+ years. While the data may yet be too sparse to be statistically significant, it is becoming evident that when an SCM effort manages and tracks to a roadmap of SCM tasks targeted at the appropriate level, it produces a high percentage of successful implementations.

2.1 Background Data

While this paper is not intended to primarily focus on the specifics of the 12 SCM Implementation efforts referenced above, it is important to provide attributes of these efforts. The attributes include:
- Industry: technology side of financial industry
- Population base: Client/Server development organizations
- Population size: range from 25-70 per organization
- Technical OS Environment: NT & UNIX
- SCM Tool: ClearCase or PVCS

2.2 Reasons for Failure

While 8 of the SCM implementation efforts succeeded based primarily on meeting the success criteria stated above, 4 efforts failed. One effort failed due to the application being decommissioned for business reasons. After some analysis of the remaining 3 efforts, the reasons for failure were derived:

- Failure 1: While the SCM Implementation Plan was prepared, it was not followed and eventually the effort lost motivation. The SCM tools were not consistently implemented and SCM procedures were not developed. The team did not consider the effort to be a project, in and of itself, so therefore did not feel the need to follow a plan. Also, most of the organizational level SCM tasks did not get completed.
- Failure 2: While the SCM Implementation Plan effort completed successfully where SCM tools and process were developed, SCM project tasks were not added to project plans and SCM tasks did not occur on a regular basis. While the SCM tool was properly implemented, it was not used properly (the process was not followed) and not all code entered the SCM tool repository in order to prepare a traceable release. Subsequent releases suffered due to regression and problems of maintenance.
- Failure 3: This effort had the same failure result as Failure 2 with the addition of the fact that once it was clear that developers where not following the SCM procedures, the SCM personnel found other positions in the company and simply left this organization. This led to additional concerns when developers were required to act as SCM tool administrators & release engineers. This can lead to the "fox guarding the hen house" scenario because, in most cases, developers were not trained in this area and, typically did not like to do this type of work. Short cuts to releases occurred as a result and typically found lacking in traceability of code back to the repository.

Other common failure scenarios observed over the past 10 years include:

- Where the need for effective SCM Implementation tends to focus on the SCM tool installation. The SCM tool installation is a concrete task that will have an immediate impact on the developers and the working environment (for better or for worse). This is typically a very tactical and short sighted event, that allows a manager to "check off" a implementation goal, but can fail in the long run without developing and following appropriate checkout/checkin, build, and release procedures.
- When the SCM task is focused at the inappropriate level of the organization. For example, trying to implementan SCM Policy at the project level without the backing of the application owner or senior management can lead to resistance to the policy, a perception that the policy is not seen as important by upper management. It may be more appropriate to focus on the SCM Policy task at the organization or application level. This typically ensures a higher level of management commitment to the SCM Policy. While grassroots efforts lead to occasional effective implementations, it is typically because of the high quality and effort of the SCM personnel.

3.0 The 3 SCM Implementation Levels

With the background data and success & failure criteria in mind, this paper focuses on developing a framework of SCM tasks for establishing Software Configuration Management (SCM). It focuses on targeting these tasks at the appropriate SCM level: establishing the SCM practice at the organization level; implementing an SCM infrastructure at the application level; and determining appropriate SCM tasks at the project level.

3.1 Organization vs Application vs Project

At this point, it is important to examine the difference between the following terminology: Organization, Application, and Project.

While most people understand the definition of an organization, it is important to understand the level within the organization that is being referred to. For clarification, are you referring to the whole company as the organization or a division within the company as the organization. In this scenario, an organization is typically a company or division which may own multiple applications and develops and produces multiple releases of each application.

When focusing on the terms, application and project, it is not uncommon for people within an organization to use these 2 words interchangeably, when, in fact, they are very different. Below are brief definitions as they relate to the discussions in this paper:

- An Application is accumulation (+/-) of code deliverables in production that make up a functioning product.
- A Project is a set of activities whose aim is to deliver a changed set of functionality (otherwise known as a release)

Some confusion lies when the beginning of an Application lifecycle (e.g., the first time the application gets developed) also coincides with the initial project.

Also, the term "product" was not included in this comparison. In relation to the above terms, a product may be considered a set of applications. For example, Microsoft Office is a product that is made up of several applications including Word, Excel, PowerPoint, etc.

3.2 The Organization SCM Implementation Level

When an organization, as a whole, has adopted SCM as an important practice, then it typically becomes easier to implement SCM at the lower levels (application and project level). It is the recommendation of the author to consider implementing the following SCM tasks prior to or, at least, in parallel with the application level SCM tasks. By implementing the SCM tasks focused at the organization level, it will improve the chances of implementing SCM at the lower levels (application and project).

The primary SCM role best suited to implement these tasks are the SCM Manager (if one exists) or an SCM champion (someone who is versed in the area of SCM and is committed to provide leadership in this area). This person(s) will work primarily with management to complete the tasks and should be prepared to ensure the meetings with management are as effective and productive as possible.

The SCM tasks at the organization level include:

- Raising Awareness of Software Configuration Management – *benefit*: this helps establish a common understanding of SCM within the organization and to ensure people are aware of the effort being proposed.
- Determining Management Commitment & Support - determine what level of management commitment exists. *Benefit*: this lets you know if management is truly serious about the SCM effort and can help you focus on ways to increase management commitment.
- Establishing an SCM group or Function - hirean SCM person or group (determine how many resources are needed and focus on where to recruit and/or train them) and establish SCM Roles & Responsibilities. *Benefit*: - having dedicated personal will increase your chances of a success SCM implementation.
- Creating an SCM Policy - establish a standard set of guidelines for implementing SCM within an organization. *Benefit*: this document, if approved by management, will show to the rest of the organization that there is commitment to SCM.
- Establishing the SCM Terminology - develop an SCM glossary or set of terminology that can be commonly used throughout the organization. *Benefit*: this helps to facilitate more effective discussion in the SCM arena. Typically within any organization, people use a variety of terms when discussing SCM. They can include version control, source management, release engineering, library management, and numerous other terms. Having standard SCM terminology can facilitate more effective discussions and progress in the SCM arena.

3.3 The Application SCM Implementation Level

Every application must have a solid and effective SCM Technology & Process Infrastructure. An application may remain viable for a number of years and through many releases. The more effective the application's SCM infrastructure, the better your chances for a more efficient, repeatable, and traceable project release process.

The primary SCM roles best suited to implement tasks at this level are the SCM Manager, SCM Engineer, and SCM Coordinator. However, participation and cooperation must occur with the Application owner and Lead Technical personnel.

The SCM tasks at the application level include:

- SCM Analysis - provide a review of the current environment (platform, tools, processes, etc), determine the level of maturity, and provide improvement opportunities that will allow for appropriate SCM planning.
- SCM Planning - provide a road map of the tasks and activities needed to implementan SCM technology infrastructure (tools & process) effectively.

- SCM Tool Selection - provide work products needed to make an objective decision on the best SCM tool for your needs. Determine SCM tool functionality, customer service, and cost requirements; evaluate tools; and determine benefits/risks of tools.
- SCM Strategy & Design - provide SCM roles & responsibilities, tool profile, environment profiles, capacity planning, training & procedure definition. Also, focus on the definition and design of tools (design, development, test, defect tracking tools) that will be integrated with the SCM tools
- SCM Technical Implementation - establish the SCM tool environment. Install the SCM tool, create repositories, import code, integrate the SCM tool with other tools, establish build procedure structure, etc.
- SCM Procedural Implementation - provide the best SCM practices (develop appropriate change control, checkout/checkin, build, release procedures, etc) for the product development.
- SCM Training - Provide training guidelines for establishing solid SCM practices. This includes SCM Overview sessions (roles & responsibilities, tools overview, procedure overview), an SCM Tool User Training, SCM Tool Admin training (vendor or in-house), and various SCM Procedure training.
- SCM Transition - provide support during the transition of staff to new SCM technology.

3.4 The Project SCM Implementation Level

The objective at the Project Level is to define a common set of SCM tasks performed during a project to produce the release. This provides control over configuration items such as requirements, design, source, executables/binaries/programs, documents, etc. and have a repeatable process for build and release.

The primary SCM roles best suited to implement these tasks at the project level are the SCM Manager, SCM Engineer, and Release Engineer. However, participation and cooperation must occur with the Project Manager, Lead Development personnel, and the Test personnel.

The goal at this level is to identify a customizable set of appropriate SCM tasks for each project (AKA, an SCM Project Plan template). This includes defining the appropriate set and size of SCM tasks per size of project. The typical SCM tasks include:

- Assign SCM personnel to the project
- Provide SCM Awareness at the project level (SCM tool used, procedures used, roles, etc.)
- Identify Change Control Board (CCB) membership
- Perform Change Control Board process and activities
- Version documents (requirements lists, designs, specifications, test reports, etc.)
- Build the release
- Branch/merge activities
- Prepare Release Notes

- Package the release
- Install the release

4.0 Approaching an SCM Implementation Effort

Approaching an SCM implementation is always a challenge. However, the key to a successful SCM implementation is to define (then follow) your roadmap (implementation path) from the beginning of the effort to completion. In a nutshell, think of the SCM Implementation effort as a project and prepare an SCM Implementation Plan.

With this in mind, consider following these steps in order to build an SCM Implementation Plan or SCM Task List.

4.1 Step 1 – Organization and Application Level or Project Level

It is very important to determine which level(s) of guidance is required (e.g., Organization, Application, Project). This will help you target which SCM tasks to review first. However, if SCM is new to you and/or the organization, it is recommended that you review all SCM tasks before determining which level(s) is appropriate for your SCM effort.

Organization and Application Level: It is important to understand that the SCM tasks in the organization level and in the application level may be placed into the same SCM Implementation plan. The SCM tasks at this level, in many cases, are a one-time-only task (e.g., you only create one Change Control procedure for an application) and specifically not intended to be rapidly repeated.

Project Level: The SCM tasks at the project level, are suited as more rapid and repeative tasks. For example, builds occur, perhaps, daily and the Change Control Board may meet weekly. Due to the different temporal difference between the tasks at the project level, they are meant to be separate from the SCM tasks in the organization or application level (e.g., instead, part of the SCM Task List which is added to the project's Project Plan).

4.2 Step 2 – Identify Tasks for the Effort

Once you have determined which level(s) of guidance you require, it is important to walk through each section and review each task. Identify which tasks that you will undertake for your particular effort according to the level of maturity of your organization or project team. In other words, try not to take on more than an organization, application, or project can handle. You may consider reviewing the C/R column in the examples below, which refer to whether the author believes a task is a **C**ore or required task for success or whether it is a **R**ecommended task.

4.3 Step 3 – Create the Plan

From the set of tasks you selected, create an SCM Work Breakdown Structure (WBS) (this could be either the SCM Implementation Plan or the SCM Task List). Note: you may customize the task name with a name more suitable or better understood by your organization. You may also include an expected output column for each task, the role responsible for that task, dependencies, and other items that will help with planning.

4.4 Examples of an SCM Implementation Plan and an SCM Task List

Below are examples of both an SCM Implementation Plan (Table 1) and an SCM Task List (Table 2).

Table 1. Example of an SCM Implementation Plan

			SCM Implementation Plan
C/R	**Phase**	**Task ID**	**Task**
R	Organization	Org1	Provide an SCM Awareness session for Management
C		Org2	Determine Senior Management Commitment/Sponsorship to SCM
C		Org3	Establish an SCM Function/Group
C		Org4	Create an SCM Policy
C		Org5	Get Senior Management approval for SCM Policy
R		Org6	Prepare SCM Terminology glossary
R		Org7	Provide an SCM Awareness session for all employees (with SCM Policy and SCM Glossary)
R		Org8	Create a common SCM organizational repository (SCM Website)
C	Analysis	Ana1	Scope the SCM Infrastructure Implementation Effort
C		Ana2	Perform Analysis of the current environment
C	Planning	Pla1	Determine SCM Technology Requirements (HW, SW, Resources, etc.)
C		Pla2	Develop SCM Infrastructure Implementation Plan
R	Tool Selection	ToS1	Review SCM Tool Candidates
C		ToS2	Demo SCM Tools
R		ToS3	Evaluate Tools (install and test)
R		ToS4	Analyze Solution Alternatives
C		ToS5	Select Tool
C	Strategy & Design	Str1	Determine Network Considerations
C		Str2	Perform Capacity Planning (Diskspace, RAM, etc.)
C		Str3	Perform Identification Process (identify all pieces that go under SCM)

C		Str4	Define Repository & Workspace Standards
C		Str5	Define Labeling Standards
C		Str6	Determine Naming Conventions for Releases
C		Str7	Define Branching & Merging Strategy
C		Str8	Determine Location of Tool, Repositories, and Workspaces
R		Str7	Define needed integration(s) of SCM tool to other tools (design, development, test, defect tracking tools)
R		Str8	Design the integration(s) of SCM tool to other tools (design, development, test, defect tracking tools)
C	Installation	Ins1	Acquire Tool
C		Ins2	Install Tool
C		Ins3	Manage Licensing
C	Implementation	Imp1	Select Applications for Conversion
R		Imp2	Evaluate/Restructure Application Code Structure
C		Imp3	Determine Access to Code (permission groups)
C		Imp4	Build outside of SCM Tool
R		Imp5	Verify Application Functionality
C		Imp6	Import Application into SCM Tool
C		Imp	Prepare Build process in SCM Tool
C		Imp8	Build in SCM Tool
R		Imp9	Verify Application Functionality
C		Imp10	Prepare Release Migration Path
R	Procedure	Pro1	Prepare Checkout/Checkin Procedure
R		Pro2	Prepare Build Procedure
C		Pro3	Prepare Release Procedure
C		Pro4	Prepare Backup & Recovery Procedure
R		Pro5	Prepare User Training
C		Pro6	Train Users
R		Pro7	Prepare Admin Training & Procedures
C		Pro8	Train Admin
R	Testing	Tes1	Verify Checkout/Checkin Procedure
R		Tes2	Verify Build Procedure
C		Tes3	Verify Backup & Recovery Procedure
C		Tes4	Verify Release Procedure
C		Tes5	Review Final System
C		Tes6	Accept System
C	Transition	Tra1	Cutover to SCM Tool
C		Tra2	SCM Technical Transition Support (2-4 weeks)

Table 2. Example of an SCM Task List (to be incorporated into the Project's Project Plan)

		SCM Task List	
C/R	**Project Phase**	**Task**	**Role**
R	Requirements & Planning	SCM Initiation to Team (tool used, process, expectations, training available)	SCM Manager, Project Team
C		Establish CCB Project Members	Project Manager, SCM Manager
C		Approve Requirements & track changes to Requirements	CCB
R		SCM Capacity Planning for project	SCM Engineer, Technical Lead
R		Prepare Application Inventory (if one does not exist	Project Manager, SCM Engineer
R		Setup Document Repository (if one does not exist)	SCM Engineer
C	Design	Establish Project Code Baseline (starting point)	Project Manager, SCM Engineer
C		Establish Branching/Merging Process for project	SCM Engineer
R		Verify the SCM Build Procedure (ensure you can build, compile, or link from the code baseline)	SCM Engineer, Technical Lead
C		Create required User workspaces	SCM Engineer, Project Team
C		Train Users in the tool (as necessary)	SCM Engineer to Project Team
C	Development	Perform Integrated/Milestone Build(s) as needed	SCM Engineer
C		Perform Release Build	SCM Engineer
C		Perform merging activities (as needed)	Project Team, SCM Engineer
C		Create initial Release Package (e.g., version control the deliverables)	SCM Engineer
R		Create draft Release Notes	Project Manager
C	Test	Populate the Test area(s) from the SCM repository	SCM Engineer, Test
C		Finalize Release Package	SCM Engineer
C		Finalize Release Notes	Project Manager
C	Release	Approve Release	CCB
C		Install Release	Release Engineer
C		Verify Release installation	Release Engineer
R		Create Maintenance Branch	SCM Engineer
R		Cleanup old workspaces & branches	SCM Engineer, Project Team

5.0 Who May Use This Paper

This paper is primarily intended for the individual or group that intends on implementing SCM into an organization, application, and/or project(s). The people who may benefit from using this paper include: SCM personnel (SCM Managers, SCM Engineers, Release Engineers), Project Managers, Product Managers, QA personnel (QA Managers or QA Engineers), and Director/VP of QA, Development, or Technology, or any equivalent roles.

The benefit of using this paper is that it will provide you with a step-by-step approach to implementing SCM.

6.0 Conclusion

After more than a decade of over 50 SCM Implementations throughout the commercial, government, military, technology, and finance sectors, the author has drawn on these experiences in an attempt to provide a practical sequence of SCM tasks focused on the organization level, the application level, and the project level. While the authors places SCM tasks into particular SCM implementation levels, it is important to stress that one needs to be flexible in allowing the SCM task to move to another level where appropriate. Also, in many instances, not all tasks need to occur in an SCM implementation effort, but if tasks are discarded, it is important to understand the risk of doing so and the impact to other SCM tasks.

Overall, this paper was written with the intention to improve your chances of success when implementing SCM. Hopefully, it can be a good starting point and will reduce the time needed to identify what SCM tasks would go into an SCM Implementation Plan or Project Plan (via the SCM Task List).

References

Charles R. Myers, Jr; John H. Maher, Jr; and Betty L. Deimel: Managing Technology Change, Software Engineering Institute, Carnegie Mellon University, (1995)

Adler & Shenhar: Adapting your Technological Base: The Organizational Challenge, in the Sloan Management Review, (Fall, 1990)

Author Index

Lecture Notes in Computer Science

For information about Vols. 1–1606
please contact your bookseller or Springer-Verlag